Britain and America Go to War

Florida A&M University, Tallahassee
Florida Atlantic University, Boca Raton
Florida Gulf Coast University, Ft. Myers
Florida International University, Miami
Florida State University, Tallahassee
University of Central Florida, Orlando
University of Florida, Gainesville
University of North Florida, Jacksonville
University of South Florida, Tampa
University of West Florida, Pensacola

Britain and America Go to War

The Impact of War and Warfare
in Anglo-America, 1754–1815

Edited by Julie Flavell and Stephen Conway

University Press of Florida
Gainesville/Tallahassee/Tampa/Boca Raton
Pensacola/Orlando/Miami/Jacksonville/Ft. Myers

Copyright 2004 by Julie Flavell and Stephen Conway
Printed in the United States of America on recycled, acid-free paper
All rights reserved

09 08 07 06 05 04   6 5 4 3 2 1

A record of cataloging-in-publication data is available from
the Library of Congress.

ISBN 0-8130-2781-0

The University Press of Florida is the scholarly publishing agency
for the State University System of Florida, comprising Florida A&M
University, Florida Atlantic University, Florida Gulf Coast University,
Florida International University, Florida State University, University
of Central Florida, University of Florida, University of North Florida,
University of South Florida, and University of West Florida.

University Press of Florida
15 Northwest 15th Street
Gainesville, FL 32611-2079
http://www.upf.com

Contents

Illustrations

Chronology

1754 French and British Americans clash in the Ohio River valley
1755 Braddock defeated trying to capture Fort Duquesne
1756 Official declaration of war between Britain and France; Minorca falls to the French
1757 French capture Fort William Henry
1758 British and Provincial forces capture Louisbourg and Frontenac, but are repulsed before Ticonderoga
1759 Wolfe's army captures Quebec
1760 The fall of Montreal and the surrender of New France
1763 The Peace of Paris hands Canada, the Spanish Floridas, and the inland wilderness between the Appalachians and the Mississippi to the British crown
1764 Revenue Act inaugurates parliamentary taxation of the colonies
1765 Stamp Act provokes determined American resistance
1766 Stamp Act repealed
1767 Townshend Duties tax various colonial imports
1770 All the Townshend Duties except the tea duty are repealed; Boston Massacre
1773 Tea Act reignites controversy over parliamentary taxation; Boston Tea Party
1774 Coercive Acts aim to punish Massachusetts, but provoke general American resistance
1775 Outbreak of fighting between British army and New England militia at Lexington and Concord; battle of Bunker Hill; American invasion of Canada
1776 Thirteen Colonies in rebellion declare their independence; British forces successful in New York campaign, but Washington's army survives
1777 General Howe's troops capture Philadelphia and defeat Washington's army at Brandywine Creek; General Burgoyne's army is compelled to surrender to the Americans at Saratoga

1778   French enter the war on the American side; the war spreads to the Caribbean, West Africa, Europe, and India

1779   Spanish enter the war as allies of the French; Britain and Ireland threatened with a Bourbon invasion

1780   The British capture Charleston, South Carolina; the United Provinces (the Netherlands) joins the war against Britain

1781   General Cornwallis's army surrenders to the French and Americans at Yorktown

1782   Admiral Rodney's victory at the battle of the Saints saves Jamaica from Franco-Spanish attack

1783   Peace of Paris; Britain acknowledges the independence of the United States; France and Spain make territorial gains at Britain's expense

1793   Britain and revolutionary France embark on a prolonged struggle

1802   Peace of Amiens brings Anglo-French war to a close

1803   War resumes between Britain and France

1805   The Essex Decision curtails American trade with the French West Indies

1806   Berlin decree attempts to close continental Europe to British trade

1807   British Orders in Council retaliate for Berlin decree; the Chesapeake Affair outrages American public opinion; Jefferson's Embargo Act

1809   Jefferson's Embargo Act replaced with the Non-Intercourse Act; new British Orders in Council prohibit American trade with France and the French West Indies

1812   Outbreak of war between Britain and the United States; American attack on Canada fails; British capture Detroit

1813   Americans destroy York, win battle of Lake Erie, and recapture Detroit; British take Fort Niagara

1814   Americans take Fort Erie, but later abandon it; British defeat Americans at Bladensburg and burn parts of Washington; Americans win battle of Plattsburg, stopping a British advance from Canada; British attack on Baltimore unsuccessful; Treaty of Ghent concluded at end of the year

1815   Before the signing of the peace is known in North America, a British attack on New Orleans is repulsed on 8 January

Introduction

Julie Flavell and Stephen Conway

In his seminal work, *A People Numerous and Armed,* historian John Shy identified the formative effect of three wars—the Seven Years' War, the American Revolution, and the War of 1812—on the British North American colonies and the new United States. In all three wars, Americans believed that their very survival as a people was at stake. In the Seven Years' War, the colonists feared encirclement if the French were able to establish themselves in the Ohio River valley and link their Canadian heartland with the smaller colony at the mouth of the Mississippi; the expulsion of the French from North America was thought to be the only adequate safeguard for the future security of the British colonies. During the Revolution, at least from 1776, the independence and continued existence of the United States was at issue; British victory would have meant a reassertion of control, or at least superintendence, from London. In the War of 1812, Britain posed such a formidable threat to the new United States that no less than national credibility and the success of the Republican experiment were felt to be at stake. The conclusion of peace in 1815 saw the threat of European intervention in American affairs virtually at an end, with the United States arriving at a position of military security that was unprecedented in eighteenth-century European international relations.[1] For the American republic, what followed was a century of isolationism.

All three wars occurred as a result of Anglo-French conflict, during which time America emerged as a key player in the European balance of power. The Seven Years' War saw Britain's Atlantic community achieve unprecedented unity in its struggle against France. Collectively, the British Isles and the British North American colonies emerged from the war with greater security than ever, although victory over the French soon brought problems as the British Parliament sought to introduce more centralized control over the expanded empire and the colonists resisted this threat to their long-cherished autonomy. The Revolution, the bloody culmination of a decade of increasingly tense relations between Britain and its North American colonies, tore the empire asunder. Loyalties shifted and new identities evolved as Britons fought to keep America. The French were transformed into allies of the insurgent colonists, and displaced loyalists ultimately established a stronghold in Canada. The War of 1812 was a further installment of conflict between Britain and the United States, coming at the conclusion of a bitter struggle with France. It revealed the extent to which the new polity in America had forged a sense of national identity among Britain's former colonies, while finally establishing the United States as a permanent presence, a trade rival to nineteenth-century Britain, and a threat to her dominions in Canada.

The essays brought together in *Britain and America Go to War* move beyond Shy's teleological—because exclusively American—account of a single nation emerging from the repeated experience of war, by approaching the period within a broader Atlantic context. Emerging Atlantic scholarship reveals that this was a critical period for the entire English Atlantic world. The geographical boundaries of English-speaking provinces in America configured and reconfigured in response to violent conflict. Established identities were undermined and new identities were created. The essays presented here remind us that outcomes, as contemporaries were very aware, were far from preordained.

The nine essays in *Britain and America Go to War* not only deal with the new international order that emerged as a result of the three wars—Eliga Gould concludes with the creation of an Atlantic state system, modeled on the European state system, between about 1795 and 1825—but also suggest what might have been, as throughout the period successive conflicts threatened to reconfigure the Anglo-American Atlantic world in unpredictable ways. The impact of war upon national identity is a particularly topical concern within this volume. Many of the essays contribute to the debate on whether armed conflict tends to promote identification with the nation or strengthen the importance of sectional divisions and local loyalties.

Bob Harris points out that much of British public interest in the Seven Years' War was generated not by interest in the American empire per se but by its role in the ongoing competition with Britain's traditional enemy, France. Peter Marshall augments this picture of a metropolis that was more concerned with its security in relation to Europe than with developing an imperial partnership with its American colonies. But Britain's refusal to recognize the growing collective importance of the colonies was not only the result of a preoccupation with Europe. It also showed a realistic appreciation of the sectional divisions that were rife in the American colonies. Julie Flavell shows how an awareness of colonial sectionalism led Britain in 1775 to venture into an American war that ultimately spread, helping to drive the former colonies into a union that was both unprecedented and fragile but that nonetheless brought them to victory and nationhood. Stephen Conway explores how, during the same period, the mobilization of manpower in Britain was an opportunity for an aspiring British middle class to assert its local leadership while simultaneously demonstrating its role in the project of advancing a British nation. Margaret Stead demonstrates that the British press accounted for the disappointing outcome of the Howe campaigns (1776–78) by depicting General Sir William Howe as a corrupt metropolitan, reminding us of how far the Americans and the British still shared ideals of citizenship and public character in this period. Yet by 1812, Christopher Bartlett and Gene Smith show us, British negative perceptions of American character had crystallized in ways that were to affect the conduct of the ensuing war. In this final Anglo-American war, the American sectionalism that was evident at the outset of the Revolution was again exploited, this time more consistently, by a British enemy.

The very essence of war, of course, is conflict between enemies. But the business of waging war also creates tensions and divisions *within* the ranks of contending parties. These essays, collectively and individually, highlight these tensions and divisions—within the British media as a civil war raged in the American colonies; between local and national loyalties in both Britain and North America during the Revolution and the War of 1812; between men and women (and men and men over women) in the British army in North America during the Seven Years' War. Peter Way challenges the image of soldiering as an all-male preserve as he demonstrates how the unacknowledged but ubiquitous presence of women continually sparked internal conflict in the British army in America. Michael Bellesiles explores how, despite victory, the conduct of the War of 1812 resulted in American disillusionment with its state militias and a greater commitment to an American professional army.

Acknowledging Shy's case for the interrelatedness of these three conflicts, the nine essays in this collection have been selected to deal with the three wars equally. Each essay deals with a different aspect of one of the three conflicts. All of the contributions can be regarded as essays in the "new military history" in that they investigate the impact of war and warfare not primarily in terms of battles and campaigns but as events or processes that had considerable ramifications for the societies that took part.

The book opens with three essays on the Seven Years' War. Bob Harris looks critically at Kathleen Wilson's work on empire and political culture in eighteenth-century England and argues that interest in empire, particularly in the North American colonies, needs to be placed in the context of "Britain's great power rivalry with France." The previous Anglo-French conflict, the War of the Austrian Succession (1740–48), had ended in stalemate, with the French victorious on land in the Low Countries and the British able to secure naval predominance. In the aftermath of the Austrian war there was much concern in Britain that French efforts were now being concentrated on maritime and commercial expansion. The prospect that the French soon might be able to mount an effective challenge outside Europe led naturally to renewed anxiety about French power and to a desire to promote national revival in the face of the French threat. The empire, in other words, became a public preoccupation as part of a broader concern about French ambitions everywhere. The Seven Years' War, seen in this light, appears less as a great struggle for imperial conquest and more as a "fight to recover national virtue" to counter an increasingly dangerous and apparently successful rival.

Peter Way focuses on the British army sent to North America during the Seven Years' War. He has already viewed this force from fresh and interesting perspectives, bringing the insights of labor history into studies of the military. In "Venus and Mars: Women and the British-American Army in the Seven Years' War" he concentrates on another area of army life that has been neglected by military historians—the often complex gender relations between the army's soldiers and the women who accompanied them. Way's essay uses the experiences of the British regular army in America to show that the nominally masculine preserve of the British military during the eighteenth century was in reality shot through with an unacknowledged female presence that sparked much internal conflict. Armies are usually depicted as male preserves and as embodying masculine characteristics. But all armies have relied on women to provide a range of services. The female camp followers of the British army in North America performed indispensable work as nurses, tailors, and laundresses, as retailers of liquor and food, and as sexual partners. Yet the presence of women in garrisons, camps, and even on campaign was disruptive, for the women were not only consumers of supplies, and therefore an added expense, but also identified as the cause of criminality and poor discipline.

The links between the Seven Years' War and the American Revolution have long been a matter of interest to historians. The bulk of the scholarship has concentrated on the ways in which the conflict changed colonial perspectives toward the mother country, with the expulsion of the French from

Canada sometimes seen as releasing the Americans from any dependence on Britain for defense. Peter Marshall focuses on British attitudes and how the war influenced the development of postwar British government policies toward the colonies. Marshall emphasizes that the war can be divided into two distinct periods. The first, from the commitment of regular troops to North America until 1758, can be characterized as a time marked mainly by defeat for Anglo-American arms and great tension between British commanders and the colonial assemblies and between the regular army and the provincial forces. In these years a distinctly unfavorable impression of the Americans was conveyed to Britons in North America and at home; the colonists were depicted as disunited, disobedient, selfish, and prone to trade with the enemy. From 1758, however, Pitt's government made concessions to the American viewpoint that facilitated the more effective mobilization of colonial manpower, and the years of victory were characterized by reduced tensions between British and American soldiers. Rather than learn the lessons of the last phase of the war in North America, however, postwar British opinion seems to have been overly influenced by the more fractious first phase. This is partly because the American contribution to the successes of 1758–60 was underreported in Britain, where the triumphs of the regular armed forces at Louisbourg and Quebec in 1758 and 1759 were given much greater coverage than the successes of predominantly provincial armies, such as the capture in 1758 of the strategically vital Fort Frontenac. Consequently, many British politicians and significant parts of the British public entered the postwar period with an image of the Americans as hopelessly divided, obstreperous, militarily ineffective, and incapable of defending themselves. The option of recognizing the benefits of Anglo-American cooperation was not pursued, because it was hardly perceived by most Britons. The colonists, who viewed the successful conclusion of the war as an indication of the strengths of imperial partnership, were understandably frustrated by the approach adopted by the metropolitan authorities in the aftermath of the conflict.

The attitudes formed during and just after the Seven Years' War were to exert a significant influence on the course of relations between the colonies and Britain during the 1760s and 1770s. Julie Flavell's essay on British perceptions of New England in 1774–75 argues that those perceptions helped to persuade metropolitan policymakers that military coercion was a viable option. Opinions on the nature of the American colonists varied. In some accounts they appear as too soft and ineffectual to offer any resistance—a selfish commercialized people lacking in military qualities; in others they are depicted as an essentially backward people, well armed and

militarily enthusiastic but deficient in professional skill. These two stereotypes, Flavell argues, reflected British distinctions between the colonists in
general and the New Englanders in particular. The colonies south of New
England were seen as more advanced and therefore as very different from
the Yankee provinces. This perception of sectional divisions had much to
commend it from a British point of view. It was not based on ignorant
wishful thinking; it reflected significant differences that existed between the
New England colonies and the rest of British North America. But the British
failed to exploit these sectional differences effectively. The idea that the
New England colonies could be separated from the other provinces, and
then militarily coerced or blockaded into submission, continued to be advanced long after the initial stage of the war. The British campaign of 1777,
which ended disastrously with Burgoyne's surrender at Saratoga, was based
at least partly on the assumption that control of the Hudson River valley
would enable the British to cut New England off from supplies and suste-
nance from the middle and southern colonies; and in August 1778 Major
Patrick Ferguson, an acute British observer, was arguing for a concerted
effort to bring the war back to New England. But, even in the first year of
the war, the British government allowed itself to be distracted. The unsuccessful southern expedition that finally came to grief at Charleston in June
1776 was predicated partly on the reasoning that the black majority in
South Carolina made that colony the "soft underbelly" of the rebellion, but
mainly on the assumption that the South generally contained many "friends
to government" who could be mobilized against Congress. The search for
loyalists similarly played a big part in the move to New York in 1776—a
move already decided upon while Howe's army was cooped up in Boston—
and it profoundly influenced the peripatetic progress of the British forces
for the remainder of the war. Yet if the British strategists had stuck to working on the differences between New England and the middle and southern
colonies, they might have found a richer vein of division to exploit.

If there were deep rifts within colonial and revolutionary North
America, there were also great differences in Britain over the conduct and
propriety of the American war. Margaret Stead's essay looks at the way in
which the British press, pamphlets, and cartoons covered the campaigns of
the Howe brothers and the subsequent parliamentary inquiry into their
conduct. When General William Howe was appointed commander in chief
of the army in North America, and his elder brother, Richard, Viscount
Howe, was made the senior naval commander in American waters, there
were high hopes in Britain that the war could be brought to a successful
conclusion. But the Howe brothers, and particularly Admiral Howe,

wanted to mix military operations with peace overtures, and as successive campaigns failed to produce victory or negotiations, criticism of the Howes mounted. The brothers were attacked by American sympathizers for their willingness to be used as instruments of government policy and by government supporters and American loyalists for their lethargic conduct of operations, which was often put down to a reluctance to deliver a knockout blow. Further criticism focused on the troops' lack of discipline and Howe's extravagant lifestyle, particularly while the army was lying idle in Philadelphia during the winter of 1777–78. The Howes, like military and naval commanders before and since, were keen to defend their reputations and feared, probably correctly, that their credibility had been fatally undermined by the persistently adverse press that had begun soon after they assumed their commands. General Howe's decision to go into print himself and defend his actions publicly tells us a lot about both his own sensitivities on this point and the assumption (on all sides) that public opinion mattered, even in the restricted world of eighteenth-century British politics. But the Howes were not the only ones damaged by media interest and criticism. Stead points out that the defense of their conduct mounted by the Howes— and particularly by General Howe—turned the spotlight on Lord North's ministry and the inadequate support that it had given to the operations across the Atlantic.

Studies of the American war tend to highlight the extensive mobilization of American manpower and resources to fight the British regular armed forces, such as those led by the Howe brothers. Less attention has been paid to the nature of the mobilization of manpower in Britain and Ireland. In truth, a remarkably large number of British and Irish males served at one time or another during the war, either in the official formations in the army, navy, or militia or in unofficial or semiofficial volunteer units. Stephen Conway's piece looks at the British volunteer corps and offers some comparisons between British and Irish volunteer activities. His essay attempts to establish the extent of volunteering in Britain—which was much greater than is usually thought—and then seeks to explain this enthusiasm for amateur soldiering. Behind the obvious military point that Britain was threatened with invasion (or at least enemy attack) from 1778, there lurked various political considerations. The volunteers were championed by the parliamentary opposition as a bulwark against a dangerously authoritarian government; more prosaically, promoting or cultivating the volunteers was a way for politicians to further their local power bases. But social explanations need to be taken into account, too. Volunteering was largely (though not exclusively) a middle-class phenomenon, and it can be seen as means by which the middling ranks asserted their importance within their own communities and the importance of those communities within their counties and regions. This localist perspective does not mean, however, that the volunteers had no national vision. While their concentration was on local defense and local reputation, they still saw themselves, at least in some instances, as part of a bigger whole. Different volunteer corps emulated one another and competed, indicating that there was nothing inherently contradictory about local pride contributing to a national effort. The British volunteer corps of the American war period are not as well known as the Irish corps established at the same time, but in this account the British volunteers emerge as similar in many respects to their Irish counterparts.

The War of 1812 can be seen as a renewal of the Anglo-American dimension of the conflict that was concluded in 1783. The essay by Christopher Bartlett and Gene Smith, focusing on Vice Admiral Sir Alexander Cochrane and his fellow Royal Navy officers and their operations, reveals how much the attitudes of British participants built on the stereotypes of the previous conflict. British conceptions of the character of the Americans influenced the nature of the war even more than they had thirty years earlier. In the Revolutionary War, British officers had often taken the view that the Americans, as rebels against legitimate authority, were not entitled to the normal protections embodied in the laws of war, hence the large-scale destruction of property that characterized the bloody struggle for American independence. In the conflict of 1812–15, the customary protections were again said not to apply to the civilian population. The idea that the Americans were the progeny of rebels and that the United States was born out of a rebellion no doubt carried weight, but the main argument against the Americans now was that as republicans and democrats they were ultimately responsible for the actions of their government. Bartlett and Smith show that American reliance on privateering also played a part in persuading British commanders that attacks on coastal towns and settlements were fully justified—as an allegedly piratical republic, the United States was viewed as beyond the pale of civilization. In another echo of the War of Independence, Bartlett and Smith show that the British government and commanders of the armed forces were keen to exploit internal divisions within the United States. The fomenting of a large-scale slave revolt was thought to be inappropriate. But many runaways were recruited into the army or marines or encouraged to settle in Canada or the West Indies. New England's lukewarm commitment to the war was also seen as a source of American weakness—although here the sectional division was a complete inversion of the situation in the previous Anglo-American conflict, when

British strategists, as we have seen, saw New England as the epicenter of the rebellion, to be cut off from the colonies further south and then starved or bludgeoned into submission.

From the British perspective on the war of 1812 we move to the American. Michael Bellesiles argues that Jackson's victory at New Orleans at the end of the conflict tended to cancel out the distinctly negative impression created by the American performance up until that point. Despite the clamor for war in 1812, and the misplaced confidence in easy victory, most of the struggle was far from glorious for the United States. Bellesiles underlines the tedium and inactivity that dominated the war experiences of many Americans in arms, leading to problems with excessive drinking and the erosion of discipline. Poor logistical arrangements added to the difficulties of the American soldiers and further lowered morale. But the lamentable performance of the American forces, and in particular the inadequacy of the militia, was overshadowed by the victory at New Orleans, which was used in the short term to justify reliance on a largely militia army. In the long run, however, it was accepted that the nation needed a cadre of professionally trained officers, and congressional appropriations for West Point increased.

In the final chapter in the collection, Eliga Gould looks at the forging of a new Atlantic state system in the aftermath of American independence, particularly following the war of 1812. This system found its clearest expression in the pronouncements of George Canning, the British foreign secretary, and James Monroe, whose eponymous doctrine was enunciated to Congress in 1823. Both the British and the Americans were unwilling to accept the reimposition by the European autocracies of colonial rule on the former Spanish possessions in Central and South America. Anglo-American agreement on this issue was not, it should be stressed, the culmination of a smooth process of adaptation by the British to the new realities of the Atlantic world. As the War of 1812 demonstrated and transatlantic trading patterns exemplified, the legacy of the colonial era lived on long after the creation of independent states in North and South America. Yet the emergence of a new system is difficult to deny. Diplomatically, at least, that system was based on equality between sovereign states. The old European assumption that the Atlantic and the American colonies constituted a separate sphere, in which the norms of European law and civilization were inappropriate or simply did not operate, was giving way to a vision of the Atlantic world as an extension of the European state system.

As this brief introduction has already suggested, there are many areas of continuity within the collection. This is inevitable in a collection whose authors—whether focusing on Britain or America—view the three wars in an Atlantic context. Perhaps the most important theme is the persistent tension between local and national loyalties within the British Atlantic world. War, while perfectly capable of promoting a sense of commitment to the nation, could just as easily entrench provincial allegiance. The challenge for enemies was to exploit local loyalties as a means of undermining national unity; the challenge for national governments and military leaders was to make local identification compatible with a wider sense of belonging.

Note

1. John Shy, "The American Military Experience: History and Learning," in *A People Numerous and Armed: Reflections on the Military Struggle for American Independence* (New York: Oxford University Press, 1976), 238–40.

I

The Seven Years' War

1

War, Empire, and the "National Interest" in Mid-Eighteenth-Century Britain

Bob Harris

The mid-eighteenth century was, for Britain, as for many other European states, a period of war and heightened international rivalry. In 1741, Britain entered a major European war—the War of the Austrian Succession—for the first time since 1713. For more than two decades, Britain and France battled one another for security and supremacy; in the end, these amounted to the same thing. In the course of this conflict, Britons were forced to ponder with unexampled urgency their relationship to the old world of Europe and the new one rising across the Atlantic. The Seven Years' War officially began in 1756 as a fight to protect Britain's colonies on the American eastern seaboard from French expansionist activities in the Ohio River valley.[1] From there, the conflict spread back to Europe and from thence across the globe. The European dimension to the war was crucial to its outcome, but for the British, under Pitt the Elder, it was secondary to the war for trade and empire. As Pitt was to express it in 1761, while defending retrospectively coalition policy toward Germany and the continental conflict, it was a case of fighting for the "new world" in the "old."[2]

Public and popular attitudes and responses to this conflict are the subject of this chapter, particularly Britain's relations to its colonies in North America. In recent years, a considerable amount of relevant work on this and related topics has appeared. In particular, Kathleen Wilson has published a series of important articles and a deservedly influential book that have served to expand our sense of how empire and imperial influences shaped eighteenth-century domestic politics and culture.[3] Why the need, then, for a further examination? Part of the reason is precisely because Wilson's views have been so influential, especially for those who are not specialists on the period; new orthodoxies deserve critical scrutiny just as established ones. Wilson's account of empire also raises several problems. Her very focus on empire has served to deflect attention from more significant realities about British responses to war in this period and to give empire an importance in public perceptions and debate in Britain that it lacked, at least in the sense in which it is depicted by Wilson. Second, the central decades of the century were crucial in forging British perceptions of empire in North America; a fuller understanding of these perceptions, and their emergence, must provide the starting point for any broader evaluation of public attitudes toward Anglo-American relations in the eighteenth century.

A major source for this chapter is the press and print. The reach of the press extended throughout Britain. News and comment about war and diplomacy dominated British newspapers, filled the pages of a growing number of periodicals and pamphlets, and provided the subjects for numerous handbills, prints, and ballads.[4] Under the impact of the midcentury wars, the press grew and further extended its influence in England, Scotland, and Ireland.[5] Even the imposition of higher taxes on newspapers in 1757 did not interrupt this growth. In 1764, an account of London newspapers dispatched through the Post Office to other parts of Britain noted that no account could be provided for daily or weekly papers; nevertheless, the number of these sent out per week could not be less than 15,000 in peacetime; in wartime, the author estimated that the figure would be around 21,000.[6] In the torrents of words printed is contained the imprint of how Britons felt about their empire and the process of imperial expansion.

The chapter has four sections. The first looks briefly at the main themes in Wilson's portrayal of attitudes toward empire. The second section examines how far and in what ways debates about empire and North America and Britain's role overseas were shaped by great power rivalry with France. The shadow cast by this rivalry over midcentury Britain would be difficult to exaggerate, and it inevitably influenced how Britons perceived and portrayed their empire. This emerges strongly in the third section, which investigates major concepts of empire current in this period. What sort of empire did Britons imagine for themselves? The fourth and final section raises the issue of religion and the role of churches in contemporary debates about war and empire. Wilson has little to say about this, something that reflects a wider view in the work of eighteenth-century political culture as something that was essentially secular in inspiration and nature. Yet the churches frequently expressed views on such issues.

Wilson's portrayal of empire's role and meanings in public debate places special emphasis on the connections between empire and the lives, fortunes, and aspirations of the expanding urban middling groups of eighteenth-century society. It attributes a similar degree of importance to the economic forces that served to bind empire together and of which members of the middling ranks were principal authors and beneficiaries. The products of empire—sugar, chocolate, coffee, tea, spices, oranges, lemons, and other fruits—were traded and consumed by an ever-expanding proportion of the population. Partly because of this, Wilson depicts empire as having joined together important mercantile groups and the growing networks of shop-keepers, tradesmen, and other stalwarts of urban middling Britain in enthu-siasm for imperial expansion and the multiplying opportunities for trade that followed in its wake.[7] Popular imperialism is, therefore, from one per-spective a political consequence of a buoyant and strongly developing econ-omy; economic progress and expansion were the sources of a vigorous and strengthening popular impetus toward empire.

Among the middling ranks, the desire to acquire territory abroad is seen by Wilson as having mirrored, and having been closely bound up with, a striving for political emancipation at home. It was empire that provided the middling ranks with a vehicle for establishing an increasingly independent and autonomous political identity. The fate of empire also helped the mid-dling sort fashion "a critique of authority which identified national, social, and moral ills with the [contemporary] distribution and exercise of political power."[8] The story of empire and the story of political reform became, in this way, closely intertwined. Unlike later versions, eighteenth-century popular imperialism functions less as a support for the state than as a source of potential opposition to it (or at least its political representatives). There is, in this respect, an interesting tension between Wilson's view of eigh-teenth-century empire and some other recent views, which see in it or its domestic and economic aspects potential sources of support for an expand-ing and increasingly intrusive state.[9]

When it comes to the precise view (or views) of empire that the middling ranks entertained, Wilson is somewhat equivocal. She writes in several places as if empire were a goal in this period. She refers, in this context, to the eighteenth-century press constructing an "accumulationist" view of empire, one that construed empire in terms of expanding trade, production, and consumption.[10] Elsewhere, however, she suggests that empire was more important as a focus for a range of other beliefs, beliefs that had less to do with empire than with Britain or what overseas territories were seen as contributing to the mother country. Thus, she writes at one point, "'Impe-rialism' in eighteenth-century Britain was clearly an amalgam of mercantil-ist, libertarian, and nationalist beliefs, given form and substance by the contexts in which they were invoked."[11] As far as the middle of the century is concerned, empire and its meanings became very closely tied up with anxieties about the health of British society and the conditions of the British polity, about the twin threats of "luxury" and "corruption," as contemporaries termed them. Wilson argues that not only was empire a major focus for these anxieties but it was also seen as an antidote to them.[12] Empire, on this view, represented the proving ground for British patriotism and public spirit. Wilson also emphasizes the anti-aristocratic and masculinist cast of this project. There are two points being made here. First, there is the marked affinity between concepts of empire in this period and the interests and aspirations of the middling ranks. Second, the contemporary definitions and understandings of empire served to underline "hierarchies of difference" within English political culture, in this case the subordinate position of women.

The emphasis in Wilson's work on trade and goods fits well with recent interpretations of eighteenth-century Britain that stress the importance of commercialization and changing patterns and habits of consumption among particularly the middling ranks.[13] It is not difficult to find plenty of contemporary support for it. Propagandists and writers on trade and the colonies had expatiated on the potential of the colonial trades from at least the later seventeenth century, and by the 1750s their increasingly fast growth was frequently remarked upon.[14] The importance of trade to Britain's national interest was also widely emphasized by opposition and ministerial supporters, by Jacobites and non-Jacobites, by English, Scots, and a significant number of Irishmen. Thomas Newton, bishop of Norwich, was therefore merely reiterating a commonplace when he declared in 1739 in a sermon preached before members of the House of Lords: "The circulation of Trade is to such a Kingdom as this, just of the same Importance as the circulation of Blood to a body natural. An Attempt upon it, is as an Arrow at the very Heart."[15]

However, if empire and the colonies were seen by a growing number of contemporaries as holding out the promise of increasing national and personal prosperity, the significance of this needs to be seen in terms of a wider context—Britain's great power rivalry with France. Wilson acknowledges this, but does not perhaps give it the degree of emphasis that it merits. As any close reading of discussion of empire and imperial issues in the contemporary press shows, it was, for most of this period, the changing conditions and intensity of this rivalry that determined levels of press interest in empire and the colonies; this rivalry also shaped closely and directly the ways in which empire and imperial issues were framed and understood.

This could be illustrated in a variety of ways, but it emerges clearly if we look briefly at coverage in the press of efforts to build up the colony of Nova Scotia following the 1748 Peace of Aix-la-Chapelle. The plan to develop the colony, which involved providing passage and land for demobilized soldiers, was one of a number of measures taken by ministers to deal with the strains created by demobilization at the end of the War of the Austrian Succession and to help Britain combat the threat from a French state, which appeared to be preparing vigorously for a resumption of hostilities. The most important pamphlet published in support of the plan was Otis Little's *State of Trade in the Northern Colonies Considered,* which was published in London in 1748. Little, who was an American merchant from Massachusetts, had come to London to lobby the Board of Trade, then led by the Earl of Halifax, to adopt the plan. His pamphlet made clear the strategic importance of the colony and the plan; Nova Scotia was a crucial barrier between Britain's North American colonies and a France actively pursuing hegemony on that continent. He left little room for doubt about the scope of French ambitions in North America: "The French have artfully extended their lines within our Colonies, not only with a Design to cut off our communication, and trade with the Natives, but to crowd such of them into the seas, as are too weak to make a Resistance, and, finally, to master the whole continent."[16] Several other themes were prominent. These included the economic potential of the colony—portrayed, as was common in such cases, as enormous—and the issue of a potential divergence of economic interests between the Northern colonies and Britain and the possibility of the colonies moving toward independence.[17] These were, however, of secondary importance compared to the issue of strategy. In Little's view, it was the threat from French ambitions on the North American continent that provided the compelling reason for reinforcing the British presence in Nova Scotia.

There is some evidence that the project aroused considerable public interest. The *Gentleman's Magazine* made efforts to provide its readers with supplementary information about the colony, which it drew, perhaps ironically, from the work of a Frenchman—the Jesuit Pierre Charlevoix.[18] The same periodical, together with many newspapers, also published a succession of letters from the new residents of the colony detailing their early experiences. The sources of these letters were mostly private individuals, while others were copies from pages of the *Pennsylvania Gazette,* at this time one of the most influential of the growing number of colonial newspapers. The early letters were enthusiastic in tone. A former blacksmith from York, for example, commented: "You'd live much better than in Old England: a country well fortified with batteries and cannon, well supplied with wood and water; plenty of salt provisions and fresh meat, and fish of all sorts; and where there is plenty of work and good wages."[19] This mood failed to last, however, and the emphasis in the letters shifted increasingly to recurrent problems with the inhabitants, who remained loyal to the French, and clashes with various groups of Indians, who were being stirred up by the French in Canada. By September 1751, the *Old England Journal*, a leading opposition essay paper, was carrying an article on the failure of the project and on the crucial contribution of the French to this.[20]

The relevant question is why Anglo-French rivalry was so influential in shaping debate about colonial and imperial issues in the mid-eighteenth century. Part of the reason, as the response to the failed project to develop Nova Scotia discussed above begins to reveal, was the looming reality of this rivalry and its frequent manifestations in international politics.[21] It also, however, reflected the specific ways in which this rivalry was portrayed and seen by contemporaries.

Contemporary views of French power and international aims were starkly drawn; they also won near universal acceptance. France was depicted as having one overriding international goal—universal monarchy or domination of Europe. It was seen as totally unvarying in pursuit of this, whether through diplomacy or war, and completely unscrupulous. France had to be watched continually and suspected; the ambition of its rulers was unquenchable; it was also a constant source of international uncertainty and instability. In 1756, one of the reviewers for the recently established *Critical Review*, commenting on a recently published pamphlet entitled *The Progress of the French, in their Views of Universal Monarchy*, recommended that

> every Briton ought to be acquainted with the ambitious views of France, her eternal thirst after universal dominion, and her continual encroachments on the properties of her neighbors, so this author has drawn together in a narrow compass, the comprehensive recapitulation of her insidious policy, and perfidious practices, with regard to Europe in general, and the welfare and commerce of this Island in particular, for upwards of a hundred years past; in order to demonstrate, that nothing but a war, vigorously carried on against her, and continued till she be utterly incapacitated for putting her wicked schemes in execution. And till this be done, it is most certain, that our trade, our liberties, our country, nay all the rest of Europe, will be in continual danger of falling prey to the common Enemy, the universal

Cormorant, that would, if possible, swallow up the whole globe itself.[22]

Britain and British power were envisaged as the major obstacle to the realization of French aims. Indeed, it was the British opposition to these aims that defined her international role and that accounted for the scope and intensity of Anglo-French rivalry.

This view of international affairs had a relatively long genealogy, having taken shape in the later seventeenth century in response to Louis XIV's foreign policy and wars.[23] In retrospect, it can seem very simplistic. By this period, it placed too much emphasis on Anglo-French rivalry as the axis on which all international events turned and too little on the distinctive aims of other important or rising powers—Prussia, Russia, and Austria. It was also a facet of a contemporary debate about foreign affairs that saw states as possessed of fixed interests, which overlooked the unpredictable and capricious elements in foreign affairs in this period.[24] Yet whatever its weaknesses or limitations, the underlying assumptions had enormous contemporary influence. We must also recognize that for many people at the time the events of the two major wars of this period only appeared to confirm and further add to their relevance. The War of the Austrian Succession began in the mold of the wars against Louis XIV's France, to prevent France from redrawing the European map, and thereby undermining the "balance of power" and British and European liberties. The French threat to British independence, liberty, prosperity and Protestantism was underlined by serious Franco-Jacobite invasion threats in 1743–44, 1745–46, 1755–56, and 1759. The '45, which presented Britons with the spectacle of invasion from the north by a mainly Highland army and a French invasion fleet mobilizing in French Channel ports, shattered any complacency about the potential threat that France and the Jacobites might pose to the Hanoverian and Protestant Succession and to British commerce and empire, a point much emphasized by loyalist propaganda.

There was, therefore, a marked continuity about the way in which French international ambitions were portrayed during this period. An important shift in perceptions of Anglo-French rivalry did, nevertheless, take place. It is this shift that helps us to see why issues of trade and empire took on ever more importance in public debate and perceptions, especially from the later 1740s. To date the beginnings of the shift precisely is impossible, but there can be little doubt that it gathered momentum from the second half of the 1740s and in particular from reaction to the capture from the French of the island of Cape Breton in the mouth of the St Lawrence river in

1745.[25] Its essence was that Anglo-French rivalry was becoming focused ever more fiercely on trade and empire. France was changing its character from a power principally seeking conquest and aggrandizement through military might to one more concerned with cultivating commerce and manufacturing. The goal may have remained the same, but the means were changing. French commercial, maritime, and imperial activity formed part of a broader scheme to remove Britain's independence and ability to prevent France from finally gaining its long-standing ambition—universal monarchy. It was a view again given added plausibility by the course of the War of the Austrian Succession, as well as by French efforts to rebuild its international power after 1748. The latter stages of this war had seen British naval power unchallenged but counterbalanced by French power on the continent and in the Low Countries especially. The Peace of Aix-la-Chapelle was seen by most people as fragile and unlikely to last. What particularly alarmed contemporaries, however, was that French efforts at military renewal from 1748 appeared to be focused on its navy. In 1751, Lord Barrington, one of the Lords of the Admiralty, complained in a Commons debate on the navy estimates: "I know I shall be told of the late great preparations of the French, and their diligent application of the marine; and I confess, that of late we have been by our Gazette pretty much amused of these accounts." Two years previously, Admiral Vernon, who saw his special role in politics as being to safeguard the interests of the navy, warned: "That an equal, or nearly equal capacity to face us at sea, will be fully sufficient to render us Tributaries to those who can already command the continent, none can deny."[26] Evidence of French hostility in North America, in the Caribbean, in India, and on the African coast only appeared to confirm the reality of the unfolding plan—to deprive Britain of the sinews of war.[27] The contest for universal monarchy, on the one hand, and peace, independence and prosperity, on the other, was to be fought out in the spheres of trade and colonial territories. Colonial rivalry was an extension or, as Marie Peters has put it elsewhere, "even an intrinsic" facet of an essentially European struggle.[28] Commerce, as William Horsley put it in 1748, had become "the new channel of power."[29]

Another concern about French activities in the mid-eighteenth century deserves brief comment here. This is the fear many Britons had about imminent French economic ascendancy and, linked to this, recognition of the vitality and achievements of the French state in promoting economic, commercial, and colonial development.[30] It is an aspect of anti-French feeling in this period that is often insufficiently emphasized, perhaps because it sits so uneasily with the equally insistent claims of contemporaries that British liberties, trade, and economic growth were inextricably interlinked. Its most powerful articulation came in the work of Malachy Postlethwayt, the influential writer on trade and economic issues.[31] In the mid-1750s, when Britain and France had resumed hostilities in the Seven Years' War, Postlethwayt was publishing stark warnings about French commercial power and expansion. In one place, he described the French as "immoderately bent upon enlarging her traffic." France was "courting commerce, with the heartiest Application and warmest Addresses that were ever yet made in a kingdom." The French Council of Commerce was praised for its efforts to develop French trade, while the French commercial challenge was portrayed as global. Postlethwayt described this commercial competition as "a Torrent."[32] French colonial administration, meanwhile, was more rational and effective than British administration. Because of this, it was feared that the French would prove invincible in North America. The message was clear: Britain needed to respond immediately to this threat. At stake were British trading fortunes as well as Britain's existence as an independent power. It is a view that helps to explain why the notion of a war to extinguish French trade was popular at various points in the midcentury. It also helps to explain why the ministry's initial steps in 1755 to combat French aggression in North America were so widely supported in Britain.

What about concepts of Britain's empire? The majority of midcentury writers, as Wilson has emphasized, accepted that the major purpose of overseas territories was security.[33] It was the colonies and the wealth they generated in the form of trade, together with the ships and seamen they employed, that provided Britain with essential sinews of war. Colonies were created by the metropolitan power to strengthen its trade and international position. This "metrocentric primacy"[34] impeded the emergence of more inclusive concepts of empire. There were important moves in this direction, a process that David Armitage has carefully mapped.[35] But what stands out is how often these moves were the efforts of colonials, colonial administrators, and provincials. The more common notions of empire remained imprecise or, perhaps more accurately, closely framed by notions of commerce, liberty, and the security of the metropolitan power. Thus, Postlethwayt's *Universal Dictionary* did not even include an entry under the term *Empire*. Under the term *Sea English,* he wrote, "That empire has always followed trade."[36]

Because its goals were security and trade, the British empire was also seen as being compatible with the interests of other European states and as a benevolent or positive force in international politics. This allowed Britain to frustrate French hegemonic ambitions and thereby to protect European liberties. It was not an empire of conquest. Calls for imperial expansion were in fact relatively rare and, in most cases, qualified. This is a point that deserves special emphasis in light of Wilson's claims to the contrary.[37] The degree of bellicosity displayed in the late 1730s—when the cry of "seize and hold" was heard in relation to the Spanish American empire—and the late 1750s and early 1760s—when British military capacity appeared almost without limits—can mislead in this context. The resort to war with Spain in 1739 was seen by most people as justified because of the failure to gain satisfaction and security for British traders in the Caribbean through diplomacy; it was a vindication of Britain's supposed naval and maritime supremacy.[38] It was also a response to threats of universal monarchy in Europe and perceptions that the Bourbon powers were winning the peace as measured in terms of the growth of trade. In 1749–50, looking back from the vantage point of the end of the War of the Austrian Succession, Richard Rolt could argue that the Anglo-Spanish war and war in Europe, in which it had quickly become subsumed, were fomented by the French to eliminate British and then Austrian opposition to the French goal of "universal empire."[39] The combined expeditions against Bourbon colonies in the 1750s and early 1760s were also represented as defensive in purpose.[40] Even the retention of Canada at the Peace of Paris (1763) was seen as defensive in purpose, although this was not a view that all contemporaries could accept. Thus, one writer declared:

> To desire the Enemy's whole country, upon no other Principle, but that otherwise you cannot secure your own, is turning the Idea of mere Defence into the most dangerous of all Principles. It is leaving no medium between Safety and Conquest.[41]

Britain was not, in most peoples' eyes, an acquisitive power. As one writer declaimed in 1755, on the eve of the Seven Years' War: "We never disturb our Neighbours with our Intrigues, we never encroach on their Territories, we never exert our Power to distress the weaker."[42]

How do we explain the unwillingness or more simply the failure of contemporaries to embrace imperial expansion as a national goal? Part of the answer we have already encountered—concepts of French power and ambition. Britons could not see past, it appears, their fears about French international goals and the character of the French state. Thus, in the final stages of the Seven Years' War, the debate about what sort of peace Britain should impose on France and Spain was, in essence, a debate about how best to create conditions in which security for Britain and its colonies would exist; most people assumed that France would continue to challenge British interests, or would do so as soon as it was able to. Some writers argued that not even possession of Canada would be sufficient to secure the British colonies in North America; the French must also be expelled from Louisiana.[43] It was also, however, a function of the other specific meanings or potential contemporaries insisted on seeing in Britain's empire in this period. Various terms existed to describe Britain's empire or identity as an international power, but easily the most frequently used and invoked was the notion of the "empire of the seas." We might argue that this was patriotic evasion in so far as it sought to disguise the territorial basis of this empire—the fact that, as Wilson points out, colonies were "crucial to the 'empire of the seas.'"[44] Yet contemporaries did clearly want to see and have Britain's empire portrayed as *sui generis,* as lacking classical or historical precedents and contemporary parallels. Classical precedents were after all a source of anxiety rather than reassurance.[45] The contemporary Spanish and French imperiums were cruel and ignoble; by contrast, British military power and heroes were marked by their humanity, as visual images of these produced in the final stages of and after the Seven Years' War sought to suggest.[46] As a maritime empire, Britain's empire was also dedicated to trade. Trade was, or could be pictured, as a benign, pacific force; it emphasized interdependency and mutual advantage.[47] Again, we could argue that this was ideological sleight of hand, the purpose of which was to leave unrevealed the exploitation on which much imperial trade rested. For present purposes, however, this is beside the point. At a more mundane level, there remained also the perception that the interests of trade were best served by peace. This was, it is true, a perception that was weakened by fears about French commercial progress, as we saw above; it was also discredited to some extent through its close association with Sir Robert Walpole and his supposedly pusillanimous foreign policy in the later 1730s. But it remained a view that had enduring force, and for good reason.[48] War may, as during the later stage of the War of the Austrian Succession and even more from 1758 in the Seven Years' War, have created new markets and destroyed the trade of foreign competitors, but it also brought merchants uncertainty and usually additional burdens, in the form of the threat from enemy privateers, taxes, higher insurance rates, embargoes on trade, and impressment.[49] In the Seven Years' War, French privateers seriously disrupted the Bristol Atlantic trade—this was a contributory factor in the rise of Liverpool to preeminence in that sphere in the later eighteenth century, and caused significant problems for Scottish merchants on both coasts.[50] In 1744–45, Britain suffered a trade recession, with the '45 proving very disruptive to commerce (and economic activity in general), especially in Scotland.

Finally, there was also the lingering perception that even the existing British colonies could be a potential source of weakness to the metropolitan power. It was an argument that appears to have been difficult to undermine completely, despite repeated reiterations in this period of the contribution of especially the rising North American colonies to British great power status. The crux of the matter was population, in particular the possibility that the colonies were a drain on population. Before the 1770s, the notion that population size was the principal determinant of national wealth and strength was axiomatic.[51] Against this background, it was easy to portray the colonies as a danger to Britain. It was a perception that Josiah Child had sought to dismiss in 1692, with the publication of his *A Discourse Concerning Plantations,* a tract that appeared in at least five separate editions during the first half of the century, the latest one appearing in 1751.[52] But it continued to resurface in debate. Thus, one colonial writer observed in 1757: "Many . . . seem to pay little regard to the Colonies in any respect, and look upon them only as a drain of people out of the nation, that might be more useful at home perhaps by which this nation may be exhausted of its people."[53] Demographic trends in the midcentury, or, more accurately, perceptions of these, may have only added to the concern. As is well known, the 1750s saw the first of two waves of publications in the eighteenth century on the population question.[54] Common to this first wave was the view that Britain's population was declining. It was a perception that only started to be eroded in the 1770s and 1780s.

The population question was part of a broader debate about the condition of society in this period, which focused on the impact of luxury. As referred to above, and as Wilson has shown very clearly, this debate was another crucial factor shaping attitudes and responses toward war and empire. Indeed, it was the strength of this relationship that was responsible for another facet of contemporary ambivalence about empire and its effects. Just as empire was a source of trade and national power, so it was easily perceived as a powerful source of luxury. Before the 1760s and the rise of the Indian nabob as a figure of popular excoriation, part of this concern focused on the consumption of the products of empire. As one writer complained in 1740: " . . . our Luxury is not confined to Europe; the whole Globe is compassed for it; the East and West Indies must be visited to supply our Pride and Vanity."[55] Others saw the problem in broader terms, picturing empire, and the trade that flowed between its different parts, as a corrupting force that portended the decline and eventual dissolution of the British state and empire. Concern about luxury intensified significantly from the 1740s; it also saw important, subtle shifts in emphasis. Luxury, it was now regularly argued, had spread throughout society, including amongst the lower orders.[56] Thomas Scott wrote in 1757 of "the numerous, repeated well-supported complaints of the vast increase, within a few years, of infidelity, of popery, of enthusiasm [a reference to Methodism], of luxury, in all sorts of vices, in the higher, in the middle and in the *lowest class of our people*" (my emphasis).[57] During the Walpolian period, opposition writers had tended to argue that the ministry and the court promoted luxury to subvert liberty and to facilitate the rise of arbitrary power. Partly because of the failure of Walpole's fall (in 1742) to produce significant political change, from the early 1740s the source of luxury was increasingly located in society, not in the corrupt machinations of Whig politicians; it was also linked, ever more insistently, to Britain's fortunes overseas. Luxury was depicted as weakening society and undermining the capacity of the British to resist the encroaching threat from across the Channel. The virtues and capacities that had made Britain a military power to be reckoned with—patriotism, public virtue, courage—were being destroyed.[58] The natural leaders of society were abdicating their proper social role in embodying and promoting, through their conduct, such qualities; in their place had emerged the "modern man of Fashion," half man, half woman, whose indulgence in frivolous, fashionable pursuits, and whose preoccupation with dress threatened to undermine natural and essential distinctions in society. John Brown, the Newcastle vicar, described the army as having become a "school, not of Honour, but of Effeminacy" governed by officers preoccupied with "Dress, Cards and Tea."[59] It was the misfortune of Admiral Byng—widely (but unfairly) blamed for the loss of Minorca to the French in 1756—to become a symbol of "unnatural" elite manners, and a focus for the fears and anxieties that these aroused.[60]

From a domestic perspective, therefore, the Seven Years' War was a fight to recover national virtue as much as it was a war to protect Britain's empire. In this context, however, it was war rather than empire that acted as the principal focus for these emotions and currents. This is something that Marie Peters has recently indicated in her examination of the attitudes and ideas of Pitt the Elder toward empire and imperial issues. As she writes:

It was bellicosity against France and Spain, rather than any particular response to their concern about commerce and colonies, that linked Pitt most strongly to the urban patriots and their commercial imperialism. But bellicosity also had a broader appeal . . . continental causes and continental heroes were . . . widely acknowledged and celebrated—the plight of Maria Theresa as well as the exploits of Admiral Vernon in the 1740s, Frederick the Great, Prince Ferdinand, and Marquess of Granby more than any admiral and at least as much as General Wolfe in the 1750s. Like Pitt's, popular bellicosity encompassed more than imperialism.[61]

The lionization of military heroes, such as Wolfe, and the condemnation of supposed villains or cowards, like Byng or Lord George Sackville (the "coward of Minden"), alert us to another set of concerns with which war and empire became inextricably intertwined in this period. These were ideas and images of glory and national honor. May 20, 1756, the day on which Byng failed to engage the French fleet under the Duc de Richelieu in the Mediterranean, was, as one writer put it, "a Day fatal to the naval Glory of the British nation."[62] Such emphases were, in turn, an ideological expression of a growing perception and attachment to Britain's great power status. Invoking a glorious past of martial valor and victory was commonplace in the 1750s. The frequency with which Elizabethan naval exploits were recalled in the context of demands for war against Spain in the later 1730s has been much remarked upon.[63] Past victories on land against the French—Agincourt, Crecy—were also urged upon contemporaries as images of a glorious past that should not be betrayed in the present. As has been suggested elsewhere, these facets of debate and feeling need to be seen in terms of a burgeoning nationalist sentiment, which defined itself in terms of threats from abroad and from within British society and politics and which was in part a response to the experience of protracted war and heightened international rivalry.[64] More relevantly in the present context, it perhaps also begins to tell us something rather significant about the social foundations and meanings of political debate in this period. Britain's overseas expansion and activities overseas were depicted as often in terms of concepts such as glory as in terms of commercial gain. As Philip Lawson has written, "Explanations of British advance overseas had to be tempered with nobler concerns and more acceptable imagery."[65] Attitudes toward trade and merchants may have become more favorable in the midcentury, but they retained an essential ambivalence.[66]

Debates about luxury and notions of glory and courage were conducted not only in the press but also through large numbers of sermons. Wilson tends to push religion to the margins of contemporary public debate. The press does provide some support for such a view, since it rarely tackled religious topics, in some cases because they were too controversial, in others because readers wanted less serious reading. Through the pulpit, however, clergymen and ministers had plenty to say about luxury (not surprisingly) and its relationship to national destiny and war, as well as repeated opportunities on which to say it. During nearly every year of war in the midcentury, as at other times in the eighteenth century, at least one day was designated by royal proclamation as a day of general public fasting. In Scotland, the general session of the established kirk also called separate fast days, as did the secession churches.[67] On these days, clergymen and ministers clearly did not speak with one voice—there were important differences in what they had to say depending on political and religious persuasions—but on the matter(s) of war they displayed remarkable unanimity.[68]

War, they told their flocks, was one of the instruments with which God punished the sinful and the wicked; it was a special sphere for the intervention of providence. The unpredictability of war was emphasized in many sermons, underlining the role of providence. "Victory," one minister urged, "doth not always attend the wisest Counsels, nor the best concerted Schemes, nor the greatest Armaments."[69] Because the outcome of war was so uncertain, and because this outcome was directly influenced by God, Britons were urged to reform their errant ways and repent of their sins before it was too late. From one perspective, what was taking place here was a further aspect of a widening of debates about luxury to focus concern more directly on religious virtue and feeling as much as popular morals.[70] The relationship was presented in different ways and with different emphases, and not just in terms of the existence of a moral universe in which God intervened through particular acts of providence to punish vice and immorality in nations. Religion and morality were inseparable; as such, religion was the essential basis of public order and virtue.[71]

Two other prominent themes of fast sermons of this period deserve particular notice. The first is that England was usually portrayed as having been singled out by providence for particular care and concern. This notion of the "elect" nation was deeply embedded in the Protestant reform traditions in England and Scotland, and it continued to reverberate through sermons and indeed "secular" concepts of national identity. Britain was the modern Israel. This carried both a promise and a warning. Just as Britain had been favored in the past with special providences—the Restoration, the Glorious Revolution—so, as had happened to the Israelites, this favor might be withdrawn. Obadiah Hughes sounded the warning very clearly in 1742:

> GOD has made Great Britain very much to resemble his ancient people; and I wish with all my soul we had not made ourselves so much like to them in another respect. I need not tell you, what I mean;

I dare to say, your own thoughts will prevent me, by suggesting the abominable immorality and profaneness, which reigns among us; our base ingratitude both to GOD and men; our perverse restlessness, and constant murmurings, notwithstanding the many blessings we enjoy, and though we are the happiest nation under heaven, if we knew and valued our mercies.[72]

This notion of an elect nation also influenced views of Britain's international role in fast sermons. Clergymen tended, hardly surprisingly, to advance notions of just war. (This is the second prominent theme.) These notions had several strands, but the most important was the emphasis on defensive war or wars to assert national rights. The fact that Britain's main enemies were Catholic powers also enabled many clergymen to import religious conceptions of international rivalry—international Catholicism seeking to destroy Protestantism—back into public debate.[73] In the Seven Years' War, the "diplomatic revolution" of 1756 gave such notions greater plausibility.

How seriously should we take such views, and how influential were they? Such questions are not easily answered. Clergymen certainly wrote and spoke as if their influence and the influence of religion were in sharp decline, although these were hardly new themes. James Hervey, rector of Weston-Flavell in Northamptonshire, asked, "Is not religion, vital religion, very much upon the decline, even among the serious?"[74] Indeed, it was this perception that provoked some preachers to take such advantage of fast days as they could, leading the *Critical Review* to discuss the "modern method" of sermonizing "ad captum vulgus."[75] The modern historian of the reaction to the Lisbon earthquake in 1755, which produced a torrent of sermonizing, tends to the view that the effects of these sermons, and the mood and anxieties they expressed, were strictly temporary, although they were recalled on subsequent fast days.[76] On the other hand, belief in providence was pervasive, among all sections of society from moderate ministers of the Church of Scotland, increasingly confident proponents of polite and Enlightened values, to those who continued to adhere to more strongly supernatural forms of Christianity, evangelical members of the Kirk, the Scottish secession churches, Methodists, and other evangelical elements within the Church of England. Supernaturalist beliefs also seem to have remained powerfully present among the populace, as J. C. D. Clark has emphasized in recent years.[77] James Burgh's powerful restatement of the role of providence in war following the Jacobite Rebellion of 1745–46, *Britain's Remembrancer, or the Danger not Over* (1746), was widely read, and it inspired a wider call for the reformation of manners in the later 1740s.[78] In 1746, Parliament gave some support to this call, passing the Profane Oaths Act, the preamble to which made explicit reference to the recent signs of divine disfavor with the nation.[79] In Scotland, the passage of this act prompted a move to institute a program of moral renewal in the Church of Scotland, which began in the West, a stronghold of the popular clergy and evangelicalism in the Kirk.[80] In 1750, following the London earthquakes, Bishop Sherlock's letter to his clergy and diocese, containing a further warning about the dangers of incurring divine disfavor and calling for moral reform, sold 10,000 copies in two days.[81] In 1755, following the much more dramatic effects of the Lisbon earthquake, John Wesley's jeremiad *Serious Thoughts occasion'd by the Late Earthquake at Lisbon* was published in at least six editions.[82] Fast days were observed throughout Britain. The fast day called in February 1756 to mark the Lisbon earthquake and the start of the Seven Years' War provoked the *London Magazine* to remark: "The public fast was observed with a becoming decency by all ranks of people. The Churches and meeting houses were thronged and there was, in appearance, an entire cessation from business throughout the city and suburbs, and all over the kingdom." Wesley commented in his journal, with more than a modicum of satisfaction: "The fast day was a glorious day such as London has scarce seen since the Restoration. Every church in the City was more than full and a solemn seriousness sat on every face."[83] The failure of a small number of Quaker shopkeepers to mark the day provoked a minor riot in the capital and a lively debate in the press about whether nonobservance of the day by the Quakers was justified by their religious beliefs.[84] In Cupar, Fife, members of one of the secession churches were prosecuted in the early 1740s for not participating in a day of national fasting.[85]

However, even more suggestive is the diary of Thomas Turner, the Sussex shopkeeper. Turner was an Anglican who embodied many of the ambivalences in contemporary reactions of trade and empire and the wider culture in which they played a growing role in the eighteenth century. He appears to have been a regular reader of the *London Gazette,* the official journal of record produced by an official in the secretary of state's department and avidly read during wartime, and his local provincial paper, the *Sussex Weekly Advertiser.* He also read the *London Magazine,* a leading monthly periodical that contained much information and comment on war and empire, including a growing number of maps and plans in the 1750s, and the influential opposition essay paper, the *Monitor.*[86] He followed closely the major events of the Seven Years' War and attended a number of celebrations of military victories hosted by the steward of the nearby estate of Halland, owned by the Duke of Newcastle.[87] He was persistently aware of his own moral shortcomings, although this did not stop him from drinking heavily on frequent occasions, gambling, or attending cricket matches. His desire, however, to reform his character and morals was equally marked; usually the activities were closely linked. He also saw his personal conduct and morals in the wider political context of the contemporary debate about luxury and its effects. It is in these different contexts that his comments on how local fast days were observed take on additional significance. On February 16, 1759, Turner recorded his thoughts, amid the growing evidence of British military supremacy in the later stages of the Seven Years' War:

> The fast in this place [East Hoathly] hath seemingly been kept with great strictness and, I hope, with a sincere and unaffected piety, our church in the morning being crowded with a numerous audience. God grant that we may every one of us reform our wicked ways and that every Briton may inspire his neighbour with a sense of religion and fear of God by his own example. For I think no nation had ever greater occasion to adore the Almighty Disposer of all events than Albion, whose forces meet with success in almost all quarters of the world, and where plenty once more rears her pleasing aspect.[88]

It is the currency of views such as Turner's that help further to explain the marked volatility of contemporary responses to war. It also helps us to understand why military setbacks in this period, such as the loss of Minorca, could trigger such upsurges of gloom and despondency, as well as alarm and anger.

People throughout Britain watched the shifting conditions and the course of war and international rivalry during the mid-eighteenth century. Interest in empire was one aspect of this; indeed, in a very direct sense, it grew from it. Questions of international power and strategy dominated perceptions and portrayals of empire; visions of advancing wealth and prosperity tended to be secondary to this. For most people, the great power rivalry with France appears to have been at the forefront of their concerns. This rivalry provided the main impetus behind attempts to think about or imagine empire, certainly for those who did not have a direct interest in the topic. One writer declared in 1757 that "however important . . . our concerns in America may be, it must be owned that the whole nation has been very neglectful of them, 'till the French opened our eyes about them."[89] The struggle against France continued to be seen as an essentially European conflict, albeit one that acquired an increasingly important imperial dimension.

The intensity of contemporary preoccupations with French aims and ambition helps us to understand why concern about empire, trade, and the colonies was so broadly based. Hostility toward France was the preserve of no single social, political, or religious group. This is not to say, as others have done, that individuals and groups among the urban middling ranks were not able, against this background, to stake stronger claims for political recognition and respectability. Partly under the impact of anxieties about the changing scope and nature of international rivalries, the ambit of patriotism was stretched and redefined in ways that had special relevance to men (and some women) of middling status, particularly merchants.[90] But care is needed when assessing the significance of this. It was one of the principal strengths of the patriotism that the French threat helped to stimulate that it provided a language that could accommodate the perceptions and aspirations of diverse social groups, both within and beyond the middling ranks. This is best seen in terms of incorporation rather than a strong or overt challenge to traditional political elites and political identities. The middling ranks were, after all, usually portrayed as a group that included the gentry and sometimes farmers; they were not exclusively urban. Older, traditional meanings continued to resonate strongly in patriotic language, as the repeated emphases on glory and national honor reveals.

Despite surges of enthusiasm for colonial acquisitions, territorial empire also seems to have meant little to contemporaries. Overseas possessions were valued primarily because of what they could contribute to British wealth and strength; they were one, and only one, manifestation of Britain's great power status. Most Britons resisted seeing, or perhaps simply could not see, their nation as an acquisitive, expansionist power. Discussion about the territorial aspects of empire was usually framed in terms of "security" or "conservation."[91] Again this may have verged on self-deception, but it is best explained in terms of the depth of concern about French aims and capability.

Concern about empire was, therefore, both more narrow and more general than Wilson implies. Responses to empire and imperial issues were characterized by volatility, ambivalence, and their often contradictory nature. This seems best explained in terms of the diverse political, ideological, and religious influences underpinning these responses. There is a sense in which these influences existed in a dynamic tension, with a shift in circumstances changing, often in very dramatic ways, the balance between them. There was, in sum, an intrinsic and fundamental instability about feelings toward and provoked by empire in the mid-eighteenth century, an instability that stemmed from the complex attitudes and emotions that shaped Britons' sense of their nation as a great power, a nation that was under direct and urgent challenge from France, a more powerful, populous state seemingly committed to Britain's elimination as a major power.

Finally, looking ahead very briefly to the next major war of the century involving Britain and its colonies—the War of American Independence—we can see important continuities with the middle of the century. Wilson wishes to see the conflict with the colonies as marking a sharp break in this context, as a period when the "libertarian, imperial dream" fragmented and collapsed.[92] Yet whatever differences did exist—notably in the way in which the threat to liberty was perceived—the similarities remain striking. The contemporary sense of an imperial crisis in the later 1770s and early 1780s bears more than a superficial resemblance to the crisis of the mid-1750s. Again, the fate of empire became a focus for an array of fears, fears that had less to do with empire per se than with Britain, its position as a great power, and the condition of society and politics. And again, it was the wider international context—the struggle against the Bourbon powers, and especially France—that was as relevant as the imperial one. Or, to put it another way, the imperial dimension was an intrinsic part, or rapidly became such, of unfolding great power rivalry. For many it was the contrast with Britain's standing at the end of the previous war that was so disturbing and difficult to comprehend and that induced them to look inwards for causes—to dysfunctions in the political system, to declining public spirit, to luxury and irreligion. Moreover, despite the loss of the colonies, elements of the old views of empire survived and pointed one of the potential ways forward to a revival of national confidence. The most important of these was the notion of the "empire of the seas." Rodney's naval victory at the Battle of the Saints in 1782 helped to restore some confidence in this empire. As "Cincinnatus" wrote in the *Public Advertiser,* "That he [Rodney] has restored to this nation the declining empire of the sea, no one can possibly deny."[93] The renewed upswing of the Atlantic economy in the 1780s and, perhaps even more, the shift in attention Eastwards helped to restore hope in Britain's commercial prospects. As far as the East was concerned, this meant India and, further afield, China, Malaya, and the East Indies. Just as great hopes had been expressed about Georgia and Nova Scotia earlier in the century, so the prospect of opening up the Pacific aroused equally unrealistic expectations. The Highland Society, meanwhile, advocated further development of the Highlands through the exploitation of the fisheries as the means to support Britain's traditional maritime power and empire after 1783, an idea that again had been strongly present in the middle of the century.[94] As Peter Marshall has shown, newer concepts of empire started to develop alongside older ones in respect to India in the early 1790s, concepts that moved away from the traditional emphasis on purely maritime empire.[95] What lay behind this is beyond the scope of this chapter. The point to be made here is that these newer concepts emerged alongside but did not submerge the older ones.[96]

Notes

1. For a lucid overview of the course of war and rivalry between Britain and its enemies in this period, see Bruce Lenman, *Britain's Colonial Wars, 1688–1783* (Harlow: Longman, 2001).

2. For Pitt's rationalization of his altered stance toward Germany from 1757, see Marie Peters, *The Elder Pitt* (Harlow: Longman, 1998), 140–42.

3. See David Armitage, *The Ideological Origins of the British Empire* (Cambridge: Cambridge University Press, 2000); Eliga H. Gould, *The Persistence of Empire: British Political Culture in the Age of the American Revolution* (Chapel Hill: University of North Carolina Press, 2000); David Milobar, "Aboriginal Peoples and the British Press, 1720–1763," in Stephen Taylor, Richard Connors, and Clyve Jones, eds., *Hanoverian Britain and Empire: Essays in Memory of Philip Lawson* (Woodbridge: Boydell and Brewer, 1998), 65–81; Gerald Jordan and Nicholas Rogers, "Admirals as Heroes: Patriotism and Liberty in Hanoverian England," *Journal of British Studies* 28 (1989), 210–24; Nicholas Rogers, *Whigs and Cities: Popular Politics in the Age of Walpole and Pitt* (Oxford: Oxford University Press, 1989), esp. 374–77; Philip Lawson, "'The Irishman's Prize': Views of Canada from the British Press, 1760–1774," *Historical Journal* 28 (1985): 575–96; Philip Lawson, "'Arts and Empire Equally Extend': Tradition, Prejudice, and Assumption in the Eighteenth-Century Press Coverage of Empire," in Karl Schweizer and Jeremy Black, eds., *Politics and the Press in Hanoverian Britain* (Lewiston, N.Y.: Edwin Mellen Press, 1989); Peter Marshall, "The Eighteenth-Century Empire," in Jeremy Black, ed., *British Politics and Society from Walpole to Pitt, 1742–1789* (Basingstoke: Macmillan, 1990), 177–200; J. P. Thomas, "The British Empire and the Press, 1763–74" (D.Phil. thesis, Oxford University, 1982); Kathleen Wilson, "Empire, Trade, and Popular Politics in Mid-Hanoverian Britain: The Case of Admiral Vernon," *Past and Present* 121 (1988): 79–109; Kathleen Wilson, "'Empire of Virtue': The Imperial Project and Hanoverian Culture, ca. 1720–1785," in Lawrence Stone, ed., *An Imperial State at War: Britain from 1689 to 1815* (London: Routledge, 1994), 128–64; Kathleen Wilson, *The Sense of the People: Politics, Culture, and Imperialism in England, 1715–1785* (Cambridge: Cambridge University Press, 1995); Kathleen Wilson, "The Good, the Bad, and the Impotent: Imperialism and the Politics of Identity in Georgian England," in Ann Bermingham and John Brewer,

eds., *The Consumption of Culture, 1600–1800: Image, Object, Text* (London: Routledge, 1995), 237–62.

4. There is no adequate summary of the evidence for this, but see my *Politics and the Nation: Britain in the Mid-Eighteenth Century* (Oxford: Oxford University Press, 2002), chap. 3.

5. See, inter alia, Jeremy Black, *The English Press in the Eighteenth Century* (Aldershot: Gregg Revivals, 1987); Hannah Barker, *Newspapers, Politics, and English Society, 1695–1855* (Harlow: Longman, 2000); Robert Munter, *The History of the Irish Newspaper, 1685–1760* (Cambridge: Cambridge University Press, 1967); Marie Peters, *Pitt and Popularity: The Patriotic Minister and Public Opinion during the Seven Years' War* (Oxford: Oxford University Press, 1980); Robert Harris, *A Patriot Press: National Politics and the London Press in the 1740s* (Oxford: Oxford University Press, 1993); G. E. Cranfield, *The Development of the Provincial Newspaper, 1700–1760* (Cambridge: Cambridge University Press, 1962). There is no modern study of the eighteenth-century Scottish press, but see M. E. Craig, *The Scottish Periodical Press, 1750–1789* (Edinburgh, 1931). The 1740s and 1750s saw considerable growth in the Scottish newspaper press, with two papers being established in Glasgow, two in Aberdeen (although one of these was short-lived), and several in Edinburgh, in addition to the already well established *Edinburgh Evening Courant* and *Caledonian Mercury*. In addition, 1739 saw the first issue of the successful monthly *Scots Magazine*.

6. Public Record Office, Kew, T1/431/103.

7. At one point, Wilson writes that the slogan of empire in this period could have been "Production at Home, Acquisition Abroad" ("The Good, the Bad, and the Impotent," 239). See also Wilson, *Sense of the People*, 158–60.

8. Wilson, *Sense of the People*, 26.

9. See, e.g., Linda Colley, *Britons: Forging the Nation, 1707–1837* (New Haven: Yale University Press, 1992); Eric Richards, "Scotland and the Uses of the Atlantic Empire," in Bernard Bailyn and Philip D. Morgan, eds., *Strangers within the Realm: Cultural Margins of the First British Empire* (Chapel Hill: University of North Carolina Press, 1991), 67–114; P. J. Marshall, "Empire and Opportunity in Britain, 1762–1783," *Transactions of the Royal Historical Society*, 6th ser., 5 (1995): 111–28.

10. Wilson, "The Good, the Bad, and the Impotent," 242; idem., "Empire of Virtue," 133.

11. Wilson, "Empire of Virtue," 154. In the same chapter, she writes that "empire was not an end in itself in the eighteenth century" (155).

12. Wilson, *Sense of the People*, 189.

13. Neil McKendrick et al., *The Birth of a Consumer Society: The Commercialization of Eighteenth-Century England* (London: Europa, 1982); John Brewer and Roy Porter, eds., *Consumption and the World of Goods* (London: Routledge, 1993); Paul Langford, *A Polite and Commercial People: England, 1727–1783* (Oxford: Oxford University Press, 1989), 61–121; T. H. Breen, "Baubles of Britain: The

American and Consumer Revolutions of the Eighteenth Century," *Past and Present* 119 (1988): 73–104.

14. See, e.g., George Burrington, *Seasonable Considerations on the Expediency of a War with France* (1743); Sir William Keith, *The History of the British Plantations in America* (1738); *A Miscellaneous Essay Concerning the Courses Pursued by Great Britain in the Affairs of Her Colonies* (1755).

15. *A Sermon Preach'd before the House of Lords in the Abby-Church of Westminster, on Wednesday, January 9th, 1739 . . . By Thomas, Lord Bishop of Norwich* (1739), 11–12.

16. Otis Little, *State of Trade in the Northern Colonies Considered* (London, 1748), 28.

17. Ibid., 15–7, 33, 38–40.

18. *Gentleman's Magazine* 15 (1750): 263–64.

19. Ibid., 42.

20. *Old England Journal,* September 14, 1751.

21. See Jeremy Black, *Natural and Necessary Enemies: Anglo-French Relations in the Eighteenth Century* (London: Duckworth, 1986), 36–63.

22. *Critical Review* 14 (1756): 265–66.

23. See S. C. A. Pincus, "Popery, Trade, and Universal Monarchy: The Ideological Context of the Outbreak of the Second Dutch War," *English Historical Review* 107 (1992): 1–29; John Robertson, ed., *A Union for Empire: Political Thought and the Union of 1707* (Cambridge: Cambridge University Press, 1995).

24. See the discussion in Jeremy Black's introduction to his *Origins of War in Early Modern Europe* (Edinburgh: John Donald, 1987), 1–27.

25. Harris, *Patriot Press,* 218–53.

26. William Cobbett and J. Wright, eds., *The Parliamentary History of England from the Earliest Period to the Year 1803,* vol. 14 (1813), 831; *Plans and Proposals Transmitted to the Committee on the British Fishery. By Several Hands* (1758), 58. Contemporary concern was well merited. Between 1746 and 1755, France and Spain launched warships with a total displacement of around 250,000 tons, while Britain launched only around 90,000 tons. See Jan Glete, *Navies and Nations: Warships, Navies, and State Building in Europe and America, 1550–1860* (Stockholm: Almqvist and Wiksell International, 1993). Because of this, Britain lost its previous naval superiority over the two Bourbon powers. It was only the fact that Spain failed to enter the Seven Years' War until 1761 that meant that this did not affect British military efforts more seriously.

27. For details of this hostility, see Black, *Natural and Necessary Enemies,* 51–59.

28. Marie Peters, "The Myth of William Pitt, Earl of Chatham, Great Imperialist, Part 1: Pitt and Imperial Expansion, 1738–1763," *Journal of Imperial and Commonwealth History* 21 (1993): 55.

29. *Daily Gazetteer,* August 14, 1746.

30. One historian who has noted this, however, is Peter N. Miller. See his *Defin-*

ing the Common Good: Empire, Religion, and Philosophy in Eighteenth-Century Britain (Cambridge: Cambridge University Press, 1994), esp. 167.

31. Malachy Postlethwayt, Great Britain's True System (1757); Malachy Postlethwayt, Britain's Commercial Interest Explained and Improved (1757). Two other contemporary writers who had similar concerns were Henry McCulloh and Josiah Tucker. See McCulloh, The Wisdom and Policy of the French in the Construction of their Great Offices so as best to answer the Purposes of Extending their Trade and Commerce (1755) and Tucker, An Essay on the Advantages and Disadvantages which respectively attend France and Great Britain, with regard to Trade (1755). See also the anonymous Reflections on Various Subjects Relating to Arts and Commerce (1752), esp. 67–74.

32. Great Britain's True System, 185, 247, 257–58, 270–71.

33. Wilson, "The Good, the Bad, and the Impotent," 239.

34. Miller, Defining the Common Good, 167.

35. Armitage, Ideological Origins, chap. 7.

36. Quoted in Miller, Defining the Common Good, 163.

37. Wilson is equivocal on this point, noting in one place, "British commentators had long insisted that Britain's greatness as an imperial nation lay in not seeking conquest, but having conquest thrust upon her" (Wilson, "The Good, the Bad, and the Impotent," 253).

38. Most commentators on the Spanish war were agreed that the war was made necessary by the failure of negotiation and the ill will of the Spanish court. Representative in this context was the Country Journal, or the Craftsman, which declared on December 8, 1739: "A Nation, which subsists in Trade, and is over-loaded with Taxes, cannot be suppos'd to chuse and wantonly enter into a War; which, however successfully carried on, must be attended with many and great Inconveniences. Necessity and self defence have forc'd us into it." Most commentators also argued that the goal of the war was security of trade and navigation. Few were specific about how this was to be achieved, although some, such as the author of Some Useful Observations on the Consequences of War with Spain (1738), advocated the seizure of Spanish territories in the Caribbean. Another favored tactic was seizure of the Spanish treasure fleets: Ministerial Prejudices in Favour of the Convention, Examin'd and Answer'd (1739), 21–22.

39. Richard Rolt, An Impartial Representation of the Conduct of the Several Powers of Europe, Engaged in the Late General War, 4 vols. (1749–50), 1:xiii, quoted in Armitage, Ideological Origins, 184–85.

40. See, e.g., A Miscellaneous Essay Concerning the Courses Pursued by Great Britain in the Affair of Her Colonies (1755); Some very Material and very Important Remarks Concerning the Present Situation of Affairs between Great Britain, France, and Spain (1755); A Letter to the Right Honourable the Earl of B——, on a Late Important Resignation (1761), 5; A Letter from a Member of the Honourable House of Commons, on the Present Important Crisis of National Affairs (1762); An Appeal to Knowledge; or, Candid Discussion of the Preliminaries of Peace (1763).

41. *Remarks on the Letter Addressed to Two Great Men: In a Letter to the Author of that Piece* (1760), 13.

42. *Jackson's Oxford Journal,* October 11, 1755.

43. See, e.g., *Reflections on the Present Posture of our Affairs in North America* (1760).

44. Wilson, "Empire of Virtue," 132.

45. See Miller, *Defining the Common Good,* chap. 2.

46. See Francis Hayman's four cavasses, *The Triumph of Britannia, The Surrender of Montreal to General Amherst, Lord Clive Receiving the Homage of the Nabob,* and *Britannia Distributing Laurels to the Victorious Generals,* painted for Vauxhall Gardens between 1760 and 1764. The paintings were designed as monuments to British glory in the recent war. As Brian Allen has noted, "They were the first genuinely popular history paintings and the public was eager to welcome pictures glorifying their contemporary history." Brian Allen, *Francis Hayman* (New Haven: Yale University Press, 1987), 70. Hayman's picture of Amherst depicted him feeding his captives who had endured weeks of siege. A parallel was explicitly drawn with great generals of antiquity. As Allen remarks, "The British public were to be left in no doubt about the validity and wisdom of British rule in the North American continent" (67). On a stone in one corner of the picture was this inscription:

POWER EXERTED,
CONQUEST OBTAINED,
MERCY SHOWN
MDCCLX.

47. On this, see Howard D. Weinbrot, *Britannia's Issue: The Rise of British Literature from Dryden to Ossian* (Cambridge: Cambridge University Press, 1993), esp. 257–70.

48. See P. J. Marshall, "'Cornwallis Triumphant': War in India and the British Public in the Late Eighteenth Century," in Lawrence Freedman, Paul M. Hayes, and Robert O'Neill, eds., *War, Strategy, and International Politics: Essays in Honour of Sir Michael Howard* (Oxford: Oxford University Press, 1992), esp. 65–66. The importance of pacific forms of patriotism in eighteenth-century Britain has tended to be overlooked in recent years, but its exponents were an influential voice in public debate, especially in the aftermath of major wars.

49. See Richard Grasby, *The Business Community of Seventeenth-Century England* (Cambridge: Cambridge University Press, 1995), 211–13, for the merchants' ambivalent response to war in the later seventeenth century. In the mid-eighteenth century, merchants were prepared to support war if they saw it as being in their interest; they were not prepared, however, to shoulder the burden of supporting Britain's war effort if this adversely affected these interests, as the issue of impressment illustrates very clearly. They were also very quick to complain if they thought the British navy was failing to offer adequate protection against attacks from enemy privateers. The volume of Spanish attacks on British merchant shipping between

1739 and 1741 created intense mercantile opposition to Walpole in the final stages of his ministry.

50. Kenneth Morgan, *Bristol and the Atlantic Trade in the Eighteenth Century* (Cambridge: Cambridge University Press, 1993), 20–21; T. M. Devine, "The Golden Age of Tobacco," in T. M. Devine and Gordon Jackson, eds., *Glasgow*, vol. 1, *Beginnings to 1830* (Manchester: Manchester University Press, 1995), 145.

51. Donna T. Andrew, *Philanthropy and Police: London Charity in the Eighteenth Century* (Princeton, N.J.: Princeton University Press, 1989), 22–25.

52. R. T. Cornish, "A Vision of Empire: The Development of British Opinion Regarding the American Colonies, 1730–1770" (Ph.D. thesis, London, 1987), 35.

53. John Mitchell, *The Contest in America between Great Britain and France* (1757), v.

54. See D. V. Glass, *Numbering the People: The Eighteenth-Century Population Controversy and the Development of Census and Vital Statistics in Britain* (Farnborough: D. C. Heath, 1973).

55. *An Enquiry into the Melancholy Circumstances of Great Britain* (1740?), 9.

56. See the comments in Nicholas Rogers, "Confronting the Crime Wave: The Debate over Social Reform and Regulation, 1749–1753," in Lee Davison et al., eds., *Stilling the Grumbling Hive: The Response to Social and Economic Problems in England, 1689–1750* (Stroud: Alan Sutton, 1992), 77–98.

57. Quoted in D. Napthine and W. A. Speck, "Clergymen and Conflict," in W. J. Shiels, ed., *Studies in Church History* (Oxford: Basil Blackwell, 1983), 239.

58. For a clear discussion of the relationship of these values to the ways in which war and actions in war were perceived and portrayed, see Gordon S. Wood, *The Radicalism of the American Revolution* (New York: Vintage Books, 1992), 100–109.

59. John Brown, *Estimate of the Manners and Principles of the Times* (1757), quoted in Philip Carter, *Men and the Emergence of Polite Society: Britain, 1660–1800* (Harlow: Longman, 2001), 131.

60. See Nicholas Rogers, *Crowds, Culture, and Politics in Georgian Britain* (Oxford: Oxford University Press, 1998), 59–64.

61. Peters, "The Myth of William Pitt," 55.

62. *An Earnest Address to the People of Great Britain and Ireland: Occasioned by the Dismission of William Pitt, Esq.* (1761), 11.

63. See Christine Gerrard, *The Patriot Opposition to Walpole: Politics, Poetry, and National Myth, 1725–1742* (Oxford: Oxford University Press, 1994), chap. 6.

64. See Colley, *Britons*, chap. 2; Gerald Newman, *The Rise of English Nationalism: A Cultural History, 1740–1830* (Basingstoke: Macmillan, 1987).

65. Lawson, "Arts and Empire Equally Extend," 140.

66. As Dror Wahrman has recently emphasized, at the heart of "Country rhetoric" remained a "deep," even "insurmountable" tension with commerce. Dror Wahrman, *Imagining the Middle Class: The Political Representation of Class in Britain, ca. 1780–1840* (Cambridge: Cambridge University Press, 1995), 70.

67. The secession churches believed in a strict separation between church and state. For this reason, they refused to recognize national days of fasting called by the state or the established church, instead calling their own days of fasting.

68. This has also been noted by Francois Deconnick-Brossard in her article "The Churches and the '45," in Shiels, ed., *Studies in Church History*, 253.

69. *A Sermon Preached in the Parish Church of St Mary, Lambeth, Upon April 11, 1744 . . . By John Denne, DD, Rector of the said Parish, and Archdeacon of Rochester* (1744), 13.

70. See the comments in Bob Harris, "The *London Evening Post* and Mid-Eighteenth-Century British Politics," *English Historical Review* 110 (1995): 1132–56.

71. See, e.g., William Byass, *A Sermon Preach'd in the Parish Churches of Storrington and Parham in Sussex, On Friday, Feb 6, 1756* (1756), esp. 19–20; Thomas Sherlock, *Nine Sermons Preached in the Parish of St James, Westminster, On Occasion of the Late War and Rebellion* (1758); James Snowdon, *The Duty of Fasting with its Appendages briefly considered. A Sermon preached at the Parish Church of St Peter, in the East, in Oxford, on Friday, February 11, 1757* (1757), 22–23.

72. *Obedience of God the best security against our Enemies: A Fast Sermon preached in Maid Lane, in Southwark, November 10, 1742. By Obadiah Hughes* (1742), 31.

73. See, e.g., T. Richards, *National Repentance urged from the Prospect of National Judgements. A Sermon Preach'd at the Parish Church of All Saints in Northampton, on February 6, 1756* (1756), 16–17.

74. *The Time of Danger, and the Means of Safety: To Which Is Added the Way of Holiness* (1757), quoted in the *Critical Review* 4 (1757): 196.

75. *Critical Review* 4 (1757): 199.

76. T. D. Kendrick, *The Lisbon Earthquake* (London: Methuen, 1956), 163.

77. J. C. D. Clark, *English Society, 1688–1832: Ideology, Social Structure, and Political Practice during the Ancien Regime* (Cambridge: Cambridge University Press, 1985), 165–71.

78. Burgh later claimed that the pamphlet had gone through between six and eight editions in London and sold between 10,000 and 12,000 copies in Scotland and Ireland. Burgh, *Youth's Friendly Monitor* (1754), iv.

79. *Journals of the House of Commons* 25 (1745–50): 49.

80. National Archives of Scotland, Edinburgh, CH2/464/3 (Register of the Synod of Glasgow and Air), fo. 363; CH2/1717/11 (Records of the Presbytery of Glasgow), 28 October 1746; CH1/3/24 (Records of the Commission of the General Assembly, 1739–48), fos. 439, 444; CH1/1/45 (Records of the General Assembly), fos. 78, 79, 444.

81. Kendrick, *Lisbon Earthquake*, 20.

82. Ibid., 156. The Eighteenth Century Short Title Catalogue contains around forty published fast sermons from February 6, 1756.

83. *The Works of John Wesley,* vol. 21, *Journals and Diaries IV (1755–65)*, ed. W. R. Ward and R. P. Heitzenrater (Nashville, Tenn.: Abingdon Books, 1992), 41.

84. *Public Advertiser,* February 7, 1756. The Quakers were attacked in the opposition weekly essay paper, the *Monitor, or British Freeholder* and defended in the anonymous *Vindication of the Quakers* (1756?).

85. National Archives of Scotland, SC20/5/2, bundle 1744–45.

86. *The Diary of Thomas Turner, 1754–1765,* ed. David Vaisey (Oxford: Oxford University Press, 1984), 347.

87. Ibid., 155–57, 161, 191–92, 194–95, 212.

88. Ibid., 175.

89. Mitchell, *The Contest,* ix.

90. See Colley, *Britons,* 85–98.

91. There were several exceptions, for example, Arthur Dobbs of Carrickfergus and John Campbell, the hack writer on trade and international affairs. For Dobbs, see Desmond Clarke, *Arthur Dobbs, Esq., 1689–1765* (London: Bodley Head, 1958).

92. Wilson, *Sense of the People,* 237–84.

93. *Public Advertiser,* May 30, 1782. For a recent discussion of public and political reactions to this victory, see Stephen Conway, "'A Joy Unknown for Years Past': The American War, Britishness, and the Celebration of Rodney's Victory at the Saints," *History* 86 (2001): 180–99.

94. See Bob Harris, "Patriotic Commerce and National Revival: The Free British Fishery Society and British Politics, ca. 1749–58," *English Historical Review* 114 (1999): 285–313; Bob Harris, "Scotland's Herring Fisheries and the Prosperity of the Nation, ca. 1660–1760," *Scottish Historical Review* 79 (2000): 39–60; Jean Dunlop, *The British Fisheries Society, 1786–1893* (Edinburgh: John Donald, 1978).

95. Marshall, "'Cornwallis Triumphant.'"

96. See also the comments in Armitage, *Ideological Origins,* 194–98.

2

Venus and Mars

Women and the British-American Army in the Seven Years' War

Peter Way

Military history has subconsciously accepted the gendered logic of warfare: that violent contestation is natural, unavoidable, defining of national character, and laudable when done by honorable men. As a result, the role of women in the military has been vitally neglected,[1] as have the ways in which notions of gender have molded camp life and impacted on warfare itself. The army was by definition a male-dominated sphere that valorized aggression in the cause of patriarchal dominance—the dynastic concerns of the king, the lineage issues of the aristocracy, and the class concerns of a hierarchical power structure. Yet warfare is an elemental human activity involving much of society in its production and reproduction. Women and children factor in as more than war's victims, historically having attached themselves to the train pulled by the war machine.

It is as sexual beings that army women are usually considered, the stereotypical camp follower being a prostitute. There is no doubt that many army women did prostitute themselves, the sexual demographics of the military making it essential. However, most women did not join in such practice, being familial and economic beings as much as sexual. Many were wives to soldiers, or at least steady partners, and often had children with them. Whether single or attached, women had to earn their subsistence, and they did this by working for the army as nurses and laundresses, by operating petty businesses such as selling liquor, or by participating in illicit trade in stolen goods. Thus, military life inevitably had domestic and economic dimensions that women had a large role in constructing. Nonetheless, women's mere presence and the sexuality they embodied for men were sparks to conflict, and army officers were right in fearing its consequences among an armed male population, if wrong in attributing most of the blame to female nature. Finally, as with all subordinate people, however much control women exerted over the personal lives, it was outweighed by the public masculine power structure of which the army was an exaggeration. This essay will explore the front line of gender relations in the Seven Years' War, where the martial masculine encountered the auxiliary feminine.

The Patriarchal Army

Classicism provided eighteenth-century women and men with a pantheon of prescriptive role models for their respective sexualities. The Roman god Mars was the apotheosis of masculine spirit, bellicose and bloody, an angry red threat in the dark night. Venus embodied the ideal of women's nature, sexually alluring, desirable and dangerous, a brilliant celestial presence in the early morning sky. These deifications of supposed innate sexual qualities separated man from woman into their ordained orbits, serving men well by closing off the public world of power, military and political, as their preserve, while relegating women to the private worlds of the heart in the home and the church. For those women who questioned this cosmos, a more terrestrial mythic figure was offered as warning: the Amazon. Eschewing the company of all men, except for the base intercourse of conception, these creatures exerted an attraction to women in their physicality and prowess in the public sphere of warfare. But such masquerading as the male came at a cost, captured in the mutilation of that defining part of womanhood, the breast, the right one of which was lopped off to facilitate the Amazon's use of the bow, phallic symbol of masculine power.[2] The Amazon was a transgressive figure, whose straddling of the defining boundary— warlike masculinity and pacific femininity—supplied a cautionary tale meant to reinforce the divide.

Gender models are not fixed, however. In more mundane terms, sexuality was recast in the early modern period as the needs of patriarchy altered. In Britain during the sixteenth to seventeenth centuries, women were seen as sexual creatures with the potential to unman the male through their insatiable desire. This stereotype began to be replaced after 1660, as new notions of gender relations emphasized sexual dichotomy, with men associated with reason and women with "sensibility," a heightened nervous and emotional responsiveness. This model allowed women to be intellectual, imaginative, pleasure-seeking, and morally superior, but conversely it suggested mental and physical inferiority. Women participated in the construction of this ideology, which at least was not as misogynistic and immutable as the older beliefs. But for all the change, women were still ideologically differentiated from men.[3]

Of course, ideology works best on the level of ideals and often breaks down as one descends through the social order.[4] Despite the pressures to conform, plebeian culture found it difficult to maintain a separation of spheres—either of the idealized, neoclassical kind, or of the enlightened dichotomy between male reason/female emotion—as powerful material forces dictated conduct more so than reified models of gender relations. D. E. Underdown argues that changes in the early modern English economy allowed women in some regions to participate more fully in the commercial economy, and that this contributed to a general anxiety about the patriarchal order that was expressed in a pervasive concern with the "scold" and dominant or unfaithful wives. This fear manifested itself in plebeian society with the policing of perceived female transgressions by witchcraft persecutions, charivaris, and the use of ducking stools.[5] Carole Shammas believes this anxiety was transported to the New World. Households deemed to be functioning improperly in the seventeenth century were policed by Puritan authorities in New England and Quaker meetings in Pennsylvania, thereby formalizing the vernacular shaming and punishment. While this undermined the patriarchal authority of individual households, it was reasserted in a unique way in the eighteenth century as the law was adapted to strengthen the powers of masters as a means of solidifying their control over servants and slaves. Similarly, Kathleen Brown argued that Virginia shared the English concerns with patriarchy, but over time the discourse of gender difference was applied to matters of racial and class dominance within a developing plantation society, providing a ready-made language of natural subordination. Patriarchy expanded in this way to incorporate the servant and slave as well as the female.[6] The New World forms of economic and social hierarchy required justification, and the language of gender provided a preexisting rationale for locating a group of people lacking the full protection of the law.

To some extent, the army provides an appropriate analogy to such exclusion, soldiers being treated as other than civil beings, denied certain rights and subject to a different legal code, with their sex being a defining aspect of their status. The military thus can be seen as an exaggerated manifestation of patriarchy, which Kathleen Brown defined as "the historically specific authority of the father over his household, rooted in his control over labor and property, his sexual access to his wife and dependent female laborers, his control over other men's sexual access to the women of his household, and his right to punish family members and laborers."[7] The army in this light approximates an extended family. The generally elite officer class exercised patriarchal authority through its control of military matériel and soldiers, by its manipulation of sexual activity, and in its presumption of the right to punish unto death through military law. Soldiers, like women and offspring, were dependent children in this family. Gender difference was used both to enjoin men to perform dangerous physical labor and armed combat and to subordinate them within a masculine lineage of authority. Simultaneously, the patriarchal army validated its unique claim on men by conceptually divorcing them from women. Conceiving of the feminine as corrupting of discipline and parasitical of resources, the army sought to eliminate women from its masculine world. Militaristic misogyny was a necessary complement to martial endeavor. Nonetheless, within this confined gendered space men and women naturally met and did what came naturally, and the latter assumed a larger role in military life than is usually acknowledged, as workers and entrepreneurs as well as wives and sexual partners. Within this world, however, as in society itself, women figure as the most oppressed, dually blighted by their condition and their imputed nature, their social and economic contributions mystified by a peculiar martial strain of patriarchy.

The experience of the regular army in America during the Seven Years' War illustrates this case. On the one hand, the pretence that the military was solely a masculine preserve and warfare purely a martial pursuit meant that the basic building blocks of civil society and private life, marriage and the family, did not figure into martial logic in any formal way. On the other hand, the army experience in this war was shot through with a female presence, while much internal conflict was sparked by such gender issues as the proper social and economic functions of women, as well as familial and sexual relations. Furthermore, it must be remembered that the army exerted more immediate, direct, and punishing control than the state did in Britain or the American colonies in the eighteenth century, and this discipline was applied to matters of gender relations as well as simple military infractions.

Mars

The army's attitude concerning women can best be discerned in its attempts to restrict their presence in garrisons. Women were seen as a negation of the military ethos, the unmartial other sexually unsuited to fighting. Furthermore, women were believed to be economically, emotionally, and sexually sapping of male power. They were a drain on resources as noncombatants;

they straggled on the march; they were disorderly and undisciplined; and they promoted vices—sex, drink, violence, crime, and desertion.[8] Such a construction of conduct between the sexes, informed as it was by prevailing gender norms, entrenched the conceptual separation of men and women; and its punitive attitude toward females, when allied to the authority of the officer class, could not but influence the real-life treatment of women by the army as outsiders and invaders of the purest manifestation of the male sphere, the military camp.[9]

Recapturing the ordinary soldier's attitude on gender matters is more difficult. Expressions of popular culture offer a means of plumbing the vernacular. Military ballads and poems tended to assume the meaning of masculinity,[10] but two elements were reiterated—bravery and the fraternity of drink culture—which provided men with essentially positive images of themselves. "A Soldier's Song" offers a glimpse into male camp culture:

> How stands the glass around,
> For shame ye take no care, my boys,
> Let mirth and wine abound;
> The trumpets sound. . . .
> Damn fear, drink on, be jolly, boys,
> 'Tis he, you, or I!—
> Cold, hot, wet, or dry,
> We're always bound to follow, boys,
> And scorn to fly.[11]

The depiction of women was more conflicted, fluctuating between the hoary misogyny of woman as parasite, scold, and flirt and the more recent sentimentality of woman as romantic ideal and embodiment of family life. The older stereotype is summed up in "The Camp Medley":

> For women are whimsical; changeable things,
> Their sweets, like the bees, they are mingled with stings,
> They're not to be got without toil, care and cost,
> They're hard to get and are easily lost. . . .
> He that is single can never wear horns,
> He that is single is happy,
> He that is married lays upon thorns,
> And always is ragged and shabby.[12]

The play *The Recruiting Officer* offered a solution to the procrustean marriage bed.

We shall lead more happy lives,
By getting rid of brats and wives;
That scold and brawl both night and day,
Over the hills and far away.[13]

Within such pronouncements on gender relations lie the core conceits of misogyny: that women scheme to get men and their resources but, once got, by nature cannot remain sexually faithful, and so the ideal society would be an all-male one of martial endeavor and bacchanalian recreation, with military life offering its nearest equivalent.

This negative construction of female identity was counterbalanced in other contemporary songs that dwelt on the ideal of love and companionship. One expression of this was the woman who promised to wait for her man. Thus in "The Soldier's Farewell," Moll, "Her hair dishevel'd, red her eyes with tears: / Her belly prominent, too plainly shews," assures her "dear William" "How blest" her fate will be if he returns. In turn, William promises:

To England soon I shall return,
With honor and with spoil;
Then banish sorrow from thy heart,
That foe to all thy charms,
For safely I shall come again
Unto thy faithful arms.[14]

Here traditional manly valor and the role of economic provider are fused to a newer romantic ideal of partnership (albeit enabled through female chastity). Another incarnation of the perfect woman was she who chose to follow her man to war. In "Bonny Lass in a Barrack," a soldier's query—"Oh bonny lass will you lay in a barrack? . . . And marry a soldier, and carry his wallet?"—is answered in the positive. "Oh yes I will go, and I'll think no more on it, / I'll marry a soldier and carry his wallet." But a woman must also commit to a soldier's life as well as to the soldier.

Oh! yes I can bear all the hardships you mention,
And twenty times more of you had but invention.
If weary and fainting I'd ever be near thee;
In pain or in sickness my presence should cheer thee."[15]

In such ballads the ideal of romantic love marked a more positive image of woman, in which the female is able to choose, to desire, and to contribute. Still, woman's love is selfless, unquestioning, and subordinate to man's self-actualization through warfare, as the male balladeer plays the ventriloquist by projecting masculine desires from the feminine mouth.[16]

Both male types—the single misogynist and the companionate mate—as well as the dualistic embodiments of the feminine—Mary Magdalene and the Madonna—were ideals. The extent to which they were made real in the British army, however, was less a direct effect of gender conventions than of the material and demographic realities of military life in a transatlantic theater of war. To assess the historic experience of men and women, the scope for family life and heterosexuality will first be examined, then the ways in which such domesticity was unhinged. Thereafter, the central role that women played in the military economy shall be addressed. Next, an examination of the consequences of sexual contestation will be made. Finally, the experiences of one particular couple, the Calhouns, will be recounted to draw the various strands together.

The Martial Family

The family in the early modern period was seen as the basis for political and social order, a metaphor for the state with the king as father and the people representing the wife and children. Within the patriarchal order, according to Susan Amussen, the family was grounded on two basic principles: wives are subordinate to husbands, and sexual relations are restricted to marriage. The head of household was insulated from most interference by the state, church, or social superiors, and he was the center of governance for most people in Anglo-America until the mid-nineteenth century. While ideology and the legal system shaped families, Amussen reminds us that families were structured more directly by their social and economic position, life cycle, and regional economic differences.[17]

These final points are important in the military context, for army life made impractical traditional families and households (that is, quasi-independent social and economic units headed by a man marked by relative geographical stability). The army was defined as an all-male institution, and marriage and families were discouraged. Those men who managed to have a family usually either lived with them and other soldiers in a communal setting or did not live with their families, especially during wartime.[18] Furthermore, the army usurped the role of paterfamilias by providing food and often shelter and by intervening in family and sexual life as a matter of discipline, even to the extreme of causing de facto divorces by ordering women from camps for infractions. The prevailing norms of familial relations, encouraged in pamphlets and from pulpits, thus did not apply to camp life. Soldiers occupied a status akin to children under the authority of their officers, which prevented the full assertion of manhood as husbands and fathers. Camp women were shorn of the full economic and legal protection (however unequal) offered their sex by the married state and thus were doubly subjugated—to the male partner and to male officers. This does not mean that families were not an important part of military life, only that they were conceived of and constructed differently than in civil society.

Military life thus militated against family life among the troops, but the army did allow some men, particularly noncommissioned officers, to take their families with them to new stations. In fact, it was almost forced to do so by the men's desire for a domestic existence if it wished to secure recruits.[19] Officers sent to Europe to recruit for the Royal Americans in 1756 were allowed money for "the passage of a small number of Women and Children, which he will be indispensably Obliged to take for the Success of the Affair and the acquisition of proper Men." The Regiment's Fourth Battalion the following June reported that 60 women and 34 children were present with its 683 privates and 100 noncommissioned officers and drummers (a male/female ratio of 13:1).[20] This record probably largely undercounted the presence of women and children, as only those who were on the official ration list would have been included.

Military campaigns annually disrupted the dull routine of major garrisons and winter quarters with massed troop movements to the front, undercutting the army's tenuous commitment to family life. For example, during Braddock's march on Fort Duquesne, no more than two women per company were allowed to march; the rest, "wives to Soldiers," were to be sent to Fort Cumberland where the governor was to "Victule" them. Any unauthorized woman caught with the army would be "Severely punished" the first time, and she would "Suffer Death" the second time.[21] Exclusionary orders must have had a profound impact on soldiers' domestic life by separating families and denying rations or work opportunities to women at the same time as the man's wage was usually removed (payment, if made, going directly to the soldier). The wives discharged by Braddock, for example, were to be subsisted with 12d. sterling per week stopped out of their husbands' pay, but as this was not sufficient to support them, the governor of Pennsylvania recommended that the Assembly "take Compassion of these poor people" and make up the difference.[22] No wonder women appear so recalcitrant in the face of orders excluding them from camp.

Thus, while it is important to remember that there was scope for family life in the army, the military environment was characterized by marked demographic inequality between the sexes, high transience, and insecurity for the domestic unit, not to mention the dangers of warfare. The resulting instability of marriage and family life, however, must be put in the context of eighteenth-century plebeian culture in England, within which the family was flexible and relationships were adaptable over time.[23] Bridget Hill argues that working people tended to exert more control over partner choice and were more likely to have premarital sex than the middling and upper classes. Thus, bastardy was common but tacitly accepted. Many did not marry in church or even legally, as it was costly; a couple could marry merely by declaring their intent to one another. Technically bigamist relationships were far from rare given the fluid approach to the marital state. While divorce was almost unobtainable, desertion and mutual separation were accepted forms of terminating marriage. Another means of ending an unhappy marriage was the wife sale, an auction often held in the market at a publicized time, in which the wife could be led in with a halter around her neck (a reference to cattle at market) and sold to the highest bidder, with witnesses and a contract usually involved in the sale, as was a disclaimer on the husband's part of financial responsibility for the woman's debts thereafter. Women's alleged adultery was a common cause.[24] Thus, care should be taken when discussing the military model of marriage, so as not to characterize it as unique, "dysfunctional," or symptomatic of pathology; the apparent instability was often only an exaggeration of accepted plebeian forms.

We can get a sense of this adaptive quality to partnerships from the lives of Elizabeth and William Scarborough. Elizabeth had lived with William, a soldier in the Twenty-seventh Regiment, in Trenton, New Jersey, "and passed there, as his Wife." When William was stationed to Fort George in New York, his wife was left to follow on, but she brought with her Jeremiah Crawley of the New York Provincial troops. Claiming Elizabeth as his wife, William quarreled with Crawley. His friends later told William that "he was making himself ridiculous, about this woman," to which he replied "that his inclinations led him so much towards her, that he would have her, if it was in his power." Jeremiah proposed they let Elizabeth choose between them; that they should "place her, in the middle of the Floor, and that each of them should go to a different door, and whichever she chose to go to, should have her." In the end, however, this proposal of free choice for Elizabeth was superceded by William's decision to give up his "wife" for a fee. Crawley produced a copy of the release, which read: "These are to certify, that I William Scarborough, doth resign up his right, and title of his Wife to Jeremiah Crawley, never to have anything to say to her, only she may pass by, as another woman . . . in paying Three Pounds four shillings, of New

York Currency." But all was not as final as this agreement suggested. When Crawley left for a few days, Elizabeth returned to William's bed, making Jeremiah both jealous and suspicious that there was some collusion between the Scarboroughs to defraud him of his bounty money. Nonetheless, he left with Elizabeth in a wagon for Albany, only to be followed by William on foot. The two putative husbands scuffled several times, then William left, Crawley claimed. William's body was found floating dead in a river, however. Jeremiah was tried for murder, but, the evidence being insufficient, he was found not guilty.[25] Whether William was murdered or committed suicide, distraught by his wife's infidelity, is unclear, as is whether Jeremiah and Elizabeth formed a lasting union. But this account suggests the tenuous nature of marriage and sexual relations within a military environment characterized by violence and a transient lifestyle.

Amazons

The household was the basis of economic activity in the Anglo-American world at this time,[26] but this could not be the case for most soldiers. Troops were dependent on the military for their quarters and subsistence, making them more like tied servants or apprentices than heads of households. There was no natural locus for petty production and rarely the means. Likewise, women were usually dependent on the army either through their partners' wages or as a result of the rations and employment offered.[27] Some women managed to evade such dependency by participating in the commercial market surrounding the army, but such initiatives were contingent on the sufferance of officers and the presence of the army, by no means guaranteed conditions.

The army placed a certain number of women on the ration roll (usually four to six per company of 100 men);[28] this meant they would be provided with food.[29] This concession obviously left many women and children without support from the military. Women on the ration list were expected to serve the army in any way required, but usually in ways associated with their gender—cleaning, cooking, and caring.[30] Women's most important jobs were associated with the army hospitals.[31] For example, as the army settled into winter quarters in 1757, each regiment in Albany was ordered to send a nurse to the hospital.[32] Sometimes, as at Crown Point in August 1760, care was taken to specify that only women without children should act as nurses, presumably to ensure that the young would be supervised in camp.[33] And by making war widows work as nurses, the army effectively provided a pension, because they lost their ration when their husbands were killed.[34] Women also washed hospital linens and provided food for the sick.[35] At Halifax in 1757, for instance, regimental officers were ordered to supply enough of their women to wash the clothes of the sick in the hospital, prompting Captain James Abercromby to detach six women from his company.[36] Women who did such duty at times only received their food in payment.[37] Normally, however, women were paid 6d. sterling per day for nursing (equivalent to a private's pay) and 1s. for washing. Thus, the women from Abercromby's company who washed linens received a shilling a day "For their trouble."[38]

Women had a necessary role to play in the military, one that was defined by their gender admittedly but was nonetheless essential to the war effort. Care of the sick validated their presence in the camps, coincidentally enabling their heterosocial existence, and brought economic benefits that were essential to themselves and their families. These benefits came with a cost, however, as it subjected them more fully to military discipline. Army women engaged in employment were expected, like soldiers, to remain on duty until relieved or else face punishment. In 1757, nurses in Albany were not to leave the hospital without a discharge from its clerk. The following year in May, it was threatened that any woman who refused to be a nurse there would "be cut off from provisions, & Drumm'd out of the corps or garrison, & never suffer'd to return."[39] Women who refused to act as nurses could not accompany their men on the expedition to Martinique, and once there, any woman that left the hospital at Port Royal without an official discharge faced being "whiped [sic] and drummed out of the regiment she belongs to, and struck off her provisions."[40]

Such orders tell us much by the type of conduct they attempt to proscribe, in this functioning as a mirror reflection of female experience, for the repeated need to enjoin women to obey orders and work in a regimented fashion suggests that women had agendas other than that of a well-functioning army. A pattern of female disobedience of orders had been set right from the beginning by the laundresses on Braddock's expedition. Unsatisfied with the 2d. wage plus provisions on offer, they reportedly entered into a "Concert . . . not to serve without Exorbitant Wages." Such mutinous behavior invoked a threat that all women who refused to serve for the set wage would be "turned out of Camp And others got in their places." In this instance, women attempted to exploit a crucial situation where their labor was needed on the eve of a very important campaign, but the fact that "A greater number of Women being brought Over Then those alowed by the Government sufficient for washing" meant that they lost the bargaining power of the labor market and were forced to yield.[41]

The army viewed the issuance of rations and payment of wages to women workers as a drain on its resources.[42] "The women, too, can very well afford by their industry to pay 2d. a day for their provisions; the idle ones that cannot are better away," maintained James Wolfe. But it was only with Canada safely won that any move was made in this direction. James Murray suggested in 1762 that in the fixed garrisons "the rations for the Ladies would be a very proper saving to the Crown" as they were of no real service. "I have Struck off many of the Ladies from the Rations" in New York City, Amherst replied, "and whatever Saving you can make in that way will be very proper, some poor Miserable Wretches would Starve without it, but those who can get a good livelihood Should do it 'tho they will not, unless they are Compelled to it."[43] The withdrawal of provisioning rights for women was made universal in North America with disbandment in 1763, a time when the army sought to economize. A general order was issued that soldiers must pay 4d. per ration (later revised to 2 and a half pence), with the codicil that "this of Course strikes off all Women & Every Other Person from whom Stoppages cannot be made" from the provision list.[44] With this order, all women and children would no longer receive rations, excepting the few nurses permanently employed by the military hospitals. For those without men to support them, this meant economic disaster; even those with a partner were confronted with the whole family now having to survive on a soldier's daily wage that had just been cut almost in half. This subversion of the subsistence of army dependents was one among a number of grievances that provoked a general mutiny in North America that autumn.[45]

The army's employment and provisioning of women could only affect a few camp females. The unfortunate others either had to depend upon a soldier partner for subsistence or had to support themselves, or a combination of both. Women cooked and sewed for the troops, acted as servants to officers, tended cattle and sheep, or worked for the merchants who sold goods to the soldiers.[46] The further away a woman moved from her prescribed role of caregiver and service provider to soldiers and into the realm of independent economic endeavor, however, the more she exposed herself to the application of military law.

Prostitution is the economic activity usually associated with camp followers, and, given the ratio of men to women, there is every likelihood that it was commonplace. The official army record has turned up surprisingly little on the matter, perhaps because it was condoned as a necessary complement to military life.[47] It is also possible that within soldier society, as in

broader plebeian culture, strong distinctions were not drawn between marriage, common-law relationships, serial monogamy, the tacit bartering of
sexual favors for money or goods, and multiple-partner "promiscuity." As
long as commercial sex was not disruptive, it was likely tolerated. One time
when this did not appear to be the case was at Schenectady in September
1758, when "the whole town of Sodom was Pulled Down and Sot on fire
Viz [?] were was a Number Womans hutes which mad great Disturbens."[48]
This incident was likely as much about the disruption that drinking and
carousing could cause in the camp as sexual escapades.

Women carved out a more visible economic presence in the sutling (re-
tailing) of goods and liquor, as did Peggy Armstrong, who ran a drinking
house at Louisbourg in 1758.[49] If done with the sanction of commanders,
such activity caused no problems; otherwise, it was subject to punishment.[50]
The sale of alcohol worried officers most, as it was seen as the main cause
of disciplinary problems. "Where as Rum and Spirits are the Distraction of
the Army," affirmed the commander at Albany, each regiment should
strongly discourage its sale. But women, despite repeated warnings, continued to sell rum. He ordered that "if Any Women belonging to the Army be
found Guilty either Selling giving away or harbouring Spirituous Liquers of
Any kind they will be Drumd out of Town."[51] At Crown Point in 1760, any
soldier caught selling liquor was to receive 100 lashes, but any soldier's wife
would be drummed out of the fort.[52] Recurring orders such as these indicate
that women paid them little heed. Despite the threatened punishments, economic need in an environment that offered women little opportunity virtually forced them to break the rules, while there is no doubting a market
existed among the thirsty soldiery.

Economic women pushed the boundaries of gender conventions, but the
army's true enemy was the female who crossed that frontier to behave in a
criminal fashion. The most common type of illicit activity practiced by
women seems to be as conveyors of stolen goods. This was almost a natural
outgrowth of their role as sutlers, with soldiers bringing property into their
shops to barter for food and drink, and questions as to ownership were not
always asked. Such activity elicited countermanding orders. Thus, Braddock ordered that any soldier, woman, or sutler caught "Stealing plundering or Wasting" provisions would suffer death. And at Oswego in 1759, it
was ordered that any soldier, sutler, or "Woomen" of the army who bought
goods without an officer confirming their ownership would be treated as a
receiver of stolen goods.[53] Such proscriptions seem to have had their usual
effect, as theft was an endemic problem and women played their part. Complaints were made in 1757 "of great Abuses & Roberys, Committed by the

Women sent on Shore to Wash" for the army on board the fleet in New York harbor. It was ordered that these women must be supervised, or face punishment and be forbidden from following the army.[54] And Joseph Burges of the Forty-third Regiment and his wife Mary were found guilty of receiving stolen goods, to wit, a hogshead of port and a cask of Madeira from a group of soldiers who stole them from a Quebec cellar. Joseph received 500 lashes from a general court-martial, whereas Mary suffered 200 strokes at the tail end of a cart and was ordered confined until "an opportunity can be had to send her out of the Garrison," simultaneously divorcing her from her husband and source of income.[55] The iron scales of military justice appeared to be weighted against the distaff side in this instance.

Venus

Female sexuality was an enemy of a different sort, officers believed, more insidious in that it was a clandestine presence, treasonously sapping martial spirit. Women's Venus-like allure unmanned the male, enslaving him emotionally and causing many discipline problems. From the army's perspective, disobedience, dereliction of duty, desertion, and violent disturbance followed in women's wake.

Sexually transmitted disease, the bane of Venus, concerned officers, who feared it would undermine the fighting capability of their troops, and they laid the ultimate blame at the feet of promiscuous women.[56] General Loudoun ordered all soldiers with venereal disease to be sent to the hospital in 1756. Three years later, all men at Oswego who had a "Venerall Disorder" were to tell the regimental surgeon immediately.[57] Whereas soldiers with such conditions were sent to the hospital, women, seen as infectious sources, were run out of camp. Thus, in August 1759, "2 Campwomen" were sent back from Crown Point and "were not allowd to follow ye army by reason of an Infectious Distemper they Carryd along with them very Comon to ye Sex in these Parts."[58]

Desertion was a more practical concern of the army. Deserters often used women's evil influence as an explanation for their desertion, as a favored defense ranking alongside drunkenness and capture by enemy Indians. Women did have a role to play in the erosion of military discipline, albeit not necessarily always that of the evil temptress. Uxorious, familial, and romantic affection could stimulate abandonment of the army. Thomas Johnson deserted the Forty-fifth Regiment at Halifax in July 1757 in an attempt to return to his family in Philadelphia. His wife had been pregnant when he enlisted in June the year before, and his captain would not allow her to accompany him. For attempting to see his child for the first time, Johnson was given a death sentence.[59] The fires of passion could also cause soldiers to forget their duty. George Merritt, who deserted the Forty-eighth Regiment in May 1759, pleaded "his Youth and his Affection for a Girl in the Country." He received 500 lashes. Similarly, Thomas Knee of the Forty-eighth cited "his Passion for a Girl in Canada" as the cause of his desertion in June 1761, a crime for which he, too, was given 500 lashes.[60]

More often, the guilty party cast the woman as the villain of the piece. Thomas Hunter of the Forty-fourth Regiment may be the most extreme case of a man claiming to be led astray by a woman. In November 1762, with the war all but over, he deserted from Montreal with his equipment, blaming drink and "the repeated Sollicitations of a Woman with whom he was intimate" who lived on the Sorel River, the same reason he had deserted once before. He was sentenced to death, but at the execution an "Accident" occurred, which led his commanding officer to pardon him. What this accident was—a snapped hangman's rope or a *mis*firing squad—is left unsaid, but Hunter did not profit from his reprieve. Abused by a sergeant and mocked by other soldiers, presumably for his dependence on this woman, he deserted yet again in January. When discovered, he remarked, "I don't care if you take that Pistol, and shoot me thro' the Head." Found guilty by a general court-martial yet again, he was executed the same day, a martyr to his emotions.[61]

A more worrisome consequence of sexuality was the violence that often eventuated. Susan Amussen has argued that violence, not sexual activity, was the key to men's identity in the early modern period. For laboring men, violence against other men remained a way of asserting social dominance, particularly for those not wholly independent like servants and apprentices.[62] Male cultural proclivity toward violence must have been exaggerated among soldiers, already in an occupation prizing violence and requiring their overt dependence.

Sexual issues often were at the root of soldiers' social violence. On October 4, 1760, for example, there was "A mighty Discord amongst the Regulars this Night Disputing who had the best Right to a woman & who Should have the first Go at her even till it came to Bloos, & their Hubbub Raised all most the whole Camp."[63] When jealousy was added to the sexual mix, it became potentially more dangerous. Thomas James, a Ranger, was charged with assaulting and insulting Captain Spry and Lieutenant Francis at Halifax in 1755. One night James violently accosted the two navy officers. When Francis drew his sword to force him off, James struck him in the head with a stick, knocking him down, and ran off. In his defense James said that his wife lodged at the Swan public house, outside of which the altercation had occurred, and he had heard "there were Men after her the whole day." Coming home that night he saw men at the Swan's door with her and assumed the worst. His sergeant deposed that James was "a very honest Man, but that since he has been married he has been at times distracted with Jealousy . . . that in a fit of Phrenzy he once hung himself up by the neck and must have quickly died had he not been accidentally relieved." James's attempt to restore his pride backfired, not only for letting his emotions master him but for choosing two officers as the means, sins for which he received 500 lashes.[64]

Amussen, furthermore, found that violence against women was an important aspect of manliness, taking the form of wife-beating and rape, with the sexual content of assaults subordinated to the exercise of physical dominance.[65] The military tradition of raping the enemy's women was long-standing but had fallen into disfavor in the eighteenth century. Still, it was enough of a concern to necessitate issuing orders threatening dire punishment for committing the offense. Thus, during the siege of Quebec in 1759, no French "peasants" were to be harmed, and "If any violence is offered to a woman, the offender shall be punished with death."[66] General orders did not prevent such rapes of enemy civilians, however.[67] Sometimes the victims of soldier-rapists were not erstwhile enemies but colonial women, as in the case of Mary Poulston of Albany, "much abused and by a Recruiting Serj[t]. of the Royal American Regiment," identity unknown.[68]

Camp women were the most common victims of rape by soldiers, however. Amussen observed that rapes usually were crimes of opportunity: females in dependent positions, such as servants, were preyed on by their superiors, or those caught alone in isolated circumstances where help was not at hand.[69] The army's communal living conditions offered much temptation and the common stationing of garrisons in thinly settled, wooded settings provided the opportunity.[70] A brutal case occurred at Crown Point in 1760. Robert Gore and John Christie, two provincial soldiers, came to the door of Mrs. Moy, a drummer boy's wife, at 10 p.m. on January 25, asking to be allowed in to warm themselves. She admitted them, but they then "stop'd her mouth & threw her on the bed that Christie then took her by the leggs & Kept them Extended while gore ravished her, threataining at the same time to Cut her throat if she made aney noise." Christie threatened to use a knife on her, then "beat her in a most Cruel manner which Gore desired he would not, but that he treated her in So inhuman a manner as made her unable to resist while he Christie ravish[d]. her." They told her to keep it a secret, and then left. At their court-martial, the prisoners pleaded that they were drunk and denied ravishing her. The regimental court, however, thought the crime so "heinious [*sic*] in nature" that it merited a greater punishment than it could order, and the case was referred to a general court-martial.[71]

Sexual violence was not restricted to adult women, as child rapes also occurred.[72] Probably much the same factors applied: the unbalanced sex ratios and consequent sexual frustration among the more numerous men; the hierarchical subordination of children; and their exposure to sexual predators within the camps. Thus, in 1758, a soldier in the Thirty-fifth Regiment was sent to the dungeon in New York for "Reveshing the Land Lords Daughter of 7 years of age and giveing her the French[?] Desease." And Urban Lewis, a Massachusetts provincial, was tried by a regimental court-martial in 1760 for "committing Violence on a child."[73]

Military Affairs

The various intersecting lines of gender expectations, lived realities, and the overwhelming power of the masculine command structure can be glimpsed in the experiences of James Calhoun, a soldier of the Forty-fourth Regiment, and his wife, May.

Their story begins at Oswego on Lake Ontario in the spring of 1760. James became incensed when a sergeant named Cameron "threw down some Rum" from Calhoun's hand, which he thought "would be prejudicial" to the soldier. Calhoun argued with Cameron, and Mrs. Calhoun joined in the squabble, prompting Mrs. Cameron to enter the fray. Both couples were confined to the guardhouse. The commanding officer, Lieutenant Colonel Eyre, sent a lieutenant to tell Cameron that "he must part with his Wife," which Cameron thought "a very hard Message, having lived with her Sixteen years & having a little Boy in the Regiment to take care of." Why Eyre took this measure is unclear. The only justification he offered spoke to the quality of her labor; he had hired Mrs. Cameron as his laundress when he arrived, but fired her shortly after for being the "worst he has ever Employed." She was in tears when released the next morning, and Cameron tried to console her by saying he would have some officers write to General Thomas Gage to get employment for her, as she had washed for him before. That day an anonymous letter was sent to the garrison major making a serious charge against Cameron.

> I cant help acquainting you of what I heard a fellow who wars a Serjints Coat Say (who is now in the Guard) that there is Eight, or ten Officers in this Garrison, who is going to write to General Gage to

have you and the Colo. brock [broke], for turning his Wife out of the Garrison, & confining; him wrongfully. . . . Sir, what I have said I luck upon as my duty to Acquaint you & being under the Military Yock [yoke].

Cameron thought that May Calhoun was behind this allegation, but the warning persuaded the commander. The colonel admitted to being "no Bishop or Pope, therefore could not take upon him to divorse the wife from the Husband, but he Swore She never Should come where he had anything of a Command." Cameron rotted in jail three months before he was found not guilty of insubordination. His wife, however, remained banished from the garrison. Whether stemming from male contestation or feminine pique, the Calhouns managed to initiate the de facto divorce of their company sergeant from his washerwoman wife. Four years later, they would again become involved in a marital dispute that would involve senior officers in the regiment and reach the desk of the commander in chief, General Gage. This time, James Calhoun would be split from his washerwoman, May.

The war was over in the late winter of 1764, but at Fort Ticonderoga in New York a new conflict was raging in which officer and enlisted man fought over the issue of access to a particular woman, and officer contested officer on proper gentlemanly conduct. Having moved on from Oswego with her husband and the Forty-fourth, May Calhoun kept cows and worked as washerwoman for the commandant, Captain Charles Osborne. Osborne had used several surplus rooms in the fort "to make the married people live as comfortable as was in my power," one of which went to the Calhouns. But after some time living with her husband, Osborne claimed that Mrs. Calhoun was "receiving such Usage from him, that's not possible to describe" and that she had sought his protection. The captain banished James to the barracks for his "Bad behaviour," while his wife remained in their apartment to prevent any further mischief. Furthermore, he was not to go near his wife, "as the woman was by his threats, put she said, in fear of her Life." Osborne was "determined not to allow him any longer to treat her in the barbarous manner he had done, or on her account make any further Disturbances in the Fortress."[74]

Initially, this seems a simple case of wife-beating. Yet all was not as it seemed. In civil society at this time the husband was allowed to chastise his wife physically, with the authorities only intruding in the most extreme situations. Thus, Osborne's interference with the Calhouns, amounting effectively in modern terms to a marriage separation and restraining order, is significant in that it points to the extent of power that military commanders exercised in the personal sphere. Osborne's justification was twofold: the women's safety, and the need to preserve the peace within the camp. Osborne's burnished front was tarnished, however, when James Calhoun's story was told.

Rather than abiding by his commander's orders, James made his way to Crown Point to complain to Lieutenant Colonel J. Beckwith (in front of the officers' mess) "that he had caut his Captain in Bed with his Wife," and that when he had confronted Osborne with this, he had been confined for ten days for disturbing the garrison. Calhoun asked Beckwith to "send his wife down the Country as he could not bear the thoughts of having her where She was."[75] Beckwith informed Osborne that Calhoun had complained "you keep his Wife from him and that he has reason to imagine you are very Intimate with her." Mrs. Calhoun was for seventeen years "the Lawful Wife" of James, who was "very unhappy at the thoughts of his Wife behaving so ill." Beckwith demanded that Osborne send her away from the fort, "as Countenancing so bad a Woman must Sooner or later Infallably bring a disgrace upon those who are Imprudent enough to Protect her against her husband."[76]

Osborne, outraged that Beckwith was "determined to believe the Word of a Soldier in preference to that of an Officer," dismissed the allegation of a sexual liaison, disparaging his commanding officer's presumption that his "fondness for the sex" might make him act so imprudently. He also blackened the character of James Calhoun, "absolutely the worst man that Lives." Osborne often had to order Calhoun to the barracks from the married soldiers' quarters to protect his spouse, but whom he had allowed to return "at the repeated entreaties of His Wife." James once broke down the door to his wife's chamber, and not long after got "Egregiously drunk," forced the same door, and, if Osborne had not intervened, would have "murdered his Wife." It was after this outbreak that James was incarcerated to await a court-martial. Osborne believed that the man's only justification was that "she is his Wife, and consequently he may brake her arms and Legs if its any diversion to him."[77] Osborne refused to send Mrs. Calhoun away, couching his defense in terms of her "undoubted right, to get her livelyhood by working for whom, and where she thought proper, while she [w]as a follower of the Army, and continued to behave conformable to order."[78] Beckwith retorted that "Calhoun has a right not only to demand his Wife, but to take her where ever he can find her to live with him if he Chooses it and no one has a right to keep her from him without his Consent or Approbation." Beckwith knew Calhoun was "a poor Drunken unhappy fellow who at Times does not know what he Does, or says, He is so distracted about his wife, who you Say lives with you as your made [*sic*] servant," but he again recommended that Osborne send her away.[79]

Concerns of patriarchy in its domestic form yielded to the more pressing demands of its martial superior. The dispute between Osborne and Beckwith seemed soon to lose sight of who exercised authority in the Calhoun quarters, as it escalated into a contest over who wielded control within the regiment: Osborne as the garrison commander, or Beckwith as the regimental colonel.[80] Their respective manhoods were at stake, and while they could not resort to violence to settle their differences, they made repeated applications to their commander in chief for patriarchal support. Things came to a head when Osborne planned to court-martial Calhoun. Beckwith feared that Calhoun was "not only like to have his Wife kept from him but in a fair Way to get a good floging [*sic*]."[81]

This struggle for patriarchal control over army dependents had everything and nothing to do with whether Osborne was sleeping with Mrs. Calhoun. Osborne had access and exhibited an unusual concern for a washerwoman, but we only have Calhoun's evidence that they were involved. The Captain's word thus had to be accepted as a gentleman, and there is a suggestion that this is what General Gage did. Beckwith, however, remained suspicious, informing Gage that he believed Mrs. Calhoun was kept forcibly from her husband and pointing out that she shared a dinner table with Osborne, unusual practice for officer and washerwoman.[82] Osborne's interference in the Calhouns' relationship, whether sexual or not, constituted a claim of domestic authority over a married couple that a civil household would not countenance.[83] Beckwith's assertion of higher authority undermined this claim and unmanned Osborne in front of his martial family, while Osborne's obstinate refusal to defer control over this matter likewise emasculated his colonel. Male honor, an honor denied James Calhoun as a soldier and member of the laboring classes, dictated that neither Beckwith nor Osborne could stand down. James thus was unmanned in a much more visceral way than either officer: a husband denied his wife, locked from his household, facing de facto divorce, and threatened with a whip. Meanwhile, as all too often is the case, Mrs. Calhoun was left silent, a void to be filled by the masculine military record. Whether she was an object of violence or illicit desire, or both, is impossible to conclude, and there remains no direct evidence to explain how she felt about the invasion of her domestic affairs. James Calhoun's masculine rage was much clearer. Regardless, the Calhouns were left asunder.

This episode, arising from a seemingly mundane domestic dispute, stripped off the redcoat that typically obscures the sexual body of military life and revealed much about the gendered world of warfare: the central role of women to the war effort; the social relations constructed by ordinary soldiers and their women; the sexual tensions that inevitably emerged in this inordinately masculine world; and the danger entailed in these tensions when they crossed the class divide between private soldier and officer, not only calling into question the proper exercise of authority but also highlighting the extent of patriarchal control in this relationship regarding matters sexual.

Conclusion

While there was no doubting that a military man was meant to be an obedient warrior, women were harder to classify. The mere presence of women belied this gender logic, making soldiers swains, husbands, fathers, cuckolds, sexual animals, and, worst of all, poorly disciplined. While human nature invited women into the camps, officers sought to purge them. But when this failed, the army moved to control and exploit them. A few females were put on the ration list, many worked as nurses and laundresses, and others were allowed to pursue commercial activities that serviced the camps. This limited sphere was as much a construction by women as by the army. Wives and daughters followed their men to war, and others were picked up along the way, making for a family life of sorts, and their continued military existence required an income, either provided by the army or pursued by the women themselves. Women thus played central social and economic roles in the military, however much officers bemoaned their corrupting influence. But when they departed too far from their allotted functions of wives and caregivers, when Venus was rising, they faced stiff punishment. More so than in civil society, women's lives were subjected to authority, one that did not hesitate to disrupt family life. Nonetheless, female subordination (like that of the male soldiers) should not blind us to their centrality to military life at this time. Camp followers (and private soldiers) are the matériel of military history. In fact, it could be said that behind every good army there is a female train, enabling the reproduction of the war effort.

Notes

1. There are exceptions to this rule. Walter Hart Blumenthal's *Women Camp Followers of the American Revolution* (1952; reprint, Salem, N.H.: Ayer, 1994) was a pathbreaking but now dated treatment of the subject. Sylvia Frey briefly examined family life in *The British Soldier in America: A Social History of Military Life in the*

Revolutionary Period (Austin: University of Texas Press, 1981), 57–63. Paul E. Kopperman detailed the army's policies on women in "The British High Command and Soldiers' Wives in America, 1755–1783," *Journal of the Society for Army Historical Research* 60 (1982): 14–34. For the British army in a later period, see Myna Trustram, *Women of the Regiment: Marriage and the Victorian Army* (Cambridge: Cambridge University Press, 1984). Holly A. Mayer's *Belonging to the Army: Camp Followers and Community during the American Revolution* (Columbia: University of South Carolina Press, 1996) documents the experience not only of women but of the entire "community" that attached itself to the Continental army.

2. For a discussion of the Amazon ideal, see G. J. Barker-Benfield, *The Culture of Sensibility: Sex and Society in Eighteenth-Century Britain* (Chicago: University of Chicago Press, 1992), xxvii, 351–54.

3. Anthony Fletcher, *Gender, Sex, and Subordination in England, 1500–1800* (New Haven: Yale University Press, 1995), 5–6, 283–84, 290–92, 296. See also Barker-Benfield, *Culture of Sensibility,* xvii–xviii, 26–27, 36.

4. In the introduction to their edited collection, *Gender in Eighteenth-Century England: Roles, Representations, and Responsibilities* (London: Longman, 1997), Hannah Barker and Elaine Chalus argue against "any simplistic application of the notion of separate spheres" (3), as gender boundaries and the division between these two ideal spaces were blurred in the eighteenth century.

5. Underdown found that the anxiety was more pronounced in urban and wood-pasture villages than in closed arable parishes, that is, the ones experiencing greater economic change. See D. E. Underdown, "The Taming of the Scold: The Enforcement of Patriarchal Authority in Early Modern England," in Anthony Fletcher and John Stevenson, eds., *Order and Disorder in Early Modern England* (Cambridge: Cambridge University Press, 1985), 116–36.

6. Carole Shammas, "Anglo-American Household Government in Comparative Perspective," *William and Mary Quarterly,* 3rd ser., 52, no. 1 (January 1995): 117–28; Kathleen M. Brown, *Good Wives, Nasty Wenches, and Anxious Patriarchs: Gender, Race, and Power in Colonial Virginia* (Chapel Hill: University of North Carolina Press, 1996), esp. introduction.

7. Brown, *Good Wives,* 4–5.

8. Looking beyond matters of discipline, the correspondence of officers provides an occasional glimpse into their personal views on women, which usually took two forms: the female as object of sexual contestation and the female as a potential pitfall to a man's career. See Christopher French Journals, vol. 2, July 13, 1763, Manuscripts Division, Library of Congress, Washington, D.C. (hereafter LC); Peyton to Loudoun, January 10, 1759, LO 6013, box 127, Loudoun Papers, North American series, Huntington Library, San Marino, Calif. (hereafter in form LO 6013, box 127).

9. This othering of women was mirrored in the shaming of soldiers who failed to behave in a manly fashion by making them wear feminine appurtenances. See Or-

derly Book, Forty-seventh Regiment of Foot, August 22, 1759, Mfm. P-212, Massachusetts Historical Society, Boston (hereafter MHS).

10. Susan Dwyer Amussen reminds us: "The social construction of manhood is less visible than that of womanhood, because the attributes of men, as of any dominant group, are naturalized, while those of subordinate groups are made deviant: the 'lenses of gender' in our society make male experience the norm." See "'The Part of a Christian Man': The Cultural Politics of Manhood in Early Modern England," in Susan D. Amussen and Mark A. Kishlansky, eds., *Political Culture and Cultural Politics in Early Modern England: Essays Presented to David Underdown* (Manchester: Manchester University Press, 1995), 214.

11. *Songs Naval and Military* (New York: James Rivington, 1779), 45–46. See also William Catton, "The Siege of Martinico: A Poem," printed sheet found in Monckton Papers, vol. 50, file 7, Northcliffe Collection, MG 18 M (microfilm reel C 367), National Archives of Canada, Ottawa (hereafter NAC).

12. *Songs Naval and Military,* 41–43.

13. Ibid., 61.

14. Ibid., 88–90.

15. Ibid., 60.

16. There are military ballads that recount the adventures of women who went to war as soldiers rather than purely as spouses of one sort or another, ballads that "feature a sturdy heroine, patriotic, adventurous, and something of a trickster." Dianne Dugaw, "Balladry's Female Warriors: Women, Warfare, and Disguise in the Eighteenth Century," *Eighteenth-Century Life* 9, no. 2 (1985): 1. I have found none that apply to the Seven Years' War in America.

17. Susan Amussen, *An Ordered Society: Gender and Class in Early Modern Society* (New York: Columbia University Press, 1988), 1–2, 94, 67; Shammas, "Household Government," 104, 109.

18. Frey found that single soldiers were the norm for eighteenth-century European armies and that states increasingly moved to restrict its warriors' rights to marriage and children. Frey, *British Soldier,* 59–61. See also Mayer, *Belonging to the Army,* 8.

19. Thus the Forty-seventh Regiment arrived in Nova Scotia in 1750 with 290 privates, 130 women, and 50 children, or almost one woman for every two soldiers, a sign that this was a peacetime garrison intended to remain in place. Stanley McCrory Pargellis, *Lord Loudoun in North America* (1933; reprint, New York: Archon Press, 1968), 31.

20. Plan for recruiting in Germany, (February 1756,) LO 2576, box 19; James Prevost, Return of Fourth Battalion Royal American Regiment, June 5, 1757, LO 3794, box 84. By comparison, Walter Hart Blumenthal found that in May 1777 the British army (including the civil branch) had a male/female ratio of 8:1, and the German troops 30:1. Mayer found a ratio of 15:1 was set for the Continental army. See Blumenthal, *Camp Followers,* 18–19; Mayer, *Belonging to the Army,* 130.

21. Pass given by General Braddock for certain females, June 9, 1755, in Samuel Hazard, ed., *Pennsylvania Archives,* vol. 2 (Philadelphia: Joseph Severns, 1852), 348; Daniel Disney Orderly Book, June 11, 1755, LC. See also Order Book, 2, July 9, 1759, pp. 59, 61, Frederick Mackenzie Collection, MG 23, K 34, NAC; General Monckton's Orderly Book, August 21, 1759, vol. 23, Monckton Papers, Northcliffe Collection (microfilm reel C 366), NAC; Edward G. Williams, ed., *Bouquet's March to the Ohio: The Forbes Road* (Pittsburgh: Historical Society of Western Pennsylvania, 1975), 56, 121, 131.

22. Robert Morris to the Assembly, June 17, 1755, in George Edward Reed, ed., *Pennsylvania Archives,* 4th ser., vol. 2 (Harrisburg: William Ray, 1900), 410. See also Monckton to Amherst, July 9, 1758, Letter Book of the Honourable Robt. Monckton, Monckton Papers, vol. 12 (microfilm reel C-365); Charles Lawrence to General Amherst, September 12, 1758, no. 647, box 13, Abercromby Papers, Huntington Library.

23. Barker and Chalus, eds., *Gender in Eighteenth-Century England,* 17.

24. Bridget Hill, *Women, Work, and Sexual Politics in Eighteenth-Century England* (Oxford: Basil Blackwell, 1989), 179ff., 6, 205–7, 215–19. See also Amussen, *Ordered Society,* 124.

25. War Office Papers, Courts-Martial Records, ser. 71, vol. 68, pp. 247–55 (hereafter in form WO71/68/247–55), Public Records Office at Kew, London (hereafter PRO). Similarly, a sergeant in the New York Regiment ran off with the wife of a sutler when he was away from Fort Edward, but only after relieving him of his money. James Abercromby to Loudoun, November 16, 1756, LO 2225, box 51.

26. Hill, *Women, Work, and Sexual Politics,* 22–23.

27. Mayer, *Belonging to the Army,* 125.

28. See, for example, Disney Orderly Book, May 18, 1755; Mackenzie Order Book, vol. 2, November 11, 1761, p. 8.

29. Pargellis states that these rations would only be forthcoming when the army was in the field, and women would have to provide for themselves when in garrison by some form of work, but I have not found this to be the norm; see, e.g., P. T. Hopson to Loudoun, February 13, 1758, LO 5574, box 120. While Sylvia Frey indicates that such women only received a half ration and children a quarter, a full ration seems to have been the norm in America during the Seven Years' War for women and no statement of policy for children was found, perhaps suggesting that children were to be provided for out of their mother's provisions. Paul Kopperman noted that women usually received full or two-thirds rations. Pargellis, *Lord Loudoun,* 326; Frey, *British Soldier,* 57; Kopperman, "Soldiers' Wives in America," 22–23.

30. For example, Priscilla Twells, presumably wife to Sergeant George Twells, was a "Necessary Woman" on board the *Eagle* in passage to America, as was Mary Randall, likely wife to mattross Joseph Randall, on the *Britannia.* F. J. Buchanan, List of Officers . . . and soldiers of the Royal Artillery on board the Eagle Galley ad

Britannia Snow, May 23, 1757, LO 5181, box 81. See also Mayer, *Belonging to the Army*, 8, 128–30, 138–43.

31. See "The Journal of Charlotte Brown, Matron of the General Hospital with the English Forces in America, 1754–1756," in Isabel M. Calder, ed., *Colonial Captivities, Marches, and Journeys* (New York: Macmillan, 1935), 169–98; Mayer, *Belonging to the Army*, 142–43.

32. George Douglass, Return of the Men of the following Regiments present in New York, July 26, 1756, LO 1359, box 30; Disney Orderly Book, October 17, 18, 1757. See also Third Battalion, Pennsylvania Regiment, Provincial Forces of Pennsylvania, August 20, 28, 1758, HM 613, Huntington Library; Orderly Book kept by Lieutenant Joseph Bull, September 22, 1759, First Battalion, New York Provincial Regiment, HM 687, Huntington Library; Mackenzie Order Book, vol. 2, February 1, 1762.

33. Orderly Book of John Thomas's Regiment of Massachusetts Provincials, August 9, 1760, John Thomas Papers, MHS; Samuel Hobart Orderly Book, August 9, 1760, LC.

34. Thus, some widows of men killed in the conquest of Quebec were sent to New York City as nurses. Monckton's Orderly Book, October 2, 1759.

35. Women did do the laundry of officers, as did the wife of Sergeant Cameron for Thomas Gage. WO71/46/97–102. Mayer found that women in the Revolution did laundry for private soldiers by the piece. *Belonging to the Army*, 140–42.

36. Loudoun, General Orders, July 27, 1757, LO 3576, box 78; Abercromby, Orderly Book, July 28, 1757, LO 3993, box 89.

37. Army policy in 1757 stated that matrons of hospitals would receive a daily ration; two years later in Oswego it was noted that women acting as nurses would be given fresh provisions. Copy of Regulation of Rations of Provisions from General Abercromby, November 28, 1757; Bull Orderly Book, September 22, 1759.

38. Abercromby Orderly Book, July 28, 1757, LO 3993, box 89. See also Disney Orderly Book, April 7, 1755, July 27, 1757; Third Battalion, Pennsylvania Regiment, Orderly Book, August 20, 1758; "The Journal of Charlotte Brown, Matron of the General Hospital with the English Forces in America, 1754–1756," in *Colonial Captivities, Marches, and Journeys*, 169–98.

39. Disney Orderly Book, October 17, 18, 1757; "The Monypenny Orderly Book," in *Bulletin of the Fort Ticonderoga Museum* 12, no. 5 (December 1969): 338, and 12, no. 6 (October 1970): 458. See also Monckton's Orderly Book, August 20, 1759.

40. Mackenzie Order Book, vol. 2, November 11, 1761, p. 8, April 15, 1762, p. 57.

41. Disney Orderly Book, April 7, 1755.

42. Paid work could cost the army significant amounts; for example, £26 11s. 6d. was paid for nurses and other expenses in caring for the sick at Forts William Henry and Edward during the winter and spring of 1757. John Duncan, Forty-fourth Regi-

ment on Account of Recruiting, &c. for the Year 1757, June 24, 1757, LO 6600, box 86.

43. Loudoun Memorandum Books, vol. 4, December 16, 1757, Huntington Library; Wolfe to Lord Sackville, May 24, 1758, in Beckles Willson, ed., *The Life and Letters of James Wolfe* (New York: Dodd Mead; London: William Heinemann, 1909), 368; James Murray to Amherst, October 7, 1762, War Officer Papers, ser. 34, Paper of General Jeffery Amherst, vol. 2, p. 131, PRO [hereafter in form WO34/2/131]; Amherst to Murray, November 28, 1762, WO34/3/182; Murray to Amherst, December 22, 1762, WO34/2/148–49.

44. Amherst to Murray, August 1, 1763, WO34/3/204; Amherst, General Order, September 22, 1763, Robert Monkton Papers, 1726–1782, Peter Force Papers (8D: 181. 18. mfm. reel 94), LC.

45. See my "Rebellion of the Regulars: Working Soldiers and the Mutiny of 1763–1764," *William and Mary Quarterly,* 3rd ser., vol. 57, no. 4 (October 2000): 761–92.

46. Hannah Smyth, for example, was a servant to Mr. Best, a sutler to the Thirty-fifth Regiment. Court of Inquiry of the Thirty-fifth Regiment, November 11, 1756, LO 2195, box 50.

47. There was a heightened consciousness about prostitution in the eighteenth century, but it was largely tolerated as a necessary release for carnal men confronted with delicate wives. Trumbach, "Sex, Gender, and Sexual Identity in Modern Culture: Male Sodomy and Female Prostitution in Enlightenment London," in John C. Fout, ed., *Forbidden History: The State, Society, and the Regulation of Sexuality in Modern Europe* (Chicago: University of Chicago Press, 1992), 98–99.

48. Moses Dorr, "A Journal of an Expedition against Canada by Moses Dorr Ensin [sic] of Capt Parkers Company," *New York History* 16, no. 4 (October 1935): 461.

49. WO71/66/422. Hill noted that women, often widows, commonly were licensed victuallers in England, while Blumenthal found that women also played a key role in the illicit liquor traffic within the British army during the Revolution. Hill, *Women, Work, and Sexual Politics,* 243; Blumenthal, *Camp Followers,* 22–25. See also Mayer, *Belonging to the Army,* 7, chap. 3 generally.

50. During the siege of Quebec, for example, it was ordered that no women were allowed to be "petty Sutlers" in the camp without proper authority; otherwise, they would be struck off the provision roll. Mackenzie Order Book, July 2, 1759, vol. 1, p. 59.

51. Disney Orderly Book, September 21, November 18, 1757.

52. Hobart Orderly Book, November 2, 1760; Nathaniel Sawtell, Orderly Book of Silas Brown's Company, Timothy Ruggles's Regiment of Massachusetts Provincials, November 2, 1760, Silas Brown Collection (microfilm reel P-212), MHS.

53. Disney Orderly Book, June 6, 1755; Bull Orderly Book, September 11, 1759.

54. Disney Orderly Book, June 12, 1757; Loudoun General Orders, June 13, 1757, LO 3576, box 78.

55. WO71/46/309–14.

56. On contemporary British attitudes toward venereal disease, see Trumbach, "Sexual Identity," 98–99.

57. Loudoun, general orders, September 2, 1756, LO 1538, box 35; Bull Orderly Book, August 29, 1759.

58. "Diaries Kept by Lemuel Wood," *Historical Collections* 19 (July–September 1882): 187.

59. WO71/66/17–18. See also WO71/41/58–60.

60. WO71/71/251–53; WO71/71/247–48.

61. WO71/72/162–64, 167–70. See also WO71/66/123–24; WO71/66/126.

62. Amussen, "'The Part of a Christian Man,'" 214, 220–27.

63. "Journal of Sergeant Holden," in *Proceedings of the Massachusetts Historical Society,* 2nd ser., 5 (1889–90): 403.

64. WO71/42/144–46.

65. Amussen, "'The Part of a Christian Man,'" 217–20.

66. Mackenzie Orderly Book, July 2, 1759, vol. 1, p. 58. See also Mackenzie Orderly Book, January 7, 1762, vol. 2, p. 20.

67. See WO71/46/306–8.

68. Proceedings of a Garrison Court-Martial, November 14, 1756, LO 2212, box 51.

69. Amussen, "'The Part of a Christian Man,'" 217–20.

70. See Court of Inquiry of the Thirty-fifth Regiment, November 11, 1756, LO 2195, box 50.

71. Captain John Wrightson, Proceedings of a Regimental Court-Martial, January 30, 1760, American series, Thomas Gage Papers, William L. Clements Library, University of Michigan, Ann Arbor (hereafter in form GP5); William Haviland, February 3, 1760, GP5. No record of such a trial survives.

72. Frey, *British Soldier,* 61.

73. Loudoun Memorandum Books, vol. 5, January 26, 1758; Orderly Book of John Thomas's Regiment of Massachusetts Provincials, February 12, 1760, John Thomas Papers, MHS. Unfortunately, in neither case is there information on the legal outcomes.

74. Osborne to Gage, February 10, 1764, GP13. The Calhouns are identified as the Cahoons in the correspondence surrounding this case.

75. Beckwith to Gage, February 13, 1764, GP14.

76. Copy of Beckwith to Osborne, February 5, 1764, enclosed in Beckwith to Gage, February 13, 1764, GP14.

77. Copy of Osborne to Beckwith, n.d. ["Sunday Morn"], and February 6, 1764, enclosed in Beckwith to Gage, February 13, 1764, GP14.

78. Osborne to Gage, February 10, 1764, GP13. See also Osborne to Beckwith, February 13, 1764, enclosed in Beckwith to Gage, February 13, 1764, GP14.

79. Beckwith to Osborne, February 9, 1764, enclosed in Beckwith to Gage, February 13, 1764, GP14.

80. Beckwith to Gage, February 13, 1764, GP14.

81. Beckwith to Gage, February 25, 1764, GP14. Osborne went ahead with the court-martial, but no records exist for the ruling on James Calhoun. Osborne to Gage, March 16, 1764, GP15.

82. Osborne to Gage, March 16, 1764, GP15; Beckwith to Gage, March 18, 1764, GP14.

83. The common law allowed men to "correct" their wives and to control their movement, a right that had eroded somewhat by the eighteenth century. Women were able to "pray the peace" against violent husbands to get some protection from the courts, much the way Osborne alleged that Mrs. Calhoun did. Still, the husband's right to chastise his wife continued to be exercised regularly. J. M. Beattie, "The Criminality of Women in Eighteenth-Century England," *Journal of Social History* 8 (Summer 1975): 86.

3

The Thirteen Colonies in the Seven Years' War

The View from London

P. J. Marshall

The importance of the Seven Years' War in Britain's relations with the thir-teen colonies has recently been powerfully restated in Fred Anderson's fine book, *Crucible of War*. "Without the Seven Years' War," he writes, "Ameri-can independence would surely have been long delayed, and achieved (if at all) without a war of national liberation."[1]

Although this is a persuasive proposition with which few scholars are likely to disagree, as is so often the case in the historiography of the revolu-tionary era, there is a marked disproportion in the attention given by histo-rians to the colonial as opposed to the British side of Anglo-American rela-tions during the war. Anderson has been able to draw on a rich vein of recent historical writing for his account of how war affected the colonies and shaped their relations with Britain. This essay is an attempt to redress the balance by examining how those responsible for directing the British war effort assessed the role of the colonies in the war and how this may have influenced British views of the colonial policies to be pursued after the war.

Historians of colonial America used to stress conflict between the colo-nies and imperial authority. There was certainly no shortage of conflicts. British military commanders in America and ministers in London railed against the inability of the colonies to combine effectively, the unwillingness of the assemblies to vote enough money and men, and their insistence on exercising control over the use made of what they did vote. British army officers resented what they saw as the failure of the colonies to provide recruits, foodstuffs and forage, quarters for troops, wagons, horses, or boats in sufficient quantities or at a reasonable price. They complained bitterly about deficiencies in the provincial troops: their failure to appear on time or to stay in the field long enough, their lack of discipline, and what they sometimes saw as their poor fighting qualities. Throughout the war it was reported that American merchants persisted in supplying the enemy in Canada or the West Indies with vital supplies in defiance of British attempts to impose blockades.

Faced with what they saw as blatant lack of cooperation, local British commanders sometimes resorted to imposing their will on the colonies. Naval officers endeavored to impress men. Army recruiting parties had a reputation for using strong-arm tactics. Commanders on occasions compelled colonial troops to serve longer than their contracted terms. Horses, wagons, and boats could all be commandeered. Towns were threatened with having troops quartered on them by force if they withheld accommodation. General embargoes on all trade were imposed on ports for long periods. Such measures were denounced throughout the colonies as arbitrary infringements of established rights and were frequently resisted. Attempts to impress seamen or recruit soldiers set off riots, and local magistrates often discharged recruits enlisted by the British army.

These conflicts have been seen as a prelude to the Revolution. This was the theme of Alan Rogers's *Empire and Liberty* and of Douglas Edward Leach's *Roots of Conflict*. Leach recounts the long history of ill feeling between regular British troops and colonial soldiers. He sees these as coming to a head during the Seven Years' War and as thus sowing the "living seeds of revolution and separation."[2]

While in no way seeking to diminish tensions during the Seven Years' War, other scholars now stress the extent to which the colonies cooperated in a great imperial war effort with which they totally identified themselves and how they saw their contributions as a matter for pride and self-satisfaction. John Shy described the war as "a time of triumph" for the colonies, "educative and euphoric in effect."[3] Fred Anderson sees the colonies as cooperating in "an imperial enterprise with an enthusiasm and vigor unprecedented in their history." Required to raise over 20,000 men for the campaign seasons of 1759 and 1760, he shows that they succeeded in putting 81 percent of them into the field in 1759 and 75 percent in 1760.[4] This followed an impressive effort in 1758. The colonies as a whole paid out over £2.5 million of which they received reimbursement from Britain of about £1 million.[5] The people of certain colonies had to shoulder a very heavy burden. Massachusetts, in particular, as well as contributing nearly one-third of all the money raised in America, kept something like one in ten of its adult male population under arms for most of the war.[6] It is hardly surprising, if somewhat ironic in view of his role in the future, that the province's new governor, Francis Bernard, should have described the people of Massachusetts on his arrival in 1760 as "better disposed to observe their compact with the crown than any other on the continent that I know."[7]

Bernard's choice of the term *compact* is not what one would expect from his later reputation as a "prerogative man," but it was a perceptive summary of the colonial view of their relationship with Britain during and after the war. The colonies envisaged empire as based on an implied compact. It was an alliance rather than a system of subordination. They saw themselves as his Majesty's loyal subjects faithfully fulfilling their part against the common enemy in the alliance with Britain, which had triumphed with the expulsion of the French from North America. As Jack P. Greene has put it, the war had intensified the colonists' "deep affection for and pride in being British," but had also "heightened their expectations for a larger—and more equivalent—role within the Empire, a role that would finally raise them out of a dependent status to one in which they were more nearly on a par with Britons at home."[8] Anderson strongly endorses this view. He, too, sees the war as giving Americans not intimations of separation but a deeper involvement with the British Empire. It was, however, an involvement in an empire in which Britain would observe its implied compact with them and repay loyalty with respect for their rights as Englishmen.[9] Francis Bernard again took on the improbable role as spokesman for colonial views. The colonies' "rights," he wrote in 1763, having been "effectually vindicated by a successful war and firmly secured by an honorable peace," "British America" now "wanted nothing more than to be well known to the mother country."[10]

Did the British draw the same conclusions from the experience of war? Did they see it as the vindication of an empire based on an alliance with the colonies, held together by loyalty in return for respect for rights? Did they welcome the prospect of Americans becoming full partners in a worldwide empire based on liberty, prosperity, and Protestantism? Americans quickly came to believe that, once the war was over, the answer was a resounding no. The posting of a large permanent garrison of British regulars in America, rigorous enforcement of the laws of trade, limitations on westward expansion, curbs on the issue of paper currency, and, most objectionable of all, the levying of parliamentary taxes on the colonies all seemed to indicate that Britain was rewarding the colonies by imposing a new status of subordination on them.

Nearly all the measures enacted after the war had been envisaged in paper plans for colonial reform going back into the early eighteenth century. There had been deep concern, amounting to a sense of crisis in official circles, about the state of the North American colonies immediately before the outbreak of fighting.[11] Even so, the war clearly made a fundamental difference. British opinion seems to have interpreted the American response to the war not as generous contributions by dutiful fellow subjects but as generally pusillanimous attempts to evade what was necessary for their own survival. Evasion could not be allowed to continue. Measures could no longer remain as mere paper aspirations. Action now had to be taken, both to solve completely new problems, such as the administration of vast additional territories or the stabilizing of a British national debt greatly inflated by wartime spending, and to deal with old problems within the existing colonies, such as defense, Indian and land policy, or trade regulation. Underlying all these was another perennial problem: uncertain colonial compliance in the past with imperial requirements. The authority of Parliament must now be invoked to enforce obedience. Empire could not therefore be based on impractical ideals of partnership and voluntary cooperation. It must be based on the effective exercise of British sovereignty.

The divergence between British and American interpretations of their respective roles in the Seven Years' War seems clear. Yet there is much about the British position that requires explanation. Why was such a pessimistic view taken of the American response to the war? As even so rigid an imperial official as Governor Bernard could recognize, a number of the colonies had made major contributions in relation to their resources. Some British politicians, such as William Pitt, seem to have recognized that, too. Pitt assured its governor that "all due attention" would be paid to Massachusetts's services.[12] Late in the war, when the colonial commitments of men and money reached their highest levels, policies under Pitt's direction were followed that were based on conciliation and a degree of partnership. As John M. Murrin wrote with perception many years ago, there were two phases to the war: the years of failure to 1757, and the years of victory thereafter. After 1763 Britain pursued the policies that had failed and ignored those that had succeeded.[13] Such an apparently perverse response merits investigation.

In the run-up to the Revolution, British political leaders are often depicted as blindly pursuing objectives that could only lead to conflict and disruption with, in Sir Lewis Namier's memorable metaphor, the undeviating rigidity of lemmings heading for the sea.[14] In retrospect, the Seven Years' War seems to have set the lemmings on an unfailing course for the cliff. On closer inspection, however, it may be that the war offered the lemmings another course, even if they declined to take it. What follows is an attempt to explain why alternative explanations of what had happened during the war did not generally prevail in Britain. This may make it easier to understand why different courses were not pursued after the war.

I

Those with experience of America commonly bewailed the lack of knowledge about the colonies that they found in men in power in Britain. The British nation was being "brought to the very brink of ruin, thro' ignorance of the object of state, the most interesting , viz. our colonies in America," wrote the Virginia agent James Abercromby in November 1756.[15] Even Lord Halifax, who was universally acknowledged to be the major British politician who had made the most extensive study of the colonies over a considerable length of time, was dismissed as a man "who deals out American facts upon very slight foundations, without the necessary enquiry; and was he not join'd in the ministry by men more ignorant than himself, he would soon be found out."[16]

As North America became a vital theater of war, those who directed the war effort from London were compelled to try to inform themselves about the colonies. The obvious official source of information available to them was the correspondence of the governors with the southern secretary of state or with the board of trade. During the war, the secretary of state and other ministers also received official correspondence from the British commanders in chief in America. With good reason, Americans came to believe that they were not likely to be well represented in Whitehall by such sources. Franklin was later to describe the imperial officials from "whom ministers chiefly have their information" as inclined to stress "their own loyal and faithful conduct with which they mix some contrary character of their people that tends to place that conduct in a more advantageous light."[17]

Taken at face value, the governors' dispatches would have created a highly unfavorable impression of how the colonies had responded to the challenges of the war, especially in its early years. Nearly all governors enthusiastically pointed out the failings of other colonies; several of them complained of the way in which their own people obstructed their best efforts to prosecute the war; and most governors were keen to expose fundamental defects in the constitutions of British America as a whole and to press for sweeping reforms that would strengthen imperial authority, particularly by bringing Parliament into play.

Robert Dinwiddie, lieutenant governor of Virginia, is a good example.

He had been quick to raise the alarm about French incursions on the Ohio and had taken wholly unsuccessful measures to eject them. He tried to pin the blame for failure both on the inertia of other colonies and on the resistance of the Virginia house of burgesses. The burgesses were "extremely obstinate and self-opinionated, and at same time infatuated, to be so unactive and indolent, when the enemy is so near our frontiers."[18] Other southern colonies would not support the efforts being made by Virginia. The two proprietary colonies, Maryland and Pennsylvania, were regarded as pariahs, both by their own governors and those of the other colonies. When the fighting began, Dinwiddie lamented that Pennsylvania, the most populous colony and directly threatened by the French and the Indians, would do nothing for its own defense.[19] Dinwiddie had heard also that the French were being supplied by British American merchants, and he believed that only through the authority of Parliament could the colonies be compelled to raise adequate funds for the war.[20]

The disillusionment of the British commanders in chief with what they found in America, the inadequacies of the support offered by the provinces, and the poor quality of American soldiers have attracted a considerable body of writing. The misunderstandings that arose from fundamentally different military cultures in the British army and the colonial forces have been sensitively explored.[21]

Edward Braddock left his superiors in Britain in no doubt as to what he thought about arrangements for prosecuting the war in America. "It would be endless, sir," he told the secretary of state, "to particularize the numberless instances of the want of publick and private faith, and of the most absolute disregard of all truth, which I have met with in the carrying on of his Majesty's service in the continent."[22] Lord Loudoun's strictures on the colonies during his command in 1756 and 1757 were much more circumstantial and carefully considered, but they were equally bleak. In a letter of August 1757, he reviewed the contributions of the colonies. The governors of Massachusetts, New York, and even Connecticut, though it was "a strange government," were all able to ensure that their provinces did their duty. South Carolina was probably doing its limited best. Georgia, North Carolina, and New Hampshire were too poor to do anything significant. The rest were all delinquent in various ways. Virginia had not fulfilled its quota. Pennsylvania had only produced half of what was required. The unspeakable Maryland was trying to keep its small contingent out of the hands of the king's general. There was "no government" in New Jersey. To make matters worse, New Jersey, Maryland, and Pennsylvania were all "under refractory Quaker influence." Finally, Rhode Islanders had turned out their governor for supporting the war effort and were "a lawless set of smugglers who continually supply the enemy with what provisions they want."[23]

Loudoun's concerns went far beyond the military failings of the colonies. He feared that America had become ungovernable.

> In all the backcountry, where we have been all the summer, the common language of the people is, that they full as lieve be under the French as the English government; and this they never fail to say, when any thing gives them the least uneasiness or displeasure.
>
> The next I have from very good authority likewise; that it is very common, for the people in the lower and more uninhabited country, to say, they would be glad to see any man, that durst offer to put an English act of Parliament in force in this country.[24]

He warned the Duke of Cumberland that the governors were "cyphers" and that "till you find a fund, independent of the province, to pay the governors and new model the government, you can do nothing with the provinces." Reforms must be pushed through now, while there was a military force to command obedience.[25]

Jeffrey Amherst, commander in chief in the last years of the war, was more circumspect in his comments. He had no regard for the provincial forces. "The disregard of orders, and studying of their own ease, rather than the good of the service, has been too often just grounds for complaint against some of the provincial officers and all their men."[26] The best that he could say of them was that "they are excellent ax men, [and] the work could not be carry'd on without them."[27]

For most British political figures, official papers were likely to have been only one source of information about America and may not have been the most important. To advance their careers, governors, senior army officers, and ambitious colonial notables all cultivated British patrons. They paid court to great men, keeping them informed of the situation in the colonies as they wished them to understand it. Major politicians were also lobbied in Britain by the supporters of colonial interests. Agents appointed by the colonies, merchant groups who traded with a particular colony, or the leaders of British religious denominations acting on behalf of their colleagues in America—all sent memoranda to ministers or sought audiences with them. They also resorted to publicizing their causes through the London newspapers.

Much of what was being fed to British informants is unlikely to have been reassuring about the state of the colonies. Officials and army officers seem to have written about the colonies in their private letters in much the same terms as they used for their official dispatches. Colonial interests in London competed for the protection of British forces by stressing their vulnerability. Georgia and South Carolina had good reason for doing so, but even Virginia and Maryland were represented by their London merchants as being "entirely defenceless both by sea and land."[28]

Pennsylvania was almost certainly the province whose affairs intruded themselves most on British political circles. It seems to have attracted a far fuller coverage in the British press than any other colony. Bitter rivalries were fought out in public in London as well as in the colony. Thomas Penn, the proprietor, sought British political allies to protect his interests. He assiduously cultivated what he called "the greatest people here."[29] In a single letter in February 1756 he described meetings with Lord Granville, Henry Fox, the Duke of Newcastle, and Halifax.[30] Other Pennsylvania voices also clamored to be heard in Britain. Those who despaired of the alleged failure of the dominant Quaker group in the assembly to sanction defensive measures on the outbreak of war launched a vigorous campaign in Britain.[31] The crown was addressed to intervene, and the addresses on the "defenceless state of the province of Pensylvania" were laid before the Commons.[32] Inflammatory pamphlets, William Smith's *Brief State of the Province of Pennsylvania* and *Brief View of the Conduct of Pennsylvania,* and numerous newspaper paragraphs warned of the dangers facing the colony. "How long must this province groan under the government of a set of enthusiasts, who will not suffer us to put forth our strength, even when the sword is at our throats?"[33] Through its agents the assembly also used the press to counter "scandalous and groundless reflexions" on it,[34] while the Quakers, the objects of particular vituperation, resorted to more discreet lobbying. The great merchant John Hanbury, Dr. John Fothergill, and the scientist Peter Collinson waited on "all who are immediately concerned in public affairs."[35] The appearance in London in 1757 of the already renowned Benjamin Franklin on a mission to represent the assembly against the proprietors added yet another competing voice. Only late in the war were rival factions in Pennsylvania able to present something like a united front to project the province in an optimistic light in the British press. In 1758 "the people" were said to be showing "a great spirit . . . to defend their country."[36]

Hard as the cacophony emanating from Pennsylvania must have been for British politicians to decipher, its overall drift was clear. A valuable colony was in disarray. This was the message being received from all over North America. French encroachments were presumed to be threatening the very existence of empire in North America,[37] and the colonial response with the possible exceptions of the New England colonies was proving to be wholly inadequate. Ministers' official and private informants uttered warnings about fundamental deficiencies in relations between the colonies and the mother country. The case for imperial intervention seemed inescapable.

II

Intervention began with the dispatch of troops from Britain. By the end of the war, British regulars had been so extensively involved in the fighting in North America that its future defense was entrusted to them apparently without any questioning. Much else was to follow from that decision. The initial response of British ministers to reports of French aggression was, however, to try to rely primarily on American manpower, which was believed to be abundant and to have proved its worth in the most striking victory of the previous war—the taking of Louisbourg in 1745 by New England soldiers. In January 1754, the Virginian Edmund Jenings was told by Lord Halifax that he understood the Virginia militia to number 13,000 and that "such a force must be sufficient for every purpose of preventing French settlement."[38] Thomas Penn reported that "it is supposed here that so great a number of Englishmen as are settled in North America would not suffer a few French to settle in the king's dominions quietly." The "greatest people here" thought that "the colonys should do something for themselves . . . and not let the whole lye on the mother country."[39]

Colonial troops in addition to saving the British taxpayer were widely thought to be better suited to war in America, an opinion reinforced by the initial failures of the British regulars. "I have often heard from very intelligent persons," wrote the Duke of Newcastle, "that the operations in those countries would be best perform'd by troops of the country; who are best used to and acquainted with the nature of the service." He added that "regular troops must not be puff'd up. . . . The Indians must be engag'd if possible and Americans must do our business."[40] American soldiers were also commonly, if usually incorrectly, assumed to be "militia," as opposed to the "mercenary" British standing army. There was, therefore, a strong ideological disposition in their favor in certain quarters. "Our American countrymen" were said to have provided a glowing example for "a British militia."[41] A member of Parliament contrasted the New Englanders with "our British mercenary soldiers"; they were the type of men who had "fought at Cressy, Nevil's Cross and Poitiers."[42]

Regular British were, however, increasingly deployed. On receiving the news of Washington's defeat at Fort Necessity, the government appointed Edward Braddock as commander in chief in America. At the insistence of the Duke of Cumberland, he was to be sent out with two regular British regiments. It was still assumed, however, that American manpower would take the major part in the operations. Braddock was to recruit his under-strength regiments in America, other British regiments were to be raised there, and provincial regiments under their own officers in the northern colonies were to undertake expeditions on their own against the French or to cooperate with regulars in Nova Scotia.[43]

The outcome of the 1755 campaign was a less than triumphant vindication of the case for British direction of the war or for the superior fighting qualities of British troops. Braddock's regulars were routed, while the New England provincials won what could be represented as a great victory at Lake George. As a "letter from Boston" in the London press put it, "The despised militia of New England have all the glory. The regulars from England have ever treated them with great contempt, but not greater than we always had for them."[44] The opposition *Monitor* insisted that the colonies should be defended by their own "brave and rough inhabitants" rather than by British "mercenaries."[45] Nevertheless, the Duke of Newcastle, who thought differently, reported that "those who govern absolutely in army affairs and military operations" still believed that regulars must be the main British force in America.[46] He was clearly referring to Cumberland, who regarded provincials as "execrable troops,"[47] and possibly to Halifax, who had come to believe that "the greatest part" of any British force must "consist of regular troops. For whatever opinions may be entertain'd of the resolution and spirit of the New Englanders, they are at best undisciplined and therefore unequal to the attack of regular troops and fortified places."[48] Following what was judged to be a poor performance by the New England troops in 1756, Thomas Penn feared that "the great dependence will be on officers and men from hence, and that those of the country will be but little employ'd. The New England army are called here disorderly bad troops, they having gone home in vast numbers."[49] A succession of commanders in chief, more senior British officers, and additional regiments of regulars were duly dispatched.

In the summer and autumn of 1756, Braddock's defeat and the devastating Indian raids that followed it were taken up by the opposition. The loss of Minorca was the main accusation against the government, but America frequently featured in the addresses to the crown or instructions to members of Parliament from counties and boroughs. The addresses repeated the language used by Pitt in December 1755 when he had castigated the government for sending only "two miserable battalions" to America.[50] The Commons was repeatedly asked to inquire into why the colonies had been left "defenceless." The Norfolk grand jury, for instance, expressed its "most anxious fears for the neglected and deplorable condition of our fellow-subjects in America" and significantly called for a militia at home, so that the "regular forces" could be sent overseas.[51] As Thomas Penn put it, "People of all sorts, the opposition most loudly, declare the colonys must be supported."[52] Ministers had no alternative to increasing the British military commitment to America. Under the short-lived Pitt-Devonshire administration, a large reinforcement of regulars was sent to America in the early months of 1757. Pitt seems to have been personally committed to sending the maximum number of regiments to America, even at the risk of weakening home defense.[53] Regulars for America had evidently become part of the program of what had been the opposition as well as of the Duke of Cumberland. Even those who regarded themselves as friends of the colonies were coming to see them not as allies capable of defending themselves but as dependants who had to be defended by Britain. The implications for the future of this change of view were ominous.

British plans for America since the outbreak of the fighting had assumed that military intervention would be accompanied by political intervention. The resources of the colonies in men and money were to be brought under effective British command. In January 1754, Halifax warned a Virginian that one of the consequences of a failure by the colonies to defend themselves would be an act of Parliament "to oblige the plantations to support as well as to raise forces."[54] In October 1754, the governors were told to raise contributions for a common fund[55] that was to be at Braddock's disposal. The agent for Massachusetts believed that "it was intended by some persons of consequence that the colonies shou'd be govern'd like Ireland, keeping up a body of standing forces there," and that there would be "an abridgment of their legislative powers, so as to put them on the same foot that Ireland stands by Poynings's law."[56] Thomas Penn reported in January 1757 that "some dutys or taxes will in a short time be laid on the colonys by act of Parliament."[57] No major reform of the way in which the colonies were governed was, however, attempted. In spite of their dissatisfaction with the contributions made to the war, ministers were evidently not prepared to risk contentious measures. The governors and the commanders in chief were left to do their best to cajole and coerce the colonies into cooperation.

III

There was a marked change of course after December 1757, as Pitt began to impose his authority over the war effort in North America. Pitt signaled his intentions for a new relationship with the colonies based more on cooperation and less on coercion by a series of measures. The northern colonies were to be encouraged to raise at least 20,000 troops for a new attempt on Canada. They were promised in return that "strong recommendations shall be made to Parliament . . . to grant a proper compensation for such expences."[58] Parliamentary reimbursement for a large part of colonial military expenditure was duly granted and was to be repeated annually for the rest of the war. It proved to be a very powerful inducement for active cooperation.

Speculation about reforms to be imposed on the colonies by act of Parliament dried up, and Pitt let it be known that he expected more conciliation and less conflict in relations between the British army and the colonies. Lord Loudoun was told that Pitt disapproved of his "preference of military to civil power" and of his "exerting too much authority over the people of the country, [and] not treating the provincial troops so well as they deserved."[59]

Loudoun's eventual successor, Jeffrey Amherst, evidently sensed what was now required. He dismayed those officers who had admired Loudoun. He is "an amiable man," one of them wrote, "but vainly fancys that he can govern these provinces by yielding and the arts of complyance." When a New York notable threatened to prosecute an officer "for pressing a slay for the publick service . . . the general in place of punishing the fellow, bowed and flatter'd and advised him." He evidently had not learned that, in America, "fear" was "a more effectual motive for action than flattery."[60] Although privately he might share many of his brother officers' prejudices, Amherst largely refrained from public controversy. He was "a great dancer" and while in winter quarters beguiled New York society with "plays, routs and assemblies almost every day."[61]

Pitt wished to see more use made of provincial officers. The principle that officers with the king's commission took precedence over officers commissioned by colonial governors was stated in 1754. A limited concession gave senior provincial officers, including generals, rank above captains but below all more senior officers in the regulars. This was much resented. Samuel Waldo, who had taken troops to Louisbourg in 1745 and was a great Massachusetts landowner, believed that, while Cumberland "had no manner of inclination to promote American officers," Pitt was sympathetic to them.[62] So he proved to be. To give "due encouragement to officers serving in our provincial corps," George II granted provincial majors, colonels, and generals rank after the equivalent British ranks.[63]

With Pitt, there was clearly a return to earlier beliefs in the potential of American manpower, together with an acceptance that this manpower could only be effectively used if American susceptibilities were observed. Whether any deeper sense of the nature of the colonies' relations with Britain lay behind Pitt's strategies for making the best of the resources of America to win the war is hard to fathom in so enigmatic a man, so given to making oracular pronouncements. His unpredictable responses to American developments after the war compound the problem. Dr. Marie Peters, whose valuable work generally stresses the limited nature of Pitt's thought about empire, suggests that he fully shared the American perception of themselves as "emigrated Englishmen" enjoying the rights of Englishmen.[64] In February 1766, he spoke of the "loyal, free and Protestant Americans."[65] Nine years later, he was to speak of "the genuine descendants of a valiant and pious ancestry, driven to those desarts by the narrow maxims of a superstitious tyranny."[66] Such people were to be cherished as valuable members of a free Protestant empire. He had the same view of the Irish Protestants, including the Presbyterians, "who were a zealous, brave and flourishing people"; their military potential too should be fully exploited.[67] Americans were not, of course, equal partners in empire. Pitt had a high view of imperial authority on such matters as economic regulation. Their assemblies were, however, genuine representative bodies, even for matters of taxation, and, as Englishmen, Americans should not be made the victims of undue exertions of military power by men like Loudoun. However incoherent, this view of empire was an alternative to the one that was to prevail after 1763. Americans may have seriously misunderstood Pitt to the point in later years of investing totally unrealistic hopes in him, but during the war the New Englanders had real grounds for holding him in "so much honor and affection" as almost to "idolize" him.[68]

The campaign of 1758 marked the turning point from the years of defeat to the years of victory. To Americans at least, these were the years in which under the wise leadership of Pitt the Anglo-colonial alliance, on which victory was built, came into being. Great numbers of provincial troops were indeed raised, and they had major roles in some of the most successful campaigns. Colonel John Bradstreet's force, which took Fort Frontenac in 1758, was almost entirely provincial. Provincials were the major part of the force that made the long slog to Fort Duquesne under Brigadier General John Forbes and were well represented at the taking of Fort Niagara.

Yet even in the years of victory, British opinion was unwilling to accept the Americans as full partners in a common effort. From the point of view of the British press and public, the heroes of North America were the British regulars and the Royal Navy, not the provincials. Moreover, much attention was given to an issue that was particularly damaging to the reputation of the colonies, trading with the enemy. Thus the euphoria of victory still could not dispel the very adverse impressions of the Americans' contribution, which had been given so much publicity in the early years of the war.

With the spectacular victories by seaborne attack at Louisbourg in 1758 and Quebec in 1759, the British army at last redeemed itself and put an end to suspicions that it could not fight in America. The taking of Louisbourg in 1758 was the turning point for the reputation of the regulars. The victory was ecstatically celebrated by illuminations, firing salutes, and feasting throughout Britain and Ireland. The captured French colors were paraded by the guards from Kensington to St Paul's.[69] The *Monitor,* which had deplored the use of "mercenaries" in America in the past, drew the conclusion that America, not "the plains of Germany," was the proper sphere for the British army.[70] The Highlanders began their long career as popular British military heroes. A letter published in the press told how they swam ashore and routed the French with their broad swords.[71] The fall of Quebec the following year produced "the greatest illuminations . . . throughout the city and suburbs that ever were known,"[72] as well as the apotheosis of General Wolfe as a British military hero killed in battle. Quebec was the focal point for a day of national thanksgiving "for the signal success of our arms by sea and land" on November 29, 1759.

Well before the end of the war, the question of trading with the enemy began to exert a malign effect on British attitudes to the colonies. From the outbreak of the war, governors and naval officers had reported that the French West Indies and Canada were regularly supplied by ships from the British North American colonies. Stories to this effect appeared in the London press.[73] The issue was brought to a head in 1759 by a report from the board of trade that focused on the huge number of colonial ships, 150 at a time, going from North America to a port of convenience in Spanish Hispaniola, called Monte Christi. From there, their bullion or supplies went straight to the French Hispaniola ports. The American ships then loaded up with French produce. Rhode Island was particularly implicated. According to the board, it and Connecticut "assume to themselves an absolute government, independant not only of the crown, but of the legislature of the mother country."[74] All this was more than Pitt could tolerate, and he sent a circular to the governors ordering them to put a stop to "this dangerous and ignominious trade" forthwith.[75] Shortly afterwards, Amherst was given

Figure 3.1. "The Death of Wolfe," by Edward Penny, c. 1764. Courtesy The Ashmolean Museum, Oxford.

evidence that judges in New York were conspiring to silence those who had information about trade with the enemy.[76] In 1762 Amherst returned to the charge with yet more evidence of "a most iniquitous proceeding in an illicit trade, by which the enemy has been furnished with provisions and stores from many parts of the continent."[77] How damaging these repeated allegations were to the standing of the colonies in British political circles was dramatically illustrated by an encounter between James Jay, agent for King's College, New York, and Lord Granville, president of the council. Jay was asking for the council's permission to launch an authorized charitable collection on behalf of the college. Granville told him that "the people in New York were a set of traitors and deserved to be hang'd instead of being assist'd." They were traitors because they had traded with the enemy. Jay found that these "horrid imputations of treason and disloyalty" were widely believed by "numbers of every rank and description."[78]

If, as seems likely, the British political public paid more attention to stories that American illegal trade was undermining the blockades of the French colonies than they did to accounts of the huge numbers of men put into the field by the colonies in the last years of the war, Americans might well have concluded that this was characteristic of the way that news reached Britain. The sources were still biased against them.

In 1759 Franklin felt it necessary publicly to correct misrepresentations about Americans that were appearing in the London press and that tended "to render the colonies despicable and even odious to the mother country."[79] Adverse comments, of which there seem to have been rather less than in the earlier years of the war, may, however, have counted for less than the dominant role that was being given to the British forces of the crown in the London press.

Through their dispatches officially published in the *London Gazette* and immediately taken up by all the newspapers, British commanders had ensured access to the press. There seems to have been no censorship or significant editing—defeats like Braddock's could feature as prominently as victories. Even the patriot press conceded that the public was "fairly and truly informed" of "all material events, the unfortunate as well as the prosperous" by the publication of "genuine, undisguised, and uncurtailed letters from our great officers by sea and land."[80] When there were victories to record, it was no doubt inevitable that they should largely be portrayed as having been won by the ships of the Royal Navy and by the regular regiments of the British army. The taking of Louisbourg and Quebec were celebrated as such. British admirals and generals became household names (Amherst was told that prints of him were "hung up at every ale house in London"),[81] while provincial generals, with the possible exception of Sir William Johnson, remained unknown. The newspaper reading public must have been left with the overwhelming impression that America had been saved not by its own but by British exertions. The colonies had been helpless victims of French and Indian aggression until they were saved by British arms.

IV

In victory, as in defeat, the war in America had been projected to Britain's political leadership and indeed a wider public in ways that belittled the colonial contribution and pointed to inadequacies in the exercise of metropolitan authority. The proposition that "Down to virtually their last detail, the reforms that followed the ending of the war reflected the legacies and lessons of the Seven Years' War as construed at the highest levels of metropolitan power" is thus unexceptionable.[82]

Yet if lessons and legacies could be clearly perceived, it was not necessarily the case that they would be acted upon. Most of the new legislation embodied proposals long discussed in Whitehall, especially in the board of trade, but never carried into execution. Ministers had been reluctant in the past to raise such issues in Parliament or to risk a crisis in the colonies. Although reform had been actively on the agenda of the invigorated board of trade under Halifax since 1748,[83] little had been achieved before all prospect of change was shelved by Pitt. War had, of course, greatly raised the stakes. The value put on the colonies in the dangerous world in which Britain found itself after the peace was much enhanced. The need to extract the maximum advantage from their trade and to ensure their future defense thus seemed to be inescapable. At the same time, Britain was facing a huge postwar debt, and there were political imperatives for any government in power to make at least a gesture toward obtaining a financial contribution from the colonies.

In the event, ministers (most notably George Grenville) took office who were not prepared to block the long-standing proposals of officials and had no inhibitions about bringing American measures before Parliament. They faced no significant opposition to any of their measures from within the main elements of the British political system. Thus the conclusion that the Seven Years' War had transformed British attitudes toward reform in the colonies seems hard to refute.

Yet it is still possible to envisage an alternative scenario. The lessons of the war were not wholly unambiguous. It had started as a war to be fought largely by Americans for limited objectives, to push the French back from the Ohio and Nova Scotia. Even when the leading role in the war was given to British troops fighting for the total subjugation of New France, the conventional wisdom of the would-be colonial reformers had been set aside for a time by the Pitt-Newcastle coalition, and the Americans had been conciliated rather than coerced. Could alternative policies have prevailed after 1763? This would no doubt have required a different political leadership in Britain after the war. The consensus of recent historical writing gives short shrift to any suggestion that the political groups that emerged as a parliamentary opposition by the end of the 1760s, the followers of Rockingham or of Pitt, now Chatham, offered an alternative that might have averted the revolutionary cataclysm. Both groups were too committed to British parliamentary sovereignty, even if with clear limitations in the case of Chatham, and both had been responsible for measures that had stoked American resentment. By the 1770s it is most unlikely that either group would have been willing to offer concessions that would have bought off American resistance. But if they had been in power after the war, would they have initiated the policies that provoked that resistance and raised the issue of sovereignty on which there could be no compromise?

It is hard to fathom how Pitt might have treated the colonies had he been in power. He attended very few debates in which American issues were discussed. He certainly accepted the deployment of the army in America in peacetime and called for a larger force to protect the British dominions there.[84] It is also likely that he strongly supported measures to enforce the Navigation Acts to which he was totally committed. On the other hand, it seems inconceivable that he could have been responsible for any measure of direct taxation, such as the Stamp Act. Above all, Pitt's evident respect for Americans' rights as emigrated Englishmen and for the established autonomies of their assemblies under British sovereign authority would surely have meant that any government in which he predominated would have been much less heavy-handed than the Grenville administration in the exercise of that authority. He spoke in an oracular way in 1763 about his doubts whether "measures of power, or force, would be proper" for "the settlement of our colonies, upon a proper foot, with regard to themselves, and the mother countrey."[85]

The Rockingham group claimed to be the heirs of Walpole and the Pelhams. The Duke of Newcastle was still associated with them. For all his infirmity of purpose and apparent lack of conviction on American issues, the duke stood for an older tradition of colonial policy. At least in the early stages of the war, he seems to have believed that Americans should as far as possible be left to fight it in their own way largely by themselves. "Until the end of his days," it has been said of him, "the duke resisted the idea that Parliament was omnipotent and could impose its will upon those in America without qualification."[86] Like other Whig politicians of his generation, he was wary of bringing American issues before Parliament. The refusal to introduce major legislation during the war shows how strongly this tradition persisted.

Members of the Rockingham connection did little to oppose the new colonial measures in Parliament after the war, and by no means all of them shared Newcastle's views about colonial issues. Lord Hardwicke's son, Charles Yorke, for instance, a keen stickler for parliamentary sovereignty, told the duke that "my notions about the Americans were *insanity*."[87] Charles Townshend, a board of trade reformer, took the lead on American issues for the Rockinghams on occasions. Even more ominously for Americans, the Duke of Cumberland was the Rockinghams' patron for a time. Yet the personal enthusiasm of Rockingham for the conciliatory policies that he introduced in 1766 seems to be beyond doubt. An administration in which he and Newcastle played dominant roles would probably have proceeded with a degree of caution on colonial issues after the war.

It would be quite vain to suppose that any British administration would have tried to reshape the empire on a new basis embodying the ideals of partnership and equality increasingly espoused in America. Ideas of parliamentary sovereignty were far too deeply entrenched across the British political spectrum. But a continuation into the years of peace of something like the coalition that had held power from 1757 to 1761 might conceivably have led to policies toward the colonies that seemed less intrusive to them and that were introduced at a less frenetic pace. The goodwill toward the empire generated by the war and the ties of commerce, migration of peoples, shared cultural and consumer tastes, and religious denominational fellowship, which were to grow so strongly in the 1760s,[88] might then have eased Anglo-American relations through the inevitable strains of the postwar adjustments. Formal imperial authority would no doubt have continued to be eroded, and governors, commanders in chief, and members of the board of trade would have continued to fulminate against this trend. Under Pitt and Newcastle, they might perhaps have fulminated to little effect, as they had so often done in the past. By 1763, it was already too late to try to put the clock back to some imaginary time when imperial authority had been obeyed. Within a few years, imperial authority would presumably have shrunk even further. American independence would have been delayed and eventually achieved "without a war of national liberation," the scenario that Fred Anderson envisages had there been no Seven Years' War.[89] In retrospect, if not to contemporaries, such a scenario from a British point of view is an attractive alternative to what was to happen.

To suppose such a scenario possible involves a high degree of wishful thinking. It supposes that Americans had not been so powerfully represented to all sections of British opinion as, at worst, people who willfully neglected their obligations, at best, as feeble victims of French aggression. It also supposes a different and most unlikely configuration of British domestic politics. The wartime coalition had broken down well before the ending of the war, and the supporters of Pitt and Newcastle never cooperated thereafter. America was obviously low in their priorities, and they put up no sort of opposition to the new policies, whatever they may have thought of them. The most that can be said is that some British politicians did have alternative interpretations as to how the war could and should be fought. These were, however, always minority views, even if they prevailed after 1757. The dominant view of American incapacity and turpitude, propagated through official channels of communication, through much of what appeared in the press and probably through personal contacts, had not, however, been dispelled. It reasserted itself after the war, when those who had labored so long to reform the British colonial system were able to win what was no doubt for them an incomplete victory. Rhode Island, for instance, kept its charter. Yet enough was done to wreck an empire. Armed with what contemporaries found a compellingly impressive interpretation of the Seven Years' War, the reformers could ensure that there would be no deviation in the lemmings' rush for the cliff.

Notes

1. Fred Anderson, *Crucible of War: The Seven Years' War and the Fate of Empire in British North America, 1754–1766* (New York: Alfred A. Knopf, 2000), xvi.

2. Douglas Edward Leach, *Roots of Conflict: British Armed Forces and Colonial Americans, 1677–1763* (Chapel Hill: University of North Carolina Press, 1986), 166. See also Alan Rogers, *Empire and Liberty: American Resistance to British Authority, 1755–1763* (Berkeley: University of California Press, 1974).

3. John Shy, *Toward Lexington: The Role of the British Army in the Coming of the American Revolution* (Princeton: Princeton University Press, 1965), 143.

4. Anderson, *Crucible of War,* 412, 805–6.

5. Jack P. Greene, "The Seven Years' War and the American Revolution: The Causal Relationship Reconsidered," *Journal of Imperial and Commonwealth History* 8, no. 2 (January 1980): 98.

6. William Pencak, "Warfare and Political Change in Mid-Eighteenth-Century Massachusetts," *Journal of Imperial and Commonwealth History* 8, no. 2 (January 1980): 52.

7. Francis Bernard to Board of Trade, August 18, 1760, Public Record Office (PRO), Colonial Office (CO) 5/891, f. 3. Bernard later set out in detail the extent of the province's contribution to the war in a letter to the board, August 1, 1764, PRO, CO 323/19, f. 14.

8. Greene, "Seven Years' War and the American Revolution," 99.

9. Anderson, *Crucible of War,* 712.

10. Francis Bernard to C. Townshend, May 18, 1763, Harvard University, Houghton Library, Sparks MSS, 4/3, p. 60.

11. Jack P. Greene, "'A Posture of Hostility': A Reconsideration of Some Aspects of the American Revolution," *Proceedings of the American Antiquarian Society* 87, pt. 1 (April 1977): 30–67.

12. To T. Pownall, December 9, 1758, in Gertrude Selwyn Kimball, ed., *The Correspondence of William Pitt, When Secretary of State, with the Colonial Governors and Military and Naval Commissioners in North America,* 2 vols. (New York: Macmillan, 1906), 1:136–43.

13. John M. Murrin, "The French and Indian War, the American Revolution, and the Counter-factual Hypothesis: Reflections on Lawrence Henry Gipson and John Shy," *Reviews in American History* 1, no. 3 (September 1973): 307–16.

14. Lewis Namier, *England in the Age of the American Revolution,* 2nd ed. (London: Macmillan, 1961), 41. This phrase was taken up in Jack P. Greene, "The Plunge of Lemmings: A Consideration of Recent Writings on British Politics and the American Revolution," *South Atlantic Quarterly* 67, no. 1 (winter 1968): 141–75.

15. James Abercromby to W. Pitt, November 25, 1756, PRO, CO 30/8/95, f. 199.

16. R. H. Morris to R. Peters, April 6, 1757, Historical Society of Pennsylvania (HSP), Peters Papers, 4:86.

17. "Fragments of a Pamphlet" [January 1766], in Leonard W. Labaree et al., eds., *The Papers of Benjamin Franklin* (New Haven: Yale University Press, 1959–), 13:80.

18. Robert Dinwiddie to T. Robinson, September 23, 1754, in R. A. Brock, ed., *The Official Records of Robert Dinwiddie, Lieutenant-Governor of the Colony of Virginia, 1751–1758,* 2 vols. (Richmond: Virginia Historical Society, 1883–84), 1:324.

19. Dinwiddie to T. Robinson, November 16, 1754, ibid., 1:405.

20. Dinwiddie to Holdernesse, September 23, 1754, ibid., 1:334–35; Dinwiddie to T. Robinson, January 20, 1755, ibid., 472–75.

21. See Fred Anderson, *A People's Army: Massachusetts Soldiers and Society in the Seven Years' War* (Chapel Hill: University of North Carolina Press, 1984). See also Leach, *Roots of Conflict,* and the material in Stanley Pargellis, ed., *Military Affairs in North America, 1748–1765: Selected Documents from the Cumberland Papers in Windsor Castle* (New York: Appleton-Century, 1936).

22. Edward Braddock to T. Robinson, June 5, 1755, PRO, CO 5/46, f. 21.

23. Loudoun to Holdernesse, August 16, 1757, PRO, CO 5/46, ff. 288–89.

24. Loudoun to Halifax, December 26, 1756, Huntington Library (HL), LO 2416.

25. Loudoun to Cumberland, November 22–December 26, 1756, in Pargellis, ed., *Military Affairs,* 273.

26. Cited Anderson, *Crucible of War,* 372.

27. Jeffrey Amherst to W. Pitt, October 22, 1759, in Kimball, ed., *Pitt Correspondence,* 2:197.

28. Petition of January 1, 1757, PRO, CO 5/18, f. 2.

29. Thomas Penn to R. H. Morris, January 27, 1756, HSP, Thomas Penn Letter Books, 4:219.

30. Thomas Penn to W. Allen, February 17, 1756, HSP, Thomas Penn Letter Books, 4:238.

31. See Alan Tully, *Forming American Politics: Ideals, Interests, and Institutions in Colonial New York and Pennsylvania* (Baltimore: Johns Hopkins University Press, 1994), 149–59.

32. R. C. Simmons and P. D. G. Thomas, eds., *Proceedings and Debates of the British Parliaments Respecting North America, 1754–1783,* 6 vols. (Millwood, N.Y.: Kraus, 1982–89), 1:140–41.

33. "Letter from Philadelphia," *Public Advertiser,* January 19, 1756.

34. "Letter from a Gentleman in Philadelphia," *Public Advertiser,* July 12, 1755.

35. Dr. John Fothergill to J. Pemberton, March 16–19, 1757, HSP, Etting Collection, vol. 29, no. 10.

36. *Lloyd's Evening Post,* July 31–August 2, 1758.

37. T. R. Clayton, "The Duke of Newcastle, the Earl of Halifax, and the American Origins of the Seven Years' War," *Historical Journal* 24, no. 3 (September 1981): 571–603.

38. E. Jenings to R. Dinwiddie, January 25, 1754, Virginia Historical Society, MS J 4105a 1, pp. 27–28.

39. Thomas Penn to J. Hamilton, January 29, 1754, HSP, Thomas Penn Letter Books, 3:289.

40. Newcastle to Holdernesse, August 26, 1755, British Library (BL), Add MS 32858, ff. 289, 292.

41. *Public Advertiser,* November 10, 1755.

42. Speech of Robert Vyner, December 16, 1754, in Simmons and Thomas, eds., *Proceedings and Debates,* 1:31.

43. Clayton, "American Origins"; Dominick Graham, "British Intervention in Defence of the American Colonies, 1748–56" (Ph.D. thesis, London University, 1969).

44. *Public Advertiser,* November 5, 1755.

45. *Monitor,* September 13, 1755.

46. Newcastle to Hartington, August 26, 1755, BL, Add MS 32858, f. 352.

47. Cumberland to Loudoun, October 22, 1756, in Pargellis, ed., *Military Affairs,* 251.

48. "Remarks on Affairs in North America," HL, LO 722.

49. Thomas Penn to R. Peters, December 11, 1756, HSP, Thomas Penn Letter Books, 5:51.

50. Pitt, speech of December 5, 1755, in Simmons and Thomas, eds., *Proceedings and Debates,* 1:110.

51. *Public Advertiser,* September 9, 1756. For the addresses, see Kathleen Wilson, *The Sense of the People: Politics, Culture, and Imperialism in England, 1715–1785* (Cambridge: Cambridge University Press, 1995), 178–85; L. S. Sutherland, "The City of London and the Devonshire-Pitt Administration, 1756–57," in Aubrey Newman, ed., *Politics and Finance in the Eighteenth Century: Lucy Sutherland* (London: Hambledon Press, 1984), 72–76.

52. Thomas Penn to R. Peters, December 13, 1755, HSP, Thomas Penn Letter Books, 4:190.

53. See letters to Loudoun from Sackville and Cathcart, February 4, 1757, HL, LO 2778 and 2858.

54. E. Jenings to R. Dinwiddie, January 25, 1754, Virginia Historical Society, MS J 4105a 1.

55. T. Robinson, circular letter, October 26, 1754, PRO, CO 5/211, f. 96.

56. W. Bollan to J. Willard, March 5, 1755, Massachusetts Historical Society, Miscellaneous Bound Manuscripts.

57. Thomas Penn to R. Peters, January 8, 1757, HSP, Thomas Penn Letter Books, 5:61.

58. Pitt to governors, December 30, 1757, in Kimball, ed., *Pitt Correspondence*, 1:136–43.

59. J. Calcraft to Loudoun, December 29, 1757, HL, LO 5140.

60. J. Robertson to Loudoun, February 3, 1759, HL, LO 6039.

61. J. Abercromby to Loudoun, February 4, 1759, HL, LO 6041.

62. Samuel Waldo to T. Flucker, May 14, 1757, Massachusetts Historical Society, Henry Knox MSS 50.

63. Warrant, December 13, 1757, HL, AB 8.

64. Marie Peters, "The Myth of William Pitt, Earl of Chatham, Great Imperialist, Part II: Chatham and Imperial Reorganization, 1763–78," *Journal of Imperial and Commonwealth History* 22, no. 3 (September 1994): 395; see also Peters, "The Myth of William Pitt, Earl of Chatham, Great Imperialist, Part I: Pitt and Imperial Expansion, 1738–63," *Journal of Imperial and Commonwealth History* 21, no. 1 (January 1993): 31–74, and the treatment of American issues in Peters, *The Elder Pitt* (London: Longmans, 1998).

65. Pitt, speech of February 5, 1766, in Simmons and Thomas, eds., *Proceedings and Debates*, 2:161.

66. Chatham, speech of January 20, 1775, ibid., 5:276.

67. Pitt to Bedford, November 21, 1759, PRO, SP 63/416, ff. 159–60; see also Pitt to Bedford, January 5, 1760, PRO, SP 63/417, f. 152.

68. E. Stiles to B. Franklin, December 30, 1761, *Franklin Papers*, 9:403.

69. *London Chronicle*, September 5–7, 1758.

70. *Monitor*, August 26, 1758.

71. "Letter from a Man of War Returned from Louisbourg," September 18, 1758, *London Chronicle*, September 23–26, 1758.

72. *Gentleman's Magazine* 29 (October 1759): 495.

73. For example, *London Chronicle*, March 28–30, 1758.

74. James Munro, ed., *Acts of the Privy Council of England. Colonial Series*, 6 vols. (London: H. M. Stationery Office, 1908–12), 4:444–45.

75. Kimball, *Pitt Correspondence*, 2:320.

76. See material in PRO, CO 5/60, ff. 52–53, 60, 170.

77. Amherst to Egremont, May 12, 1762, PRO, CO 5/62, f. 4.

78. P. J. Marshall, "Who Cared about the Thirteen Colonies? Some Evidence from Philanthropy," *Journal of Imperial and Commonwealth History* 27, no. 2 (May 1999): 59–60.

79. Benjamin Franklin to *London Chronicle,* May 9, 1759, *Franklin Papers,* 8:340–56.

80. "Cato the Censor," reprinted in *London Chronicle,* September 26–28, 1758.

81. West to Amherst, February 10, 1759, PRO, WO 34/77, f. 8.

82. Anderson, *Crucible of War,* 559.

83. James Henretta, *"Salutary Neglect": Colonial Administration under the Duke of Newcastle* (Princeton: Princeton University Press, 1972), 297–318.

84. Pitt, speech of March 4, 1763, in Simmons and Thomas, eds., *Proceedings and Debates,* 1:440–41.

85. Newcastle to Devonshire, August 11, 1763, BL, Add MS 32950, f. 71.

86. Henretta, *Salutary Neglect,* 342. See also Paul Langford, "Old Whigs, Old Tories, and the American Revolution," *Journal of Imperial and Commonwealth History* 8, no. 2 (January 1980): 114–15.

87. Newcastle to Rockingham, January 25, 1766, BL, Add MS 32973, f. 275.

88. P. J. Marshall, "Britain and the World in the Eighteenth Century, II, Britons and Americans," *Transactions of the Royal Historical Society,* 6th ser., 9 (1999): 1–16.

89. Anderson, *Crucible of War,* xvi.

II

The American Revolution

4

British Perceptions of New England and the Decision for a Coercive Colonial Policy, 1774–1775

Julie Flavell

> The Word general puts me in mind of a General, your General
> Clarke, who had the Folly to say in my hearing at Sir John Pringle's,
> that, with a Thousand British grenadiers, he would undertake to go
> from one end of America to the other, and geld all the Males, partly
> by force and partly by a little Coaxing. It is plain he took us for a
> species of Animals very little superior to Brutes.[1]

Thus, a year after the peace, did Benjamin Franklin humorously recollect the contempt for the colonial soldier that was part of the London scene at the eve of the War of Independence. Indeed, a conviction of colonial ineptitude was a contributing factor in the coming of war. As one historian put it, "It was apparently inconceivable . . . that the Americans had either the will or the ability to resist the British military."[2] There is no doubt that the assurance of victory heartened ministers as they chose a coercive response to the latest round of colonial resistance. British complacency on this score fits in with a picture of the government at the start of the conflict as out of touch with the true state of affairs in the colonies. The government's "decisive failures of understanding" regarding the mood in the colonies in 1774–75 comprehended not only politics but also military considerations, specifically an underestimation of colonial fighting capacity and an overestimation of the extent of Loyalist support the British army could expect.[3]

But a miscalculation that led to such a disaster for Britain deserves a closer look. After all, the American Revolution was the only significant uprising within the eighteenth-century empire that the British failed to suppress. The British army of the period was a small one by European standards, but it nevertheless prevailed in colonial conquests and military domination of its peripheries by exploiting native divisions—the rival dynasties of India, the religious conflicts of Ireland, the clan rivalry of Scotland. So why did the British ignore the Cassandra-like warnings of General Harvey and others in 1775—pointing to the fact that the conquest of America would involve an extent of territory greater than Scotland, Madras, or Ireland—and allow hubris, this once, to lead to their downfall? Why, to paraphrase Harry Truman's comment on the prospect of all-out war against China, did they allow themselves to be dragged into the "gigantic booby trap" of war in North America?

This chapter recalls that the American Revolution began as a New England uprising. It examines British assumptions surrounding the prospect of a war limited to that region in 1774–75. In so doing, it helps to make sense of the British slide to war. New England was the most distinctive province in British North America. Both metropolitans and the colonists to the south shared a view of New England as one of the empire's underdeveloped peripheries, whose rusticity and warlike proclivities invited comparisons with troublesome Scotland. On both sides of the Atlantic, New England was the most disliked and least trusted section of British North America on the eve of war.

British strategists assumed that in a war confined to New England, colonial sectionalism would play a part in a British victory. New England's distinctiveness could be used to detach it from the more valuable and better integrated colonies to the south. But after 1776, the British shifted the theater of war southward, anticipating that another kind of division—the political one of Loyalist versus Patriot—would work in their favor. Ultimately, however, they found themselves attempting to dominate a territory whose vastness overextended their resources, and whose significant sectional differences—which were to prove much more enduring than the political animosities that had sparked off the war of independence—were more easily put aside while they found themselves opposing a common British enemy. By choosing to exploit political divisions rather than sectionalism, the British helped to drive the former colonies into a union that was both unprecedented and fragile but that nonetheless brought them to victory and nationhood.

The Idea of War in New England

It is well known that the experience of the Seven Years' War had left British officers with the conviction that the Yankee was a "poor species of fighting man."[4] But it also left a conviction that an armed challenge to British rule was more likely to come from New England than from anywhere else. In 1763, British officials considered retaining a garrison at Crown Point, in New England's hinterland, in order to guard "against any Disobedience or Disaffection amongst the Inhabitants of the Maritime Provinces [New England], who already begin to entertain Some extraordinary Opinions, concerning their Relations and Dependance on their Mother Country."[5] The idea that New England was meditating independence from the empire cropped up again from time to time during the subsequent decade, and in 1776 Lord Mansfield asserted in the House of Lords that the "Northern Colonies" had been plotting independence since the Peace of Paris.[6] After August 1774, when General Thomas Gage realized that he was facing not a Boston mob but armed opposition from all over New England, he presumed a war confined to the "conquest of New England." The king, in late 1774, made his well-known comment, "The New England governments are in a state of rebellion, blows must decide whether they are to be subject to this country or independent."[7]

This assumption of a limited war was shared by observers in the Atlantic world. By autumn 1774, when the prospect of an armed confrontation in America had reached the public sphere, commentators pictured a local New England uprising. An observer in London, anticipating the effect of the Coercive Acts in America, declared that "the New England Men . . . will not tamely receive the Yoke. Blood will be shed." A South Carolina merchant wrote of "the Horrors of a Civil War in N. England" in early 1775. James Duane of New York wrote in December 1774, "If we proceed to Extremities the principal Burthen of a War they [the people of New York] think will fall upon New England without any effectual Succor from their Neighbours."[8]

In 1774 and early 1775, British policymakers were presuming that if war broke out in the colonies, it would be a localized New England conflict. Containment was a realistic policy for both economic and geographical reasons. New England was the poorest and most crowded region within the mainland American colonies. Since midcentury, when the Connecticut Valley had at last filled up, migrants had been streaming into Pennsylvania and beyond. By the late colonial period, Massachusetts and Rhode Island had urbanized to the extent that they were importing food.[9] New England on its own, as Major Patrick Ferguson pointed out, could not hold out for long; its people "have always found difficulty in subsisting without foreign Supplys, & their very numbers which enable them to assist powerfully in any enterprise from Home, would be the Means of hastening their Submission."[10]

Of Britain's provinces in North America, New England was seen as the most vulnerable economically. Britain's most valued mainland American colonies were Virginia and South Carolina. New England, by contrast, was increasingly seen as a troublesome rival.[11] In September 1774, General Gage commented to Dartmouth, "These People esteem themselves of much greater Benefit to Great Britain, than it is believed by many that they would be found to be, upon a critical Examination. The Fisheries in which they are Rivals, Pot-Ash, Lumber and Iron, and Shipping, all of which is either exported to Britain, or other Places under the Protection of Britain has made them opulent, were they cast off and declared Aliens, they must become a poor and needy People."[12] By contrast, Major Ferguson noted that the wealthy tobacco colonies of the Chesapeake region were the only assets by which the Americans could "lure to their assistance the powers of Europe" in a war with Britain.[13] Geographically, New England was vulnerable to encirclement; her ports could be bottled up, and her backcountry could be cut off by controlling Lake Champlain and the Hudson. No wonder that Gage suggested in a private letter to Lord Barrington in August 1774 that if it came to a war with New England, "you wou'd be able to overcome them, no doubt, in a year or two."[14]

The danger was that an insurrection might receive support from the wealthier colonies to the south. British officers in America in 1774 and early 1775 considered the development of a Continental Congress in military terms. It was not only a source of further constitutional debate and trade stoppages but also a potential source of funds for a New England army. Writing from Boston, Gage warned Dartmouth in December 1774 that "the aim of the hot Leaders here has been to have a Body of Troops in Pay, and under their Direction, and to perswade the other Colonies to contribute towards the Expence"; thus far, noted Gage, the Congress had not agreed.[15] Gage reported that the New Englanders were confident of the outcome of a fight between themselves and regular troops: "Many of their Leaders I apprehend mean to bully and terrify, and others to push Matters to extremity, puffed up by the Hopes of Assistance from the whole Continent, and the Certainty of the immediate aid of the four New-England Provinces, which they flatter themselves are alone sufficient to withstand all the Force of Great Britain."[16]

Historian Jeremy Black has criticized the British for not acting quickly enough after Lexington and Concord to prevent the collapse of royal government in the southern colonies.[17] But as Sir John Fortescue tells us, contemporary military advisers saw spreading the war as a mistake.[18] In early 1776, General Howe criticized acts that expanded the war. Of Dunmore's clumsy attempt to rouse Virginia's slave population the previous year, he remarked, "It is to be presumed the southern rebels would have been less able to defend themselves, had they not been roused up by the conduct of their governors, who have not, I fear, the means of suppressing them." Howe had not been consulted about the expedition to the Carolinas, which had been supported by Lord North as much for reasons of political expediency as for any compelling military objective. He gave Lord Dartmouth his reaction to the scheme in plain terms: "I am free to own my opinion to your Lordship which has been to leave the southern provinces in the fullest persuasion of their security until the rebels should have been defeated on the side of New York." He continued, "our utmost strength should be exerted to accomplish it before designs of less importance are taken up inconsistent with the general plan of operations for the ensuing compaign."[19] For British military personnel, the expansion of military operations outside of New England after April 19 was by no means a foregone conclusion. The possibility of confining the war to New England persisted as a viable alternative throughout 1775.[20]

When Lord North proposed in early 1775 that Massachusetts Bay was in a state of rebellion, Edmund Burke ridiculed his stubborn persistence in thus distinguishing that colony, pointing out that other colonies—notably Virginia—were equally forward in protesting British legislation, "and that therefore it was plain it was not Boston, but America; and if you meant a war with the whole, you ought with your eyes open to prepare for that, and not for a skuffle at Boston."[21] Historians have joined in this indictment of the North administration's fatal short-sightedness, and events proved Burke correct. But, of course, all this is with the benefit of hindsight. Privately, the opposition had doubts as to whether colonial unity could survive for long. Rockingham himself believed that the colonies were so notoriously unable to agree among themselves that the best they could achieve was a temporary unity in opposition to British measures.[22] And New England was recognized throughout the Atlantic world as the most distinctive and least integrated of the mainland regions.

New England's Image in the English Atlantic World

Sir Henry Clinton, in his account of "The American Rebellion" published after the war, began with a sketch of "the military face of the theater of the war, and the ability of its inhabitants to defend it" at the outset of the conflict, revealing how the metropolis perceived New England in contrast to the other colonies in 1774–75. The states to the east of the Hudson River, he began, teem with a robust and hardy race of men, who are seated in general in a mountainous and a strongly defensible country, accessible, however, from the sea by numerous bays and inlets, which afford most excellent harbors for shipping. The other[s] . . . to the south and westward of that river are somewhat less difficult for military operations . . . ; and the white inhabitants (who from constitution and climate are less qualified for war than their northern neighbors, and in the five more southern provinces are inferior in number to the blacks) cannot be so readily or in such force collected for their internal defense, from the comparative inferiority of their armed strength and their more scattered situation, having but few towns and living in general on their respective plantations.[23]

Clinton's description of the thirteen colonies on the eve of the war with Britain reflects the fact that as John Murrin has pointed out, the most conspicuous regional division in the colonies was "New Englanders" versus "everyone else."[24] Everything to the south of New England was often referred to as the "southern colonies."

Within the eighteenth-century English Atlantic world, New England was ascribed several distinct characteristics. Its formative Puritan heritage was well known; its lifestyle was reputed to be rustic; the manners of its people lacked gentility; its seaport trading people were frequently depicted as enterprising sharpers.[25] In the commentary of both wealthier colonists to the south of New England and British officers, New England's Puritan heritage was viewed as having long since degenerated into a hypocritical, sanctimonious pose (though it could take on the unlovely form of fanaticism at times).[26]

New England manners were deplored in identical language by metropolitans and colonial elites south of Connecticut. From New York, we find a merchant in 1763 ordering that his son never be sent to Yale because he might imbibe "that low Craft and cunning so Incident to the People of that Country, which is so interwoven in their constitutions that all their art cannot disguise it from the World tho' many of them under the sanctified Garb of Religion have Endeavored to Impose themselves on the World for honest Men." Virginian George Washington found the leveling tendencies of New Englanders distasteful, and noted, "They are an exceedingly dirty and nasty people." A South Carolinian member of Congress, Edward Rutledge, said of the New Englanders, "I dread their low Cunning, and those levelling Principles which Men without Character and without Fortune in general Possess, which are so captivating to the lower Class of Mankind."[27]

British officers in New England described the people in the same language. Lord Percy reported in 1774, after a month at Boston, "The people here are a set of sly, artful, hypocritical rascals, cruel & cowards. I must own I cannot but despise them compleately." A few months wrought no improvement in his mind: "The People here are the most designing, Artfull Villains in the World. They have not the least Idea of either Religion or Morality." In 1777, Captain John Bowater, who was stationed in Rhode Island, used similar terms: "The Natives are such a Levelling, underbred, Artfull, Race of people that we Cannot Associate with them. Void of principal, their whole Conversation is turn'd on their Interest." A "sad set of presbyterian Rascals they are" was his conclusion.[28]

John Adams was mortified to learn at the First Continental Congress just how his "Countrymen" (as he called them) were regarded to the south. Admittedly, he wrote, New Englanders wanted "Art and Address": "Our N. England People are Aukward and Bashfull; yet they are pert, ostentatious and vain, a Mixture which excites Ridicule and gives Disgust." He confessed, "They have not the faculty of shewing themselves to the best Advantage, nor the Art of concealing this faculty." Adams attributed this to "the little Intercourse We have with strangers, and to our Inexperience in the World."[29] New Englanders of substance were far less likely to invest in a metropolitan education for their youth, or finish their upbringing with a Grand Tour, than were well-to-do colonists to the south.[30] Their manners and speech were not as consciously patterned on metropolitan standards. Bostonian Josiah Quincy, reaching London in November 1774, gained an audience with Lord North, who afterward (in words that echoed those of John Adams) pronounced him "a bad, insidious man, designing to be artful without abilities to conceal his design."[31] Clearly New England manners struck the same note of discord throughout the Atlantic world.

New Englanders were also recognized as a people who, because of the poorness of their soil, were obliged to resort to conduct that was a "blemish on their Integrity," in other words, smuggling—hence the accusations of "low Craft and cunning," which were so frequently leveled at them.[32] *Artfulness* and *cunning* were terms that were also applied to Scots traders during the period.

But Clinton referred to yet another quality—the New Englanders were more "qualified for war" than the colonies to the south. In the eighteenth century, New Englanders were seen as the most militarized of Britain's North American colonists, not only in their collective capacity to prepare for war, but in their individual capacities as fighters. This martial image was established early in the eighteenth century, when New Englanders began to see themselves as adept at wilderness fighting. New Englanders compared themselves favorably with colonists to the south in this respect and also with British regular soldiers, although the latter were also sometimes the objects of grudging respect.[33]

That the other colonies shared this perception of New England can be seen from the alarm that the prospect of a New England army aroused in the early stages of the conflict with Britain. Samuel Adams, upon arriving at the First Continental Congress, confided to Joseph Warren, "There is . . . a certain degree of jealousy in the minds of some, that we aim at a total independency, not only of the mother-country, but of the colonies too; and that, as we are a hardy and brave people, we shall in time overrun them all." John Adams recalled that in the first weeks of the meeting of the second Continental Congress, there was a party favoring a petition to the king, a party "jealous of independence," and "a third party, which was a southern party against a northern and a jealousy against a New England army under the command of a New England general." This southern concern did not merely reflect regional pride. Adams noted that most southerners were "fearful of New England's imperial ambitions." In June 1775, he reported that some other members of Congress were concerned that New England, "full of Veteran Soldiers," would "conceive Designs unfavourable to the other Colonies." Connecticut congressman Eliphalet Dyer described "the fear of [the southern colonies] lest an Enterprising eastern New England Genll proving Successfull, might with his Victorious Army give law to the Southern & Western Gentry."[34]

Loyalists made much of this prospect in arguments opposing the rebellion. Tory propaganda warned that "The Northern colonies, inured to military discipline and hardships" would "carry devastation and havoc" over the colonies to the south. Blaming New England for the start of hostilities, Jonathan Boucher cautioned the southern deputies to the Congress in a public letter that echoed the words of Sam Adams: "See ye not that after some few years of civil broils all the fair settlements in the middle and southern colonies will be seized on by our more enterprising and restless fellow-colonists of the North? O 'tis a monstrous and an unnatural coalition," prophesied Boucher "and we should as soon expect to see the greatest contrarieties in Nature to meet in harmony, and the wolf and the lamb to feed together, as Virginians to form a cordial union with the saints of New England."[35]

These worries seemed to be justified by New England actions in the first months of war. After the start of hostilities at Concord, the New Englanders acted quickly and aggressively to avoid being cut off and isolated by their enemies. They did not always wait for the sanction of a continental or provincial congress. Clinton noted that shortly after news of Lexington, several Connecticut regiments appeared in the neighborhood of New York, "animating the disaffected in that city," disempowering the moderates, and leading to the election of New York delegates to the Congress.[36] News of the unauthorized seizure of Ticonderoga by Grants settlers and Connecticut militia filled many members of Congress with consternation. It was followed by calls from the New England backcountry to invade Canada forthwith.[37] In Philadelphia, three months after the start of the conflict, James Tilghman reported nervously to William Baker that "everything seems verging towards anarchy." Pennsylvania riflemen who went to join the patriot forces at Boston "sent a Memorial to the Congress, expressing their Expectation that, as they were leaving their Lands & Possessions on the public service, they sho'd be protected from the Violences of the Connecticut People." These were now [in Wyoming] openly declaring that "they shall pay no regard to the Decision of the King & Council, if it should be against them, & that they will possess the Country by force." Tilghman's words chime in with a letter sent to Brigadier General Robertson in late May 1775, reporting, "The affair at Lexington has given such ideas of New England prowess that the Americans will listen to no terms but such as they themselves shall dictate." New Englanders in Congress, he continued, were blocking discussion of compromises such as Chatham's proposal and North's conciliatory offer. New Yorkers, he reported, "hate the New Englanders."[38] John Adams heard a congressman from New York express dread of the New Englanders, like Boucher describing them as "Goths and Vandalls." [39] It was clear that some colonists—like the British officers in Boston—feared at the outset of hostilities what might be unleashed by funding a New England army.

Clinton's description of the "populous and hardy eastern colonies" in his account of the war reveals that British officers shared this perception of New England as the most militarized region of the North American colonies, "more qualified for war" than the colonies to the south. British officers stationed in Boston in 1774–75 believed that they were dealing with an armed citizenry. Lord Percy, assessing the likelihood of an armed confrontation in September 1774, reported, "What makes an insurrection here always more formidable than in other places, is that there is a law of this Province, wh[ich] obliges every inhabitant to be furnished with a firelock, bayonet, & pretty considerable quantity of ammunition."[40] A military report submitted a month before Lexington and Concord described the "habitual use of the firelock" that prevailed in the province, asserting that the locals were "sure of their mark at the distance of 200 rods."[41] General Howe, planning the campaign of 1776 from his Boston camp (a campaign he still thought of as limited to New England), spoke of "the young men of spirit in the country" who made up much of the rebel army, and "who are exceedingly diligent and attentive to their military profession."[42]

The British shared with New Englanders the view that the Yankees understood irregular wilderness warfare. Lord Germain compared the British rout at Lexington and Concord to Braddock's defeat at the hands of experienced French and Indian irregulars, arguing that the regular army needed to augment its training in light infantry tactics in order to wage war in America.[43] In summer 1775, Burgoyne put to Lord Rochford the impossibility of stirring from Boston camp, outnumbered as they were, and "against such an enemy, who in composition and system are all light troops."[44] Percy, assessing the capacity of the New Englanders after hostilities had begun, commented, "They have men amongst them who know very well what they are about, having been employed as Rangers agst the Indians & Canadians, & this country being much covd w. wood, and hilly, is very advantageous for their method of fighting." [45]

The New Englander as a soldier is not usually considered by historians exploring the colonial transition from Puritan to Yankee or discussing the development of New England's regional identity.[46] Although the impact of participation in the colonial wars on New England's culture and society has been explored in several perceptive studies, the fighting qualities of the New England male have remained largely the domain of literary histories.[47] But for their contemporaries in the English Atlantic world, the militarized character of New England's people was a significant regional trait. In the eighteenth century, metropolitans viewed England's peripheries within an interpretive scheme that stressed "regional cultures at different levels of civility."[48] Theorists such as Adam Smith invoked models that depicted human society as evolving through stages that could be distinguished by their increasing complexity. Degree of militarization figured prominently in the assessment of a people's level of development. As civilization advanced, the military obligations—and capacity—of the citizenry declined.[49]

New England's militarized image stemmed not only from that region's participation in the colonial wars but also from the perception that it was less developed than the other colonies to the south. British officers and colonial elites from New York southward clearly saw New Englanders as underdeveloped, and this was apparent by their comments on New England manners, leveling social arrangements, religious practices, and, I suggest, warlike character. Although New England was the most distinctive of the mainland American regions in the eighteenth century, to metropolitans and colonists to the south this was not the well-defined New England identity that was to be celebrated by Jedediah Morse and others in the early Republic.[50] The notion of New England as typifying an ideal of republican austerity still lay in the future. In the late colonial period, qualities that were later to be described in terms of approval as "steady ways" or virtue were seen as merely rustic.

That New England's regional identity within the English Atlantic world was determined by its perceived level of civility as much as by its unique characteristics is exemplified by the comparisons with Scotland that were pervasive in the late colonial period and beyond. These comparisons persisted despite the obvious differences between these two British provinces and despite New England's enthusiastic participation in the virulent Scotophobia that emerged after the mid-eighteenth century. Comparisons stressed characteristics such as widespread literacy, religious devoutness, and rusticity of manners.[51]

Both regions shared many of the traits that metropolitans identified with provincialism during the century: for example, "Presbyterianism" in its metropolitan sense, and the high literacy rate that was associated with intensely Protestant societies. In both places, refinement was seen to be confined to a few towns and cities that were surrounded by a barbarous countryside. Glasgow was in the midst of the wild highlands, and Boston was on the coast of a barely settled frontier. For both regions this provincialism was intensified by geographical remoteness. The relative isolation of Scotland and New England meant that within the British world the lingering practice of prosecuting witches was last seen in those places.[52] Clinton's reference to New England's geography in his description of the people ("a robust and hardy race of men, who are seated in general in a mountainous and a strongly defensible country," and who in part by virtue of their climate are better qualified for war than the colonists to the south) echoes remarks contemporaries made about the highlanders of Scotland, in which their warlike disposition, their ruder manners, and their distinctive culture were attributed to the isolation and hardship incurred by living in mountainous regions, where civilizing influences were delayed.[53]

Ian Christie once said of the North administration, "Perhaps the ministers thought in terms of Culloden, the last occasion when a civil conflict had been fought and when a backwoods army of highlanders had been cut to pieces by regulars in one decisive action."[54] This comparison seems simple, but it comprehends a great deal. In terms of tactics alone, New England and Scotland were vulnerable to encirclement, had mountainous terrain, and had a limited food supply. In broader cultural terms, the militarized citizenry of each made both armed resistance and a military response from the center of empire more likely.

British Policymakers and New England

Many metropolitan and colonial elites described New England's underdevelopment in negative terms. But British radical Whigs who supported the Patriot cause saw New England—with its yeomen farmers and relative absence of slavery—as the ideal of American life, not the deviant region.[55] Richard Price, considering the importance of the American Revolution a year after its conclusion, posed Connecticut as the best example of the kind of society the new nation could produce:

> The happiest state of man is the middle state between the savage and the refined or between the wild and the luxurious state. Such is the state of society in Connecticut . . . where the inhabitants consist, if I am rightly informed, of an independent and hardy yeomanry, all nearly on a level, trained to arms, instructed in their rights, clothed in home-spun, of simple manners, strangers to luxury, drawing plenty from the ground, and that plenty gathered easily by the hand of industry and giving rise to early marriages, a numerous progeny, length of days, and a rapid increase; the rich and the poor, the haughty grandee and the creeping sycophant, equally unknown.[56]

We can recognize in Price's eulogy the same qualities that many contemporaries attributed to New Englanders, though they used less flattering terms: the leveling, underbred, and warlike Yankees. For Price, the city-hater, it was New England's countryside that comprehended everything of worth in the province.

But detractors of New England usually saw things in the reverse. Urban New England nurtured at least some gentility, while the interior was rustic and crude. London merchant Richard Oswald—whose trading interests brought him in contact with many American colonists—described New England in these terms. The "Farming or Inland Inhabitants of New England" he described as small farmers who were socially equal. "But upon the Sea Coasts, & in the Towns, such as Boston & other Maritime places the Case is quite otherwise, where Trade flourishes, & where Considerable Estates have been acquired, & are transmitted in Succession from Father to Son, in the Same Profession, & is what we call the Mercantile Interest of

these Provinces, which is entirely different in its nature & consequences,"
can boast "a number of Gentlemen, of good Education & manners."[57]

In London, the perception of New England as less developed and less
integrated culturally was evident at the level of policymaking. Oswald suggested to Lord Dartmouth in February 1775 that the government might
attempt to detach Virginia from New England by sending a "Person of
Address" to Virginia to represent to the elites of that colony how far New
England's interests conflicted with their own. In a lengthy document outlin-
ing the appeal such an envoy might make, Oswald recommended the following opening comments:

> You may believe the People at home of all ranks, as well as his Majs
> Ministers were not a little surprised to see the Colony of Virginia enter
> into this Combination with these Fanatics to the Northward. A Royal
> Colony . . . whose principal Inhabitants are no less distinguished in
> their Education & manners from the others on the Continent; And
> where one meets with the Descendants of the Oldest Families in the
> American Dominion, . . . I say we could not but be surprised at home
> to see Gentlemen of your Rank and Character connect & Combine
> yourselves in this detested Confederacy with a Mob of Northern Yeo-
> men.

Oswald's envoy was to suggest to the Virginians that they might assume the
West India trade heretofore dominated by the "Confederacy of Smuglers in
Boston, [and] Rhode Island," whom he described as a "Race under such
proverbial discredit here as well as elsewhere that nothing could be more
astonishing at home than on hearing you had entered into a Treaty with
them on the footing of Brethren & Fellow patriots." The envoy was also to
suggest that without Britain's restraining presence, the "lawless and licentious" northerners would probably turn on the colonies to the south.[58]

North never sent the emissary Oswald advised, but beginning in early
1775 he did send out unofficial feelers to the colonies south of New England. Through these he attempted to convey to leading moderate colonists
from Pennsylvania, New York, and the Carolinas that the government
sought reconciliation. One of his agents, Thomas Drummond Lundin, better known as Lord Drummond, who posed as an unofficial spokesman for
the British government, met with moderate members of Congress in January 1776, chiefly from New York, Pennsylvania, and South Carolina.
Drummond avoided the New England delegates, and when discussion en-
sued over what would happen if Massachusetts rejected a plan that was

supported by both the colonies to the south and the Ministry, Drummond reported that John Jay was certain that public opinion would demand a break with the licentious New Englanders, rather than involvement in a civil war "merely," as Jay put it, "to humour a Set of People who were obnoxious to them."[59] After May 1775, anxious to determine the reaction of the elite elements of colonial society from New York southward to his conciliatory proposal, North monitored private post from those colonies carried by the packets.[60]

In London, colonists of patriot sympathies from Pennsylvania, New York, and South Carolina found they could gain access to Lords North and Dartmouth, and later Germain, during 1775.[61] By contrast, Bostonian Josiah Quincy, reaching London in November 1774, was obliged to resort to a stratagem to gain an audience with the chief minister. Benjamin Franklin, commenting on North's conciliatory proposal in early March 1775, asserted, "All the Colonies but those of New England, it is given out, may still make Peace for themselves, by acknowledging the Supreme unlimited Power of Parliament: But those are absolutely to be *conquered*."[62] Franklin's account of North's intention in offering his conciliatory proposal had a cynical ring to it. But North declared that he did intend to offer concessions to the colonies through his proposal, possibly even to open talks.[63] First, however, he needed to ensure that the colonial spokesmen he would be dealing with would not be those whose terms were utterly unacceptable to a British government. Such were the radicals of Massachusetts.

The North administration, in singling out New England in 1774 and early 1775, should not be accused of perversely ignoring the extent of colonial resistance. Of Britain's provinces in North America, New England stood out as a misfit. Southerners agreed with the metropolitan view that they were more valuable to the empire and altogether better integrated. Yet by the eve of independence some New Englanders were arguing that "the northern colonies generated more wealth for the mother country than the plantation colonies," rejecting the metropolitan view of New England as an unprofitable competitor.[64] All of this foreshadowed the economically grounded sectional rivalry that was to occur between New England and the southern states, both during the war and afterwards.

Sectionalism, which was to be the bane of the new Republic, was a lasting division that lay open to British exploitation. But in the months and years following Lexington and Concord, British commanders and ministers were diverted from their original strategy. Ultimately, Howe turned southward to Philadelphia. The middle colonies appeared to be the soft underbelly. Less bellicose than their northern neighbors, their conquest would assist in isolating and subduing the New Englanders without the effort of an invasion. And with a large Loyalist population, they offered a division of another kind—a political one—to exploit. But the political division of rebel versus Tory proved much more ephemeral than sectional rivalry. As the war gradually spread throughout America, the British army found itself fighting against a background of war-weary civilians who just wanted the fighting to end. And by spreading the war, the British army helped to unite its enemies throughout America's very different colonies. Not until after the peace in 1783 did British policymakers revert to exploiting sectional rivalries in the new Republic, a strategy that they adhered to through the War of 1812.

At the outset of the War of Independence, metropolitan policymakers envisioned a war confined to New England. Indeed, a limited conflict was critical if they were to prevail over such a vast territory. Behind the various dimensions of the metropolitan assessment of New England as a military problem in 1774–75, an assessment that embraced geography, economics, and manpower, is revealed the metropolis's recognition of that region as a distinct and deviant province whose long-standing differences with the other colonies could play a part in resolving the imperial crisis.

In 1778, Major Patrick Ferguson, writing to General Clinton, suggested that British strategy should revert to the idea of an invasion of New England. The Continental army, he pointed out, would be obliged to march to its defense; the region's own militia would be tied down in the same cause; and its large population and relatively small food supply would mean that shortly, "without effecting the Distruction of their Towns, . . . in place of treating of terms the Republicans would be obliged to beg for bread." The fact was that New England could not carry on a war by itself; it lacked the resources. As with earlier commentators in 1774–75, this British officer was calculating that if New England were thus singled out, the other colonies would ultimately decide to leave it to its fate. Certainly a prolonged war confined to that region must have strained colonial solidarity, as New England would have been compelled to appeal for support from the south. An attack on New England, Ferguson explained, "being the Object of jealousy & dislike throughout America, the other Provinces may hereafter more readily acknowledge the justice of our Choice & recollect our having at some hazard to our Country, left them the Queit [sic] possession of their Towns & settlements." [65] Three years into the war, Ferguson resurrected the issue of whether warfare itself could be the instrument with which to sever a deviant and troublesome region from the more integrated mainland colonies and restore imperial harmony.

Notes

1. Verner W. Crane, *Benjamin Franklin's Letters to the Press, 1758–1775* (Chapel Hill: University of North Carolina Press, 1950), 263n.

2. David L. Ammerman, "The Tea Crisis and Its Consequences through 1775," in Jack P. Greene and J. R. Pole, eds., *The Blackwell Encyclopedia of the American Revolution* (Oxford, 1991), 208.

3. John Derry, "Government Policy and the American Crisis, 1760–1776," in H. T. Dickinson, ed., *Britain and the American Revolution* (London, 1998), 62. Piers Mackesy noted, "British Ministers have been accused of obstinate blindness to the quality of the rebels." See Piers Mackesy, *The War for America, 1775–1783* (1964; reprint, Lincoln: University of Nebraska Press, 1992), 30; Michael G. Kammen, *A Rope of Sand: The Colonial Agents, British Politics, and the American Revolution* (Ithaca: Cornell University Press, 1968).

4. John Shy, "A New Look at the Colonial Militia," in *A People Numerous and Armed: Reflections on the Military Struggle for American Independence* (New York: Oxford University Press, 1976; reprint, Ann Arbor: University of Michigan Press, 1990), 40.

5. John Shy, *Toward Lexington: The Role of the British Army in the Coming of the American Revolution* (Princeton, N.J.: Princeton University Press, 1965), 66.

6. R. C. Simmons and P. D. G. Thomas, eds., *Proceedings and Debates of the British Parliaments Respecting North America, 1754–1783,* vol. 6 (April 1775 to May 1776) (White Plains, N.Y.: Kraus International, 1987), 379; John R. Cuneo, *Robert Rogers of the Rangers* (New York: Oxford University Press, 1959), 188, 238.

7. Shy, *Toward Lexington,* 407, 410–11; K. G. Davies, ed., *Documents of the American Revolution, 1770–1783,* 21 vols. (Dublin: Irish University Press, 1972–81), 7:176, 180; Ian R. Christie, "The British Ministers, Massachusetts, and the Continental Congress, 1774–1775," in Walter H. Conser Jr. et al., eds., *Resistance, Politics, and the American Struggle for Independence, 1765–1775* (Boulder, Colo.: Lynne Rienner, 1986), 339.

8. Staffordshire Record Office, Dartmouth MSS, D(W) 1778/II/1148, E. Vanderhorst to Dr. Samuel Cooper, February 16, 1775. Permission to quote from these letters has been granted by the Head of Archive Services, Staffordshire Record Office. Henry Laurens to John Laurens, Westminster, March 11, 1774, in George C. Rogers Jr. et al., eds., *The Papers of Henry Laurens,* 11 vols. (Columbia: University of South Carolina Press, 1974), 9:351; James Duane to Thomas Johnson, New York, December 29, 1774, in Paul H. Smith et al., eds., *Letters of Delegates to Congress, 1774–1789,* 14 vols. to date (Washington, D.C.: Library of Congress, 1976–), 1:281.

9. Ralph Davis, *The Rise of the Atlantic Economies* (London: Weidenfeld and Nicolson, 1973), 273.

10. Major Patrick Ferguson to Sir Henry Clinton, August 1, 1778, in Howard H. Peckham, ed., *Sources of American Independence: Selected Manuscripts from the Collections of the William L. Clements Library,* 2 vols. (Chicago: University of Chicago Press, 1978), 2:309.

11. Jack P. Greene, *Imperatives, Behaviors, and Identities: Essays in Early American Cultural History* (Charlottesville: University Press of Virginia, 1992), xii; P. D. G. Thomas, *Tea Party to Independence: The Third Phase of the American Revolution, 1773–1776* (Oxford: Oxford University Press, 1991), 206–10.

12. General Gage to Lord Dartmouth, Boston, September 12, 1774, in Clarence Edwin Carter, ed., *The Correspondence of General Thomas Gage with the Secretaries of State, and with the War Office and the Treasury, 1763–1775,* 2 vols. (New Haven, 1931, 1933; this edition 1969), 1:374.

13. Major Patrick Ferguson to Sir Henry Clinton, August 1, 1778, in Peckham, ed., *Sources of American Independence,* 2:310.

14. Cited in Shy, *Towards Lexington,* 410.

15. General Gage to Lord Dartmouth, Boston, December 15, 1774, in Carter, ed., *Correspondence of General Thomas Gage,* 1:387.

16. General Gage to Lord Dartmouth, Boston, October 30, 1774, in Carter, ed., *Correspondence of General Thomas Gage,* 2:381. For examples of letters of Patriots suggesting that New England could conduct a war on its own, see letter of William Lee to Josiah Quincy Jr. in Philadelphia, or to Samuel Adams in Quincy's absence, London, April 6, 1775, Samuel Adams Papers (microfilm, New York Public Library), reel 1, and Joseph Warren to Arthur Lee, February 20, 1775, in Paul P. Hoffman, ed., *The Lee Family Papers, 1742–1795,* 8 reels (Charlottesville: University of Virginia Library, 1966), reel 2.

17. Jeremy Black, *War for America: The Fight for Independence, 1775–1783* (Stroud, Gloucestershire: Sutton, 1991), 31, 83–88; Jeremy Black, *War and the World: Military Power and the Fate of Continents, 1450–2000* (New Haven: Yale University Press, 1998), 135.

18. Sir John Fortescue, *The War of Independence* (London: Macmillan, 1911; reprint, Greenhill Books, 2001), 26–27.

19. General William Howe to Lord Dartmouth, January 16, 1776, cited in Troyer Steele Anderson, *The Command of the Howe Brothers during the American Revolution* (New York: Oxford University Press, 1936), 118. On the government's failure to consult Howe regarding the southern expedition, see Thomas, *Tea Party to Independence,* 267. Lord North sought an expedition to the more loyal colonies in the south in hopes of an easy victory that would "lessen domestic criticism of the conduct of the war." Black, *War for America,* 87.

20. Thomas, *Tea Party to Independence,* 259. In August 1775, for example, General Murray outlined for Lord Germain a prospective campaign that involved the conquest of New England alone. Mackesy, *The War for America, 1775–1783,* 35.

21. Speech of Edmund Burke in the House of Commons, February 6, 1775, in Simmons and Thomas, eds., *Proceedings and Debates of the British Parliaments Respecting North America,* 5:361.

22. Rockingham to Dartmouth, November 1769, Sheffield City Library, Wentworth Woodhouse Muniments: Rockingham Papers, R1–1244.

23. William B. Willcox, ed., *The American Rebellion: Sir Henry Clinton's Narrative of His Campaigns, 1775–1782* (New Haven: Yale University Press, 1954), 10–11.

24. John M. Murrin, "A Roof without Walls: The Dilemma of American National Identity," in Richard Beeman et al., eds., *Beyond Confederation: Origins of the Constitution and American National Identity* (Chapel Hill: University of North Carolina Press, 1987), 343. See also Jack P. Greene, "The Constitution of 1787 and the Question of Southern Distinctiveness" in *Imperatives, Behaviors, and Identities,* 331.

25. Merrill Jensen, "The Sovereign States: Their Antagonisms and Rivalries and Some Consequences," in Ronald Hoffman and Peter J. Albert, eds., *Sovereign States in an Age of Uncertainty* (Charlottesville: University Press of Virginia, 1981), 229.

26. Margaret Ellen Newell, *From Dependency to Independence: Economic Revolution in Colonial New England* (Ithaca: Cornell University Press, 1998), 102–3.

27. Murrin, "A Roof without Walls," 343; James Kirby Martin and Mark Edward Lender, *A Respectable Army: The Military Origins of the Republic, 1763–1789* (Arlington Heights, Ill.: Harlan Davidson, 1982), 45; Edward Rutledge to John Jay, Philadelphia, June 29, 1776, in Smith et al., eds., *Letters of Delegates to Congress,* 4:338.

28. Lord Percy to Henry Reveley, Esq., Boston, August 8, 1774, and Lord Percy to the Rev. Thomas Percy, Boston, November 25, 1774, in C. K. Bolton, ed, *Letters of Hugh Earl Percy from Boston and New York, 1774–1776* (Boston: Charles E. Goodspeed, 1902), 31, 44; Capt. John Bowater, Rhode Island, April 4, 1777, in M. Balderston and D. Syrett, eds., *The Lost War: Letters from British Officers during the American Revolution* (New York: Horizon Press, 1975), 122–23.

29. John Adams to Abigail Adams, August 3, 1776, in Smith et al., eds., *Letters of Delegates to Congress,* 4:611.

30. The practice of sending young men abroad to complete their education was growing in the colonies south of New England, particularly Pennsylvania and South Carolina. William Connely, "Colonial Americans in Oxford and Cambridge," *American Oxonian* 29 (1942): 6–17, 75–77.

31. P. O. Hutchinson, *The Diary and Letters of His Excellency Thomas Hutchinson, Esq.,* 2 vols. (London, 1883–86), 1:299–301.

32. Henry Laurens to Henry Laurens Jr., Westminster, April 5, 1774, in Rogers et al., eds., *The Papers of Henry Laurens,* 9:377–78; Speech of Captain Luttrell in the House of Commons, January 23, 1775, in Simmons and Thomas, eds., *Proceedings and Debates of the British Parliaments Respecting North America,* 5:295.

33. Richard Slotkin, *Regeneration through Violence: The Mythology of the*

American Frontier, 1600–1860 (Middletown, Conn.: Wesleyan University Press, 1973), 227–29; John Ferling, "The New England Soldier: A Study in Changing Perceptions," *American Quarterly* 33 (1981): 37–40.

34. Samuel Adams to Joseph Warren, September 25, 1774, in Harry Alonzo Cushing, ed., *The Writings of Samuel Adams,* 4 vols. (New York, 1904–8; this edition New York, 1968), 3:158; Merrill Jensen, *The Founding of a Nation: A History of the American Revolution, 1763–1776* (New York: Oxford University Press, 1968), 610–11; John Ferling, *A Wilderness of Miseries: War and Warriors in Early America* (Westport, Conn.: Greenwood, 1980), 169; Eliphalet Dyer to Joseph Trumbull, Philadelphia, June 17, 1775, in Smith et al., eds., *Letters of Delegates to Congress,* 1:499.

35. Ferling, *A Wilderness of Miseries,* 169; "To the Honble. The Deputies in Congress from the Southern Provinces," in Jonathan Boucher, *Reminiscences of an American Loyalist, 1738–1789* (Port Washington, N.Y.: Kennikat Press, 1971), 131–32, 134.

36. Clinton, *The American Rebellion,* 15.

37. Edward P. Hamilton, *Fort Ticonderoga: Key to a Continent* (Boston: Little, Brown, 1964; this edition published by Fort Ticonderoga with permission of the Massachusetts Historical Society, Fort Ticonderoga, N.Y., 1995), 110; Michael A. Bellesiles, *Revolutionary Outlaws: Ethan Allen and the Struggle for Independence on the Early American Frontier* (Charlottesville: University Press of Virginia, 1993), 120–21.

38. Staffs. Rec. Off., Dart. MSS., D(W) 1778/II/1399, James Tilghman to William Baker, Philadelphia, July 30, 1775 (copy); [ ] to Brigadier General Robertson, May 25, 1775, Reports of the Historical Manuscripts Commission, *Dartmouth MSS* 2 (14 Report, APP., Part X, 1895), 316.

39. L. H. Butterfield et al., eds., *Diary and Autobiography of John Adams,* 4 vols. (Cambridge: Harvard University Press, 1961), 2:107.

40. Lord Percy to the Duke of Northumberland, Boston, September 12, 1774, in Bolton, ed., *Letters of Hugh Earl Percy,* 38.

41. Intelligence of Military Preparations in Massachusetts, undated, enclosed in Lieutenant General Gage's letter of March 4, 1775, to Dartmouth, in Davies, ed., *Documents of the American Revolution,* 9:65.

42. General William Howe to Lord Dartmouth, January 16, 1776, cited in Anderson, *The Command of the Howe Brothers,* 116.

43. Mackesy, *The War for America,* 78. John Dickinson made the same comparison in a speech to Congress in May 1775, warning that, as in 1755, the British regulars might return in force to convert their disaster into a victory. "John Dickinson's Notes for a Speech in Congress" (May 23–25?, 1775), in Smith et al., eds., *Letters of Delegates to Congress,* 1:375.

44. Cited in Anderson, *The Command of the Howe Brothers,* 82.

45. Lord Percy to General Harvey, Boston, April 20, 1775, in Bolton, ed., *Letters of Hugh Earl Percy,* 52–53.

46. See, e.g., Joseph A. Conforti, *Imagining New England: Explorations of Regional Identity from the Pilgrims to the Mid-Twentieth Century* (Chapel Hill: University of North Carolina Press, 2001).

47. Slotkin's study, *Regeneration through Violence,* deals with the subject at some length. A briefer discussion is found in Ferling, "The New England Soldier: A Study in Changing Perceptions." Studies of the impact of the French and Indian Wars on New England's culture and identity include Fred Anderson, *A People's Army: Massachusetts Soldiers and Society in the Seven Years' War* (Chapel Hill: University of North Carolina Press, 1984); Nathan O. Hatch, "The Origins of Civil Millennialism in America: New England Clergymen, War with France, and the Revolution," *William and Mary Quarterly,* 3rd ser., 31 (1974): 407–30; Kerry A. Trask, *In the Pursuit of Shadows: Massachusetts Millennialism and the Seven Years' War* (New York: Garland, 1989); Harold E. Selesky, *War and Society in Colonial Connecticut* (New Haven: Yale University Press, 1990).

48. Ned C. Landsman, "Border Cultures, the Backcountry, and 'North British' Emigration to America," *William and Mary Quarterly,* 3rd ser., 48 (April 1991): 255.

49. Lawrence Delbert Cress, *Citizens in Arms: The Army and the Militia in American Society to the War of 1812* (Chapel Hill: University of North Carolina Press, 1982), 29.

50. Conforti, *Imagining New England,* 9.

51. "Extract of a Letter from a Gentleman in General Abercrombie's army, dated Camp at Lake George, August 24," *London Chronicle,* December 21–23, 1758, and reply by Benjamin Franklin, "To the Printer of the London Chronicle," May 9, 1759, reprinted in Leonard W. Labaree and William B. Willcox, eds., *The Papers of Benjamin Franklin* (New Haven: Yale University Press, 1959–), 8:340 ff.; Henry F. May, *The Enlightenment in America* (New York: Oxford University Press, 1976), 181; John Melish, *Travels through the United States of America in 1806, 1807, and 1809, 1810, 1811* (Belfast, 1813), 101 ff.; John Morison Duncan, *Travels through Part of the United States and Canada in 1818 and 1819,* 2 vols. (New York, 1823), 1:106 ff.; Andrew Hook, *Scotland and America, 1750–1835* (Glasgow: Blackie, 1975), 91.

52. Ned C. Landsman, *From Colonials to Provincials: American Thought and Culture, 1680–1760* (New York: Twayne), 26, 41, 50.

53. Samuel Johnson, *A Journey to the Western Isles of Scotland: Johnson's Scottish Journey,* ed. Finlay J. Macdonald (London: Macdonald, 1983), 63–65; and see Peter E. Russell, "Redcoats in the Wilderness: British Officers and Irregular Warfare in Europe and America, 1740 to 1760," *William and Mary Quarterly,* 3rd ser., 25 (1978): 635, 639–40, for British officers' descriptions of Scottish Highlanders as particularly adept at fighting in mountainous terrain.

54. Christie, "The British Ministers, Massachusetts, and the Continental Congress," 342.

55. Colin Bonwick, *English Radicals and the American Revolution* (Chapel Hill: University of North Carolina Press, 1977), 45.

56. Richard Price, "Observations on the Importance of the American Revolution, and the Means of making it a Benefit to the World" (1784), reprinted in Bernard Peach, ed., *Richard Price and the Ethical Foundations of the American Revolution* (Durham, N.C.: Duke University Press, 1979), 208.

57. Staffs. Rec. Off., Dart. MSS, D(W)1778/II/1165, Richard Oswald, "Sketch of an Examination at the Bar of the House," enclosure in a letter of Oswald to Lord Dartmouth, February 27, 1775.

58. Staffs. Rec. Off., Dart. MSS., D(W) 1778/II/1139, Richard Oswald, "Thoughts on the State of America," enclosure in letter of Richard Oswald to Lord Dartmouth, February 9, 1775.

59. Milton L. Klein, "Failure of a Mission: The Drummond Peace Proposal of 1775," *Huntington Library Quarterly* 35 (1971–72): 347–49, 352, 354–57, 360–61, 363, 370, 379, 380.

60. Julie M. Flavell, "Government Interception of Letters from America and the Quest for Colonial Opinion in 1775," *William and Mary Quarterly*, 3rd ser., 58 (April 2001): 403–30.

61. Julie M. Flavell, "American Patriots in London and the Quest for Talks, 1774–1775," *Journal of Imperial and Commonwealth History* 20 (1992): 335–69.

62. Benjamin Franklin to Charles Thomson, London, March 13, 1775, in Labaree and Willcox, eds., *The Papers of Benjamin Franklin*, 21:521–22.

63. Thomas, *Tea Party to Independence*, 205, 216, 251, 267–68.

64. Newell, *From Dependency to Independence*, 278.

65. Major Patrick Ferguson to Sir Henry Clinton, August 1, 1778, in Peckham, ed., *Sources of American Independence*, 2:307–10.

5

Contemporary Responses in Print to the American Campaigns of the Howe Brothers

Margaret Stead

This study of responses in the British media to the American campaigns of Sir William and Richard, Viscount Howe during a critical phase of the War of American Independence exemplifies the increasing concern of the British nation with politically and nationally sensitive issues during the second half of the eighteenth century. It demonstrates that aristocrats with key political and military roles in national affairs were becoming more accountable to the middling ranks of British society than has sometimes been suggested,[1] and it argues that such accountability was politically significant. Opinion published in the media was avidly read and discussed, not only by politicians and the enfranchised but also by wealthy and articulate men of movable property and literate artisans and tradesmen, many of whom lacked direct representation in Parliament but, as citizens, were free to petition and address the crown. Politicians of all parties increasingly recognized the propaganda value of ephemeral forms of print and encouraged journalism conducive to their political ends.

The work of Robert Harris has shown how foreign affairs, particularly war and commercial and territorial rivalry with France, led to increased involvement and even vigorous intervention of the press in the politics of the 1740s.[2] To be commercially viable, the press must represent the views of a substantial cross-section of the wider political nation. Significantly, Harris regards the press at that time as a link between the two worlds of the court and Parliament and of the tavern and tradesmen's club, arguing that, by virtue of this connection, the press did not lack influence in Parliament and at court.[3]

By examining the development of a popular stereotype in print and its relationship to political debate and government policy, this article argues that such publicity was an influential feature of the eighteenth-century press. Within six years of the end of the Printers' Case,[4] press reporting of parliamentary business and the subsequent discussion in print of the issues it raised were already valued, particularly by antiministerial parties, since an overwhelming government majority was assured by the votes of well-rewarded placemen who supported the administration. Publicity in print was seen as a way of reinforcing public opinion and potentially influencing political events.

The criticism and derision that the Howes attracted as commissioners and military commanders at this critical juncture in the relationship between Britain and America may well have contributed to the erosion of public confidence in Lord North's administration. At the very least, it is important to recognize such publicity as a prominent factor in contemporary political discourse.

In her study of the social contexts of print culture, Kathleen Wilson emphasizes the ongoing dual role of the printed media throughout most of the eighteenth century in reflecting and encouraging readers' involvement in national concerns such as trade, war, and imperial expansion. She argues the centrality of print in "giving form and substance to the political nation." Her analysis of the influence in Britain of support for Admiral Vernon following his defeat of the Spanish at Porto Bello in 1739 demonstrates how the press and the market for political artifacts were of central importance in initiating and sustaining the extraparliamentary politics focused on him, and that this support came from a substantial cross-section of British society. She emphasizes the significance of opposition propaganda during the American War as a weapon in the struggle between opposers and supporters of government policy in America, arguing that North's policies were subjected to particular strain because of national response to the trial of Admiral Keppel in 1779.[5]

My analysis of reactions to the campaign of the Howe brothers in the press and in satirical prints similarly focuses on the significance of propaganda for the lives and reputations of prominent individuals during the American Revolution. There are parallels between the cases of Keppel and the Howe brothers in that all were members of Parliament, commanders of the armed forces, and Rockinghamites. Keppel was more hostile than the Howes to the government's American policy. The indecisive engagement with the French fleet off Ushant under his command took place in the summer of 1778, and the demand for his court-martial was centered on press reports published between the following October and December. The case was tried in February 1779, and his acquittal was rapturously celebrated in March 1779.

The most critical publicity surrounding the Howes' command occurred between June 1777 and their occupation of Philadelphia during the winter of 1777–78. In the close metropolitan community where members of fashionable society mixed with men of middling rank in club and coffeehouse, people knew each other personally and reputation mattered. Consequently, the fabrication of a derogatory public image in their absence so incensed the Howes that they insisted on a parliamentary inquiry to vindicate their American campaign and expose what they perceived as ministerial responsibility for the lack of resources available to them. Sir William Howe expounded their grievances in Parliament on April 29, 1779, and the inquiry took place in June 1779. The popularity of Keppel's vindication may have encouraged the Howes to insist on addressing this forum, knowing that full reports would reach those responsible for or readers of the propaganda that had distressed them.

Both these inquiries demonstrate interaction between national events and media publicity, an association that is further illustrated by the contrast between the treatment of the Howe brothers by the press and the eulogies that greeted Cornwallis on his return to England after his disastrous capitulation at Yorktown in 1781. Despite his failure to understand the vulnerability and isolation of his forces following an impetuous outrunning of his supplies and support, Cornwallis was fêted in Britain as a hero. Public perceptions of all these men had been influenced by stereotypes created in print.

From the outset of their American commands, the Howe brothers were in an invidious position, being appointed peace commissioners and joint commanders in chief of the armed forces in May 1776, but arriving in America with restrictions on their negotiating capacity within days of the Declaration of Independence. Nevertheless, the British media held them accountable to the political nation.

Sustained vindictiveness and ironic comment, as distinct from complaints about lack of precise news, came from Almon's press[6] and the *St. James's Chronicle.* The *Gazetteer,* which represented the interests of London citizens, particularly merchants, confined itself to reporting news and rumor about the Howes. The *Public Advertiser,* critical of Lord North, but strongly anti-"patriot" and anti-American, printed occasional satirical comments on Sir William's inactivity, such as a spoof news item on August 19, 1777, that "a great number of Feather Beds, stuffed Coaches, several Phial Bottles full of Lethe, and other Soporifics" was ready to be shipped for the use of General Howe and his army. While ready to attack "peevish patriotic incendiaries"[7] over their complaints about delays in information, the *Morning Post* commented on December 17, 1777: "Lord and Sir William Howe have each a salary of 20£ a day annexed to their office of Commissioners; no wonder therefore if they should be more inclined to treat for peace with the sword than by negotiation." It was prepared, also, on January 1, 1778, to publish an open letter to Lord North signed "Gustavius Vasia," which perpetuated the charge of the Howes' personal greed. The *London Chronicle*, which prided itself on its objectivity, confined its copy almost exclusively to information conveyed in letters from America, official gazettes, and reports of parliamentary debate. By contrast, the provincial press showed little interest in personal attacks, which suggests that much adverse propaganda was generated at the metropolitan center of British political life.

The Establishment of a Stereotype, 1775–1777

The brothers were vulnerable to criticism and satire in two respects: their performance as commissioners and commanders in the field, and their personal lives. As members of Parliament with a command in America, their activities were scrutinized by their constituents. Sir William's accountability to the electorate is illustrated by a letter from Samuel Kirk, a grocer in his Nottingham constituency, dated February 10, 1775, when his constituents had learned that Sir William had agreed to serve in America. Kirk expressed their "discontent and disappointment" that Howe was "prepared to embark for America to enforce the Acts," which he had assured them in his election promises he would vote to repeal: "The most plausible excuse that is made among us, is, that the King sent for you and what could you do?" Howe's placatory reply illustrates his awareness of the need for voters to accept that he was acting patriotically: "My going thither was not my seeking. I was ordered, and could not refuse, without incurring the odious name of backwardness to serve my country in distress." He suggested that Americans who did not support the crown were "the few"; for fear of punishment they would soon conform to the laws, which must be obeyed "for the well-being of this empire."

This correspondence may not have been widely known outside the constituency when it took place, but its arguments were sufficiently familiar to be extended by another Nottingham constituent,[8] writing under the pseudonym "Nottingham." The *London Evening Post* of March 5, 1776, carried Nottingham's first "Letter to Lord Howe" at a time when the newspapers were reporting parliamentary debates concerning the employment of German mercenaries. He expressed the violent opposition of the town's commercial community to the government's American policy, questioning the Howe family honor in terms of Lord Howe's perceived duty as a senior officer:

> The war which your Lordship is about to undertake, is a choice of disgrace. . . . Perhaps indeed you will not, you dare not, and apprehend you have no right, to consider the means or the ends of your commission, but that as a soldier you are bound to execute whatever commands you may receive. If this is your opinion, and if it is justly founded, you are much to be pitied. . . . But how happens it, my Lord, that soldiers and commanders, of great name and note . . . have with disdain rejected commissions which disgraced them as Englishmen and soldiers?

The argument echoes the letter to Sir William from Kirk implying that Lord Howe lacked the courage and integrity to follow his convictions.

Subsequent use of Kirk's letter sustained publicity for Howe's supposed halfheartedness over several years. It appeared in the *London Evening Post* of April 23, 1778, with a prefatory note signed "B" calling attention to Howe's duplicity, and it was reprinted in the 1779 pamphlet by Joseph Galloway, *Reply to the Observations of Lieutenant General Sir William Howe,* and again in 1780 as an appendix to *Three Letters to Lieutenant General Sir William Howe* by Israel Mauduit. Justified or not, the insinuations were printable and thereby judged credible to the politically minded public.

Their plausibility can be substantiated from other accusations that Sir William lacked devotion to duty and failed to seize opportunities. As early as May 12, 1776, a print, "Noddle Island, or How are we decieved"[sic] was published,[9] satirizing the evacuation of Boston (Fig. 5.1). It demeans the action as absurd by depicting an exaggerated female headdress in which the armies oppose each other from beflagged forts.[10] American flags depict a crocodile and a crossbow and arrows, symbols of danger from the colonists, while the flags of their British opponents are an ass and a fool's cap and bells. Already Howe's strategy was being questioned in a medium of light entertainment. The personal jibe ensured that the print would be appreciated even though the event was embarrassing to Britain. It probably also reflected public dissatisfaction with the account of the engagement in the *London Gazette,* which was regarded by the parliamentary opposition as misleading.[11] The public was already wary of half-truths.

Such skepticism of Sir William Howe's ability as a military strategist sometimes appeared justified. Captain Johann Ewald, Field Jäger Corps,

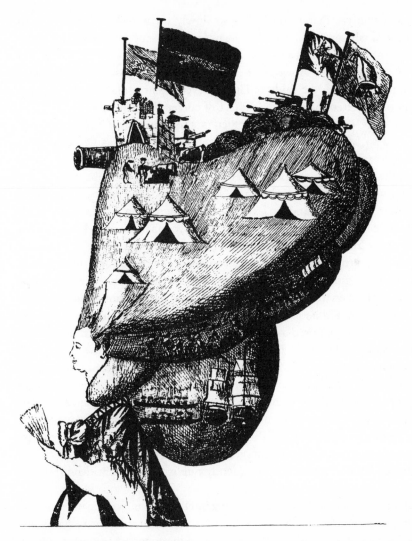

Figure 5.1. BMC 5335. "Noddle Island—or How. Are we decieved" [*sic*]. M. Darby, Strand. 12 May 1776. Copyright © The British Museum.

was trenchantly critical of his judgment after Forts Washington and Lee had fallen to the British army in December 1776. Although Cornwallis pursued Washington's troops to the edge of Brunswick, Howe ordered him to halt. Both British and Hessian leaders agreed that the consequent eight-hour delay was folly, since Washington's forces, taking advantage of this unexpected opportunity, escaped across the Delaware to mount a successful attack on Trenton.[12] Ewald commented in his journal, "It became clearly evident that the march took place so slowly for no other reason than to permit Washington to cross the Delaware safely and peacefully. I was assured that Lord Cornwallis had orders from General Howe to proceed in such a way. The two Howe brothers belong to the Opposition Party. Therefore no more need be said."[13] Though events lent it plausibility, such an opinion reflected the damaging effect of current innuendo.

Thomas Paine's second pamphlet in the *American Crisis* series, addressed to Lord Howe and dated January 13, 1777, was derogatory on another level.[14] It attacked the unpopular proclamations that had accompanied the commissioners' peace overtures, contrasting the behavior of Lord Howe with that of his elder brother, George Howe, who had been extremely popular in America and was killed at Ticonderoga in 1758. Paine, in an attack echoing Kirk's, accused Howe of a sycophantic attitude toward an unworthy king who was attacking his formerly loyal people. "You may issue your Proclamations, and welcome, for we . . . scorn the insulting ruffian that employs you. America, for your deceased brother's sake, would gladly have shewn you respect, and it is a new aggravation to her feelings, that Howe should be forgetful, and raise his sword against those who, at their own charge, raised a monument to his brother.[15] But your master has commanded, and you have not enough of nature left to refuse."

Opinions expressed in the *American Crisis* contributed to insinuations surrounding the Howe brothers already current when the *Gazette*'s official reports of their 1777–78 campaigns were published; these would appear to readers to be confirmed by newspaper reports. David Syrett suggests that the Howes' actions in the Philadelphia campaign were considered ponderous and indecisive, and they enraged some of the brighter officers serving in America.[16] Their letters were frequently published in the British press and read privately among friends.

Paine accused Sir William of lacking intelligence as a commander and as being uncommitted to the action necessary to achieve decisive gains; his leisure pursuits were trivial; he was wasting his country's resources, and he plundered the cities he occupied. Around the end of February, when the *American Crisis* series was being read in Britain, these four elements of its propaganda were also current in the antigovernment press. Nottingham continued his letters to Lord Howe in the *London Evening Post* in March and April 1776. He insisted that terms were negotiable, insinuating that personal grievances stood in the way of Howe's devotion to duty and arguing that he had assumed he would take acceptable terms to America, but found himself "expected to impose a despotism by conquest." Even the excuse credited to him, that he had been deceived by ministers, was derogatory. A further letter suggested that his actions were promoting the interests of the Bourbons whom his brother had helped to defeat, and demanded that he negotiate terms dictated by justice and liberality, rejecting a mission that would lead to war rather than peace. Nottingham predicted that his service would be required ultimately to defend the country against Bourbon attack, a worthy commission for a Howe. Even before Lord Howe sailed for America, therefore, he was regarded by some opposition supporters as the weak-willed and gullible tool of a deceitful government.

Nottingham's repeated reference to the distinguished reputation of the Howe family implied that the brothers were not the men of honor and admirable leaders that George Howe had been.[17] His choice of pseudonym was itself symbolic: by association derived from Sir William Howe's seat in Parliament, he was included in the strictures. It also suggested that the writer's opinions were held by influential supporters among his constituents to whom, though the family was highly regarded, its present members were accountable.

This series of letters shows how earlier public sentiment could inform and reinforce current insinuations. Their plea for regard to personal reputation and family honour suggests a target readership to whom the Howe family were sufficiently known for these to matter. The brothers stood accused by one section of the media of lacking the traditional gentlemanly attributes of honor and keeping one's word. However different might have been the reality in society, these values sustained the public image of the English nobleman and could be invoked in the rhetoric of public debate. One element in the success and persistence of this critical public construction of reputation was its careful targeting of vulnerable areas where personal pride was at stake. An army's commission was to serve king and country with the utmost dispatch, a duty that demanded from common soldiers and generals alike the abrogation of personal freedom and the right to life itself. Sir William Howe might be deemed to have failed, despite his actual gains, by evading the rigorous performance of his duty.

It is difficult to establish how widely the stereotype was accepted. On January 7, 1777, the *London Chronicle* published an extract of a letter from an officer in the king's troop, headed "New York 26 November 1776," which praised both brothers for their contribution to the successes of the army and navy, emphasizing the men's loyalty to their general, and saying that "they would cheerfully keep the field the whole winter, without murmuring, if he thought proper to employ them." For the contemporary reader, even this compliment might have implied Howe's reluctance to use the men's eagerness to advantage.

Representations of the Campaign of 1777–1778 in the British Media

Between June 1777 and April 1778, the stereotype of the Howe brothers gained added dimensions. On June 3, the *London Chronicle* reported that General Howe had left New York with as many troops as could be spared, "to make an attempt on Philadelphia via Chesapeake Bay." Lack of further information from America fueled press criticism on grounds of waste of time and resources and lack of commitment. In June and July, even the pro-government *Morning Post* expressed irritation at the brothers' dilatoriness in sending reports and suggested that they should be recalled, arguably a device to distance the ministry from responsibility for confusion arising from lack of information about official policy and its implementation in the American campaign.

The opposition press repeatedly questioned the activities of the "lost" fleet and troops throughout the autumn. The *London Evening Post* insinuated on October 28 that ministry runners were "fabricating little lies of the day to keep up the spirits of the people" and that, if the ministry were revealing all they knew, Sir William's present actions were falling short of acceptable standards, since he had promised on July 5 that he would inform Germain when he reached his destination: "Sir William must either have made a long voyage, be entirely lost, or he is not a man of his word." The writer further attacked the policy of the British commander as unlikely to subdue America: "Howe can set fire to every town upon their coast, and is able to plunder and burn the handsome *city of* Philadelphia. So might a few people set fire to London, or any town in the kingdom. But would any fool say, this is conquering Britain? . . . If the gaining of Philadelphia, as the courtiers say, in all probability will put an end to the war, why did not Howe continue his march to it through the Jerseys? It were as easy . . . to obtain it that way, as to go a round about way to it by Chesapeake Bay.

This argument reinforced damaging accusations: that Sir William was prepared to set fire to and plunder the areas in his path and that his strategy was dilatory and inept. A commander was expected to control his troops in accordance with the conventions of war. What could legitimately be termed "foraging" was a practical necessity for an army living off the land, as the British were compelled to do at 3,000 miles' distance from their source of supply. But troops were difficult to control when ranging the countryside away from their base, and in the propaganda war one side's "forage" was its opponents' "pillage," and accusations could be substantiated by examples that were difficult to refute. This was an area in which Sir William Howe was particularly sensitive and tenacious in his own defense.[18]

One firsthand account suggests that such reports were exaggerated, even false. An unpublished document of the Moravian Church recorded, for the Unity's central organization at Herrnhut, its members' responses to the arrival of Howe's troops in Philadelphia:

> About the latter end of September the whole City was in a most violent agitation. The sudden departure of the Congress, and the carrying away of the cannon and ammunition of War, put the populace into the utmost confusion. . . . We who remained were chearful [sic] and undaunted; nor did we find ourselves deceived in our hope; for the royal Army took possession of the City in the best order & in stillness; General Howe having forbidden his troops on pain of death, to molest the inhabitants, or to take from them by force the value of a penny.[19]

Such an account, written by people with no political ax to grind, gives a very different impression of the occupation of the city from those that were partisan or politically motivated.

Accusations of dilatoriness and reluctance were more widespread than those of inhumanity, many of which probably originated from the pens of Americans hoping to foment disaffection. Even the *London Chronicle*, which had a policy of presenting news without comment and confined expressions of opinion to articles and correspondence, published an uncharacteristically satirical contribution on September 13, 1777.

> Extempore, on reading that, as soon as one General *appeared* on the Back Settlements [General Burgoyne], another *disappeared* on the Coast of the Jerseys.

> Our Gen'rals, noted for disasters
> Are like to *Polluxes and Castors;*
> No sooner does one *star* arise,
> Than in a cloud another *Flies,*
> And hides his rays the lord knows where;
> Both lights are too much for one sphere,
> But if they mingle not their light,
> We'll bid the "Western World" good night.

On November 4, the *London Evening Post* denigrated a report of the arrival of the *Isis* with dispatches from the Howes and the imminent publication of a *London Gazette* by printing a satirical "Gazette" and the following verse:

All joy to great Caesar, the Howes are found
Safe and sound
On Christian ground;
And if they go on at the rate they have done,
As sure as a gun.
By losing one town, and by getting another,
Lord Howe and his brother,
In a century more,
Will have made our affairs ten times worse than before.

Once again the stereotype had been reinforced by satire.

The *St. James's Chronicle* was similarly satirical, but with a flavor that accorded with its local and aristocratic readership. The following extract is from a paragraph entitled "Postscript. Intelligence Extraordinary," which appeared on November 20, 1777, on the same page as two letters, one expressing disappointment with the achievements of the campaign, the other hinting that reports of success in Philadelphia had been exaggerated:

It is reported that a very diligent Search and Enquiry has been made after the Howes, in order that the Minister might, in his Speech of the Day, be able to give the People some Satisfaction about the Safety of our Fleet and Army. Nothing has been discovered of them in America, and much Industry has been used in Knightsbridge, where an Army has before lurked in Disguise, but without Effect. It was thought unnecessary by some to examine the Serpentine River, but as many of our Ships in this War have been sent into Creeks and Places where Ships of Burthen never were before, there was a majority for making a Search there. The Diligence of the Ministry has not omitted making Enquiry at the Lost and Found Office in Holborn, but without Success.

This sophisticated satire probably included topical references now inaccessible, but like the *London Evening Post*'s satire, it implied an inept and embarrassed ministry and reflected an unflattering perception of the Howes' apparent disappearance. Malice proliferated when there was no firm news to counterbalance it; the Howes had reason to be incensed by the portrayal in the London press of their campaign to capture Philadelphia.

These accounts in the *London Evening Post* and the *St. James's Chronicle* suggest that, though different in appeal and market, both represented a readership receptive to opinion or innuendo against the Howes. While the letters in the *Post* appealed to critics in the middling orders, the *St. James's Chronicle* ridiculed the absence of news with a malice redolent of gossip in the clubs of St. James's. Neither would have been tenable as propaganda in a society where their implicit values of polite behavior did not apply and personal aspersions had less impact. The extracts from the *London Chronicle* show that even a less politically motivated newspaper occasionally indulged in such satirical comment.

The hostile press made little allowance for the patchy nature of information and government's need to give a cautious reception to news from unofficial sources before the commanders' dispatches arrived. As reports of successful action around Philadelphia remained unconfirmed, exasperation was expressed in the *Morning Post* on November 12:

> Ministry are in no small distress at not receiving a confirmation of the Liverpool news; they are still in hopes that this week may produce something in their favour, and enable them to meet Parliament without fear of the witty sarcasms prepared for them by the Minority. Lord George Germaine, after a *painful* attendance in continual expectation of official advices of the action said to have happened between General Howe and Washington, has left town for a few days, to recover the fatigue of a week's vain watching. . . . The defeat of Washington and the possession of Philadelphia are facts, which the Ministry have not the least doubt about. . . . Let therefore, those peevish, *patriotic* incendiaries restrain the licentiousness of their pens, and tongues, least [*sic*] a few days, perhaps a few hours, should cover them with confusion.

The *Morning Post* of November 14 relied on receipt of a *New York Gazette Extraordinary* for news of the action in Chesapeake Bay. Announcing military activities at Brandywine Creek, the *Post* gave the reasonable explanation for the nonreceipt of dispatches, that General Howe was in pursuit of Washington and that the *Gazette* accounted for news to the 25th of September. Dispatches detailing action at Brandywine Creek and the subsequent advance to occupy Philadelphia were not received until December 2.

The public construction of reputation in late eighteenth-century British society was furthered by the production of fashionably collectable satirical graphic prints, many of them more sophisticated than "Noddle Island." Like the satirical element in newspapers, they were intended primarily for amusement; both needed to entertain the reader in order to survive financially. The printmakers created collectable topical images that were potentially influential,[20] as this selection from examples featuring the Howe brothers illustrates.

"The Flight of the Congress"[21] is one of the few remaining prints that overtly attack the Americans. It was published on November 20, 1777, following word that the Continental Congress had left Philadelphia in anticipation of the arrival of British troops. By focusing on American fear of British forces, it recognizes Sir William Howe's achievement only indirectly. The accompanying verse celebrates the success of Britain aided by German mercenaries, emphasizing the reprehensible actions of America: the Declaration of Independence, the rejection of George III, and the approach by Congress to the French king.[22]

All the named congressmen are portrayed as animals appropriate to their personalities, with attributes familiar from fables and emblems. The Lion, king of the beasts, is roaring, "How," in recognition of Howe's approaching army as the cause of the flight, so that the satire represents the regal British Lion putting to rout the recalcitrant faction among the colonists. By the use of this satirical device, the general is deprived of status. The satire is primarily concerned to support the affirmation of constitutional monarchy and British authority over America, symbolized by the ignominious departure of the Congress, rather than to recognize the military achievement of the commander.[23]

On October 10, 1777, when the British were awaiting confirmation of unofficial preliminary accounts that forces commanded by the Howe brothers had occupied Philadelphia, a particularly incisive print, "The Conference Between the Brothers HOW to get rich,"[24] was published that reinforced familiar images of their self-indulgence (Fig. 5.2). The mood of the political nation as reflected in the British press could swing rapidly in response to a happy coincidence of news. It was anticipated that the British would rapidly defeat Washington's forces, despite rumors of French reinforcements. The mood at the time of the satire's publication was probably close to that reflected here:

> From the present admirable disposition of the King's forces in America, it should seem evident that the rebellious game of the Provincials is nearly over; for whenever we hear of Washington's being brought to a regular action, which nothing but a miracle being wrought in his favour can much longer prevent, from that moment we may safely date the termination of the unnatural insurrection, and the re-establishment of order, and good government on the other side the Atlantic.[25]

Such optimism was congenial to satire: when affairs in America appeared to be going well, commercial advantage could be gained from affirming familiar personal stereotypes in satirical prints.

Figure 5.2. BMC 5399. "The Conference Between the Brothers How to get rich." W. Williams, Fleet Street. 10 October 1777. Copyright © The British Museum.

The probable source of "The Conference" was an innuendo that had appeared in a routinely reported speech by John Wilkes, who still had a popular metropolitan following, in the debate on the Civil List on April 16, 1777. This was published in a volume of his speeches on July 9, 1777, by which time the new volume of the *Parliamentary Register* would also have been available.

I observe, Sir, in the Civil List accounts on the table, an article, "Lord Howe and Sir William Howe, commissioners *for restoring peace in America* 100£ per week each, arrears, 1,742£". . . . The *peaceful* mode adopted by the two brothers, according to my calculation, will not soon *restore peace in America,* but it will possibly be the period of the Trojan war, ten years at least, so that we may compliment the Howe family with above one hundred thousand pounds free gift, at the rate of 100£ per week each brother, besides the settled pay and perquisites as officers.[26]

By questioning the Howes' motives in a manner calculated to raise a laugh in Parliament and later amuse the reader, Wilkes provided an eminently suitable subject for "The Conference Between the Brothers HOW to get rich." As Dorothy George suggests, the satirist was attacking the Howes "for dishonesty and inactivity," but this satire gained its topicality by referring to a malicious jibe that had recently been going around London society.[27] It provides evidence for a close connection between what was said in Parliament and the subjects of satirical prints, confirming their commercial appeal to every social group with an interest in politics.[28]

The iconography of the print is more complex than might appear from its clear general intention. The Devil dominates a unifying circle of five hands; his pointing fingers, turned outwards from his body, identify the brothers as his own. The portrayal of the Devil, tempter and deluder, encouraging the brothers to continue the war uses an image associated in political graphic satire with the myth of Lord Bute as purveyor of advice destructive of the state.[29] Where the Devil was involved, there was politically motivated activity injurious to Britain's interest, a connotation that would be understood by association.

George's contention that the cabbages imply perquisites, since "cabbages" were pieces of cloth pilfered by tailors, is convincing, because the print was produced in London where Wilkes's jibe would be known, with its serious implication that the Howes were being given money falsely legitimated under the Civil List and pilfered from the people. They are being hawked by a man from the community in which the "cabbages" have grown, who addresses the Howes by name, probably a suggestion that gullible taxpayers of Britain, through their parliamentary representatives, are providing perquisites from state funds as long as the brothers continue the war.[30] By this argument, the print was centered in recent preoccupations of British taxpayers rather than in the American campaign itself.

The cameo of the sedentary Howes recurs in "A Picturesque View of the State of the Nation for February 1778,"[31] an illustration in the February issue of the *Westminster Magazine* available at the end of January (Fig. 5.3). This periodical circulated among people who knew the Howes' predilections and habits as members of the aristocracy. When the frontispiece was commissioned, stories would be current in London society that officers of the occupying forces were very comfortable and entertained in Philadelphia.[32] The satire, prepared in anticipation of the forthcoming debate on the state of the nation, supported the opposition by calling the ministry to account for the expense and ineffective outcome of campaigns in America,

Figure 5.3. BMC 5472. "A Picturesque View of the State of the Nation for February 1778." *Westminster Magazine,* February 1778. Copyright © The British Museum.

and expressed the nation's apprehension at well-founded rumors that France and Spain would carry the war to Europe.

The stereotype was being sustained in newspapers despite the availability of news of military action around and in defense of Philadelphia. On January 10, 1778, the *London Evening Post* carried three derogatory items. One related to Sir William Howe's mistress, "whom he bought of her husband for a contract," complaining that the country must pay the piper and pay for pimping. A second quoted letters from Philadelphia alleging that, far from moving against the enemy, General Howe was comfortably quartered in Philadelphia. The third was an "extempore Epigram" on the *Gazette Extraordinary,* which derided the victory at Mud Island and hinted that General Sir William Howe wished to be recalled. Both the *St. James's Chronicle* and the *London Evening Post* reported on January 10 an accusation by the Dowager Lady Howe that Ministry hacks were responsible for abuse against her sons, which had appeared regularly in the press. True to form, however, the *Post* kept the stereotype before its readers. On January 24, it contained the following paragraph: "As much has been said against General Howe for choosing Philadelphia for his winter quarters, a correspondent vindicates him on the following prudent principles: Where should the *Brothers* winter, says he, but at *Philo delphi;* particularly as it is washed by the *Delay-war?*"[33]

Although only a background element in the "State of the Nation" satire, the ideograph, which recapitulated the Howes' reputation for high living and reluctance to engage Washington, was a potent symbol of the wastefulness of the American campaign.[34] Two of the nine headings in the "explanation" of the engraving summarized the stereotype.

VI. The good ship Eagle laid up and moved some distance from Philadelphia, without sails or guns and shewing nothing but blank portholes, all the rest of the fleet invisible, nobody knows where.

VII. The two Brothers napping it, one against the other, in the City of Philadelphia, out of sight of fleet and army.[35]

Versions of this print were marketed without the explanation. Probably some were intended for sale in America as part of the continuing transatlantic market in topical publications, of which Paine's writings are another example; some bore captions in French or Dutch for sale in Europe. As a result, the unflattering stereotype of the Howes became widely recognized. A broadside written by Hopkinson, a native of Philadelphia, dated about 1777, is quoted by Granger:

Howe with his Legions came,
In hopes of wealth and fame
What has he done?
All day, at Faro play'd,
All night with whores he laid,
And with his bottle made
Excellent fun.[36]

It accords with the depiction of the Howe brothers in Philadelphia in the two satires that portray their life there, and can be assumed to have been known in London, possibly as early as October 1777 when the first was published.

Westminster Magazine's drawing included the flagship *Eagle,* lying idle outside Philadelphia, "without sail or guns and shewing nothing but naked portholes." The accusation that the rest of the fleet was "invisible, nobody knows where" was a convenient fiction; the fleet was continuing to ensure supplies to the forces and had successfully supported the army in the clearing of the Delaware.[37] This information was available in Britain, since the *Eagle* arrived in Falmouth on January 5 with news that Mud Island and other river forts had been taken on November 15. On January 8, 1778, the *St. James's Chronicle* gave an account of its reception in London. "A Gentleman who has received a Letter from Lord Howe himself, brought by the above Packet, read part of it publickly this Day in Garraway's Coffee-House, in which, after mentioning the River Delaware being clear &c. his Lordship says, that he was preparing to sail with his Fleet for Rhode Island."

Although such information combined news with hearsay, it was well authenticated and potentially able to counteract accusations of expensive inactivity. The reality accessible to perceptive British readers was very different from the satirical stereotype, suggesting that the commanders' behavior was such as would have been acceptable for men of their social status in other circumstances. According to Jackson, the enforced period in winter quarters in Philadelphia produced a daily routine of elegance and culture shared enthusiastically by Philadelphian loyalist society; it followed conventions no different from the pursuits of the wealthy at home.[38]

Ample evidence reached the country during January that the British forces in America were consolidating their position in the face of difficulties. The *London Gazette Extraordinary,* which reported Lord Howe's account of the naval actions against Mud Island (i.e., Fort Mifflin) and the subsequent strategic evacuation of Red Bank by the rebels, was published on January 9, 1778. It claimed that the enemy's shipping was no longer protected, that the river passage was sufficiently accessible to British vessels, and that removal of the barriers (chevaux de frises) could be undertaken at "a more favourable season."[39] Meanwhile, the *London Evening Post* denigrated the *Gazette's* account, declaring the official statistics incredible. On January 24, a letter addressed to Lord North, signed "A Real Whig," disparaged the conquest of "a paltry muddy island of no consequence to the Americans," and belittled any prospect of further action by Howe.

Major John André's firsthand account of the capture of Mud Island paints a very different picture. He describes preliminary action between October 23 and 25 to facilitate attacks on Red Bank and Mud Island, and sustained battery attacks from November 10 to 14, which were met by strong defensive action. On November 15,

> the "Vigilant" . . . was brought up and moored between Providence and Mud Island. A sloop carrying six eighteen-pounders was moored close to her. These with the Batteries ashore, and the "Somerset," "Isis," "Roebuck," "Pearl," and a galley below the chevaux de frise

kept up an incessant cannonade the whole day. The Rebel floating
Batteries fired a great deal on the ships. The Grenadiers of the Guards
were on Providence Island in readiness to storm had it been required.

At . . . [sic] o'clock at night the Rebels evacuated the fort and set fire
to the barracks. They left in it twenty-eight pieces of cannon, several
of which were good and unspiked. The place was very much battered,
every gun dismounted, a great many dead bodies were found, scarce
covered, in trous de loups or ditches. Ten other pieces of cannon were
afterwards found sunk in a scow.[40]

This diary brings into perspective "The Takeing of Miss Mud I'land,"[41]
a graphic satire that suggested that British actions in the Delaware during
the occupation of Philadelphia were trivial (Fig. 5.4). The taking of Mud
Island on November 15 was the successful outcome of a three-day action
following careful preparation, though this was not made clear in the official
dispatches.[42]

The satire, produced in London from information available there, concurs with the official account of the placement of British ships:[43] *Isis* at the
front, bearing the brunt of the opposition; *Somerset* approaching up one
channel and *Roebuck* on the other side, with *Vigilant* round the back of the
island. *Eagle*, Lord Howe's command ship, is indicated at the center front,
serving merely to show that this was a naval exercise.

Vulgarity and sexual innuendo are used to portray the aggressive American virgin, "Miss Mud I'land," defending her territory by blasting the British attacker with a salvo of wind. She is sitting astride a cannon, but the
alternative interpretation of the salvo from the cannon's mouth is where the
derision lies. Probably the satire was a response to firsthand accounts describing the ferocity of the rebels' cannonade on November 14, which
would have been read in clubs and coffeehouses.

The conquest of the fort was portrayed in Britain as exemplifying a futile
war of petty incidents rather than as a victory. Suiting the critical atmosphere preceding the state of the nation inquiry, it supported antiministerial
complaints that resources were being unwisely employed in petty actions
against a stubborn adversary. Newspaper opinion reflected this state of
mind, and the Howe brothers' reputation suffered further.

As news of the arrival of the *Eagle* packet reached London, the *St.
James's Chronicle* of January 8, 1778, reported:

She brings advice, that on the fifteenth of November the Fort on Mud
Island was taken with the Loss only of five Men killed and four
wounded, and that the several Forts in the Delaware were all, when
she sailed, in Possession of his Majesty's Troops. . . .

Figure 5.4. BMC 5402. "The Takeing of Miss Mud I'land." W. Humphrey, 227 Strand, undated. Copyright © The British Museum.

There is no Officer come in the above Ship from General Howe, or his Brother, Lord Howe, but there are official Despatches to the Admiralty and Lord G. Germaine, which are in the ordinary Way, and therefore contain nothing more than the taking of the Forts abovementioned, there having been no Action between the two Armies.

The *London Evening Post* of January 10 was even more dismissive, quoting a letter from one of Sir William's officers: "What has been done in the Delaware has opened a communication with the ships; but otherwise it is of no consequence, not being worth the trouble, and time it has taken." The only conclusion another correspondent draws from the reduction of

Mud Island by the forces under General Howe is that "the Americans have gotten out of the *dirt,* and left the English in it."

Together, these newspaper reports reflect despondency in Britain between the news of Burgoyne's capitulation and the reopening of Parliament after the Christmas recess. In these circumstances news that naval actions had opened the Delaware sufficiently to ensure better supplies to the army overwintering in Philadelphia made little impact on the British public. The Howes' achievement received scant recognition in the press, letter writers being occupied with comment on Burgoyne's capitulation. The parliamentary opposition was demanding a debate on the current situation and the expense of the war. "Miss Mud I'land" fitted the nation's mood.

There was evidence in the newspapers, even as dispatches arrived from Philadelphia, that the Howe brothers were discontented. They felt they had not received adequate ministerial support to sustain an effective campaign and would become scapegoats for government incompetence; they resented the way they had been portrayed in print. They therefore renounced their command, Sir William departing for England on May 24, 1778.

It is not clear from the parliamentary records how much confidence the ministry retained in the Howes at the end of their American campaign; their position was invidious when viewed from London, as a result of Sir William's haste and the ambiguity of Lord Howe's position. The latter had particularly objected to the appointment on February 17, 1778, of a new Peace Commission in which the brothers would be subordinate to the Earl of Carlisle,[44] since they were then in America and their appointment as commissioners had never been rescinded. It was unlikely that they would accept this loss of status without complaint, and indeed they refused to serve under Carlisle.

Political Implications and Repercussions of the Campaign

Responses in Parliament to the Howes' performance in America showed little of the bias evident in opposition publications. During the debate on the king's speech, which began on November 18, 1777, Governor Johnstone "spoke strenuously on the merit of Lord Howe as a commander."[45] The debate on December 2 concerning the setting up of a committee to consider the state of the nation included discussion of the Howes' position as peace commissioners. Edmund Burke referred to their difficulties, arguing that ultimate responsibility for conciliation had lain with the ministry rather than with the two commissioners.[46]

In Lord North's introduction of his Conciliatory Propositions on February 17, 1778, he confessed his misgivings about the American campaign, implying criticism of Sir William Howe in that he had thought Howe's victories more decisive than they had been.[47] His remark confirmed impressions that the commander was a poor strategist, and fueled the invective of critics who believed he had not tried to defeat Washington's army. North's attitude demonstrated the British government's failure to appreciate the realities of waging war at a distance, where all supplies must come by sea and any shortfall must be met by living off the resources of a hostile land.[48] This lack of understanding was at the heart of Sir William's bitterness and determination to justify his campaign strategy by means of a parliamentary inquiry.

Critical letters sent to America by Germain had offended the brothers, particularly Sir William, by their coldness. The ill feeling between the two men was regarded by Lord North and the king as irreconcilable and a stumbling block in the way of a future campaign, since Sir William would be difficult to replace.[49] Such antagonism does not appear to have extended to Lord Howe, who, after his brother had been replaced by Sir Henry Clinton on May 8, completed a further mission against d'Estaing at Sandy Hook between July 11 and July 22, 1778, before returning home. He later served as admiral in the defense of Gibraltar, arriving with reinforcements in October 1782. Despite his readiness to take offense,[50] in December 1778 the king, always a strategist, considered appointing him as head of the Admiralty Board. Lord North was asked on February 4, 1779, to sound out Lord Howe with the offer, which he refused.[51] The brothers remained in agreement over the necessity for an inquiry, Sir William contending that the ministry had let them down and that ministerial influence lay behind the adverse press comment that their command had attracted in Britain.

The parliamentary inquiry took place in 1779, and the brothers had a formidable adversary in Joseph Galloway. Throughout the British occupation of New York he had provided information about loyalist support,[52] and during the occupation of Philadelphia he had worked with Sir William Howe as "Superintendent General of Police in the City, and its Environs, and Superintendent of Imports and Exports to and from Philadelphia." Galloway's circumstantial evidence before Parliament, therefore, appeared authoritative in press reports, and his opinions carried more weight than his lack of military expertise should have justified. He also became involved wholeheartedly in pamphleteering, attempting to prolong British interest in the American campaign by claiming that the war could have been won speedily and that the colonies still need not be lost. He contended that government-dictated strategy up to mid-1778 had been sound but inadequately carried out by indolent commanders.

Galloway's importance as a propagandist against the Howes arose from his detailed testimony in Parliament[53] and his published letters to Sir William Howe.[54] The publicity that both enjoyed in newspapers, periodicals and magazines such as the *Monthly Review* reached those who were closely involved in military affairs and politics and knew the participants, as well as many who would not be sufficiently well informed to assess their credibility.

In 1780 Sir William Howe's response appeared in a pamphlet that summarized his evidence to the parliamentary committee and included observations on Galloway's pamphlet, insisting that "the southern expedition, by drawing off General Washington and his whole force, was the strongest diversion that could have been made."[55]

Though Sir William was Galloway's primary target, Lord Howe did not escape criticism. In his 1779 *Letter to the Right Honourable Lord Viscount Howe, on his Naval Conduct in the American War,* Galloway criticised Howe's supposed unwillingness to act against privateers and American merchant shipping and to support the British land forces. He blamed both commissioners for lack of determination in face of Congress, arguing that the Peace Commission could have succeeded and holding Howe responsible for its limited assurances and failure to convince the Americans of the justice of British government. His assertions against both brothers echoed in print as suspicion and assumption and have never been finally dismissed.

It is difficult to assess, retrospectively, the influence of these pamphlets and reviews. Being specialized and discursive, they had a more limited circulation than did satirical graphics and antigovernment newspapers, but they were less ephemeral. The impact of this saga went far beyond the immediate events and the heartfelt grievances they aroused at the time. The Howes' insistence on a parliamentary inquiry to justify their military strategy and highlight what they saw as ministerial lack of support provided a source of doubt about the ministry's handling of the war.[56] Sir William Howe's impassioned defense in Parliament and pamphlet demonstrates his belief in the ability of print to reach the people on whom he depended for his ultimate reputation.

On one level, criticism of the Howes, particularly in satire of all descriptions, pandered to sensationalism and exploited the perpetual desire of society to denigrate and pillory its public figures. On a deeper level, satire became an instrument in the political battle between the government and its opponents who sought to end North's ministry by publicizing what they perceived to be inept handling of the American campaign.

The extensiveness and variety of politically motivated propaganda, and the tenacity with which it was created and maintained, provide evidence of an increasing conviction in the government and in British society that public opinion mattered. Because readers, including politicians, believed there was a political function for expressions of opinion such as those outlined here, they became significant events in themselves, a potentially influential element in the protracted process by which Lord North's ministry ultimately lost credibility.

Notes

1. Analyses of the culture of the political and intellectual elite such as that of J. C. D. Clark, *The Language of Liberty, 1660–1832: Political Discourse and Social Dynamics in the Anglo-American World* (Cambridge, 1994), while valuable in their own terms, do not account adequately for changes in British society now being widely acknowledged by other scholars.

2. Robert Harris, *A Patriot Press: National Politics and the London Press in the 1740s* (Oxford, 1993). See particularly chapter 1 for the relationship between press and politics, commercial requirements, and readership.

3. Ibid., 254–56.

4. The significance of the Printers' Case is discussed in P. D. G. Thomas, *John Wilkes, a Friend to Liberty* (Oxford, 1996), chap. 8. Harris emphasizes the increase and significance of press repercussions following the regular reporting of debates. Bob Harris, *Politics and the Rise of the Press: Britain and France, 1620–1800* (New York, 1996), 40–41.

5. Kathleen Wilson, *The Sense of the People: Politics, Culture, and Imperialism in England, 1715–1785* (Cambridge, 1995), 36–43, 140–65, and chap. 5, esp. 253–62.

6. John Almon also published the writings of his friend, John Wilkes, a strong supporter of America in the early years of the Revolution.

7. *Morning Post,* November 12, 1777, p. 2.

8. "Nottingham" wrote as a supporter of the Howe family and opponent of the government's American policy. The pseudonym implied that he was Sir William's constituent. The letter was one of a series, the first in February on Howe's appointment to the naval command in America, the last in late April, when he sailed.

9. *British Museum Catalogue (BMC)* 5335, illus.1.

10. Mary Darly produced a series of satires of a fashion of 1776 and 1777, including *BMC* 5330, "Bunkers Hill, or America's Head-dress," and "Miss Carolina Sullivan, one of the obstinate daughters of America, 1776" (Library of Congress 701). Such satires were for amusement rather than propaganda.

11. George cites *London Chronicle,* May 9, 1776, and Walpole's *Last Journal* (1910), 1:540, where he wrote, "nobody was deceived." *BMC* 221.

12. Rodney Atwood, *The Hessians: Mercenaries from Hessen-Kassel in the American Revolution* (Cambridge, 1980), 84–86.

13. Captain Johann Ewald, *Diary of the American War: A Hessian Journal,* trans. and ed. Joseph P. Tustin (New Haven, 1979), 30.

14. Thomas Paine, *The Political and Miscellaneous Works of Thomas Paine,* 2 vols., ed. R. Carlile (London, 1819). It was intended for British and American readers: "As I send all my papers to England, this, like Common Sense, will find its way there" (1:25).

15. The Howes' elder brother, George, was revered as the hero of Ticonderoga. Massachusetts contributed to a memorial to him in Westminster Abbey. *Cassell's Biographical Dictionary,* 520.

16. David Syrett, *The Royal Navy in American Waters, 1775–1783* (Brookfield, Vt., 1989), 80.

17. M. M. Boatner refers to George Howe as "a man who scorned the luxurious habits of other British officers while in the field, who liked the colonists." *Biographical Dictionary of the American War of Independence 1763–1783* (New York, 1867–69), 520. Lord and Sir William were known to enjoy a more conventionally aristocratic lifestyle.

18. In 1780, in *Narrative of Lieutenant-General Sir William Howe etc. entitled Observations upon a Pamphlet,* Howe wrote that, though contented that his professional conduct should be criticized, "I feel myself hurt as a man when I am accused of inhumanity."

19. "Congregational Accounts to the Unity Elders' Conference at Herrnhut, Saxony, of the Congregation at Philadelphia from the month of August 1777 to June 1778." Archive of the Moravian Church, Fulneck, Yorkshire, packet 357.

20. As Diana Donald has demonstrated, the late eighteenth century saw a market for caricature prints among a wide spectrum of British society. See Diana Donald, *The Age of Caricature: Satirical Prints in the Reign of George III* (New Haven, 1996), 2–9.

21. *BMC* 5401, November 20, 1777, Wm. Hitchcock, 5 Birchin Lane. Not illustrated.

22. Benjamin Franklin, Silas Deane, and Arthur Lee, the three commissioners sent to negotiate a treaty, were already established and popular in France. *World Almanac of the American Revolution,* ed. L. E. Purcell and D. F. Burg (New York, 1992), 91–92, 153.

23. True also of *BMC* 5340, "News from America, or the Patriots in the Dumps," *London Magazine,* November 1776. Here Howe's name appeared only as a signature on the document.

24. *BMC* 5399, October 10, 1777, W. Williams, Fleet Street, illus. 2.

25. *Leeds Mercury,* October 14, 1777, quoting London, October 9.

26. *The Speeches of John Wilkes, one of the Knights of the Shire for the County*

of Middlesex, In the Parliament appointed to meet at Westminster the 29th day of November, 1774, to the prorogation, 2 vols. (1777), 2:42–43.

27. Wilkes was well liked by City representatives in London; in the February 1776 election for Chamberlain he polled 1,137 votes to Hopkins's 1,456. *London Chronicle,* February 4, p. 187.

28. Patronage may have been involved through the connection between Wilkes and Almon, who still provided material for the *London Evening Post* and published the *Parliamentary Register.*

29. Lord Bute became a traditional image used in satirical prints in 1766, 1774, and 1775 to suggest "Scotch influence" in British politics.

30. This interpretation assumes that the background sketches of ships and tents, along with growing cabbages, are symbolic of the Howes' commission and attitude toward it, not representations of locations in America or of local loyalist support for the British army in Philadelphia, which then would be unknown in London. John W. Jackson, *With the British Army in Philadelphia, 1777–1778* (San Rafael, Calif., 1979), 91.

31. *BMC* 5472, illus. 3.

32. Fox, defending the Howes in the Commons, February 11, 1778, referred to inevitable public criticism of commanders either for indolence or overindulgence: "Whoever should succeed to the present gentlemen in command, would just meet with the same fate." *Parliamentary Register,* 8:363.

33. *Philo* has connotations of a lover, as in *philander,* a reference to Sir William's reputation with women, and *delphi* may be an ironical comparison of Sir William with Apollo, god of music and poetry, to whom is attributed perfection of manhood. The British held frequent plays, performed by the officers. Sir William Howe is described as "a fine figure, full six feet high and well proportioned . . . his manners were graceful and dignified and he was much beloved by his officers." John F. Watson, *Annals of Philadelphia, being a collection of Memoirs, Anecdotes and Incidents of the City and its Inhabitants from the Days of the Pilgrim Founders* (Philadelphia, 1830), 687.

34. For background to the social and recreational activities of the British forces, see Jackson, *With the British Army,* esp. 104–6 and 212–19.

35. *Westminster Magazine,* 6 (February 1778): 64. See also *BMC* 5:285.

36. Bruce Ingham Granger, *Political Satire and the American Revolution, 1763–1783* (New York, 1960), 172.

37. By January, Washington's activities from Valley Forge made it difficult for local people to bring provisions, and foraging expeditions were hazardous. Naval support provided a lifeline. *Hessian Journal,* ed. Tustin, 118.

38. Jackson, *With the British Army,* "Convivial Interludes," 212–20, and "Meschianza," 244–48.

39. For an account by a Hessian common soldier who observed the two events, see J. C. Dohla, *A Hessian Diary of the American Revolution,* trans. and ed. B. E. Burgoyne (Norman, Okla., 1990), 58–59.

40. *André's Journal; an authentic record of the movements and engagements of the British Army in America from June 1777 to November 1778 as recorded from day to day by Major John André*, ed. Henry Cabot Lodge (Boston, 1903).

41. *BMC* 5402, W. Humphrey, 227 Strand, illus. 4. Undated, probably early 1778. The "takeing" of Mud Island between November 12 and 15, 1777, was reported in the *Extraordinary Gazette* of January 9, 1778.

42. For accounts of the action, see Jackson, *With the British Army*, 74–78, and Dohla *Diary*, 58–59.

43. It concurs even more precisely with Jackson's well-researched account. This suggests that eyewitness reports were widely available.

44. Carlisle was a young man who had recently realized that he preferred an active political life to a reputation as a dandy.

45. *Parliamentary Register*, 8:4.

46. Ibid., 78.

47. Ibid., 282–83.

48. For an analysis of the difficulties facing the British army in a hostile environment, supplied from Britain by sea and dependent on local supplements, see R. Arthur Bowler, *Logistics and the Failure of the British Army in America, 1775–1783* (Princeton, 1975), 239–50.

49. Sir John Fortescue, *The Correspondence of King George the Third from 1760 to December 1783*, 6 vols. (London, 1928), 4:10, no. 2156, 4:15, no. 2161.

50. Horace Walpole, a malicious and prejudiced observer of society, portrayed Lord Howe as touchy and mercenary. "Lord Howe suspended his resentment for six weeks, waiting to be pacified by some more lucrative offer." *Journal of the Reign of King George III, from the Year 1771 to 1783 by Horace Walpole, Being a Supplement to His Memoirs*, 2 vols., ed. Dr. Dolan (London, 1859), 2:45.

51. Fortescue, *Correspondence*, 239, no. 2485, 266–67, nos. 2518 and 2519.

52. Ferling has argued that Galloway consistently overestimated loyalist numbers, to the disadvantage of the British government, who relied on him. John E. Ferling, *The Loyalist Mind: Joseph Galloway and the American Revolution* (University Park, Pa., 1977), 40–47.

53. *Parliamentary Register* carried a full account of the inquiry, including Galloway's responses under questioning by Germain and others. Probably the pamphlet version appeared first, as it was reviewed promptly.

54. Both printed in London for J. Wilkie, 1779. Reviewed in *Monthly Review* 61 (September 1779): 228.

55. *The Narrative of Sir William Howe in a Committee of the House of Commons on 29th April, 1779, relative to his conduct during the late command of the king's troops in America, to which are added some observations upon a pamphlet entitled "Letters to a Nobleman"* (1780), 62.

56. Sir William was unpopular with the ministry. Germain received regular complaints from him that the campaign was not being properly resourced, a charge that he always refuted. The reputations of both men suffered as a result of logistical problems inherent in attempting to conduct a war in America.

6

"Like the Irish"? Volunteer Corps and Volunteering in Britain during the American War

Stephen Conway

The British "amateur military tradition"—part-time soldiering most famil-iarly exemplified by the Local Defense Volunteers or Home Guard of the Second World War—has attracted scholarly interest in recent years.[1] While much of the attention has concentrated on the nineteenth and twentieth centuries, the eighteenth century has not been ignored. Linda Colley has highlighted the importance of the volunteer military associations formed across England during the 1745 Jacobite uprising, and she has also looked at volunteer corps in the French Revolution of the 1790s—as have other historians, notably J. E. Cookson.[2] The Irish volunteers of the time of the American War of Independence have likewise been studied in some detail in a clutch of articles, essays, and books.[3]

Little has been written, by contrast, on volunteering in Britain during the American Revolution. This essay will begin by indicating the scale of volun-teer activity in England, Wales, and Scotland between 1778, when the first corps came into existence, and the end of the war in 1783. This is a neces-sary first step, not least because the importance of British volunteering dur-ing this conflict has not been generally appreciated. Attention will then be turned to explanations. It would be inappropriate to think in terms of a single, monolithic volunteer movement; volunteer activity took many forms and needs to be placed in a number of contexts. The emergence of volunteer corps, it will be argued, cannot be understood simply in military terms. Volunteering was not just a response to the threat of enemy invasion or incursion. At least some volunteer units saw themselves as performing a police function, maintaining order in turbulent times. There was also a political dimension to volunteering that requires illumination. And volun-teer activity needs to be seen in relation to broader social trends—particu-larly the increasing assertiveness of the "middling sort," associational activity as a means of expressing that assertiveness, and the claims of urban centers, where a notable quantity of the associational activity occurred, to greater recognition. By examining volunteering in this period, the importance of local loyalty can also be seen as well as the complex ways in which it was linked to wider national allegiances. The final part of the essay will offer a comparison of British and Irish volunteering in the American Revolution. The Irish volunteers have so dominated the historiography, and their political role has so often been emphasized, that it would be easy to assume that they were very different from the volunteer bodies that emerged in England, Wales, and Scotland. But in many ways—though by no means all—the British and Irish volunteers were remarkably similar. Contemporary Britons were well aware of at least some of the similarities—either because they feared Irish example or because they wished to follow it. As a Scottish clergyman explained to an English correspondent in May 1782, the volunteer corps formed in his country "two or three years ago" were "like the Irish."[4]

I

When the extent of volunteering in England, Wales, and Scotland during the American Revolution is considered, precision or anything remotely approaching it is unfortunately impossible. The figures available to the historian are limited. Herbert Butterfield, seeking to shed light on this subject many years ago, cited an estimate in the papers of the commander in chief of the army, General Amherst, which suggested that by the end of 1779 there were 150 companies in England alone, each comprising at least fifty men.[5] But this is just a snapshot of the situation at a particular moment, not a comprehensive picture. Furthermore, it almost certainly relates only to corps approved by the government, and therefore it understates the number of volunteers even at that time. Many companies did not seek official sanction and the government arms that went with it,[6] which means that their existence is not always apparent from surviving archives of the central departments of the state. Only by combining the records of central government with fugitive reports in newspapers, local authority documents, and private collections is it possible to gain an impression of the extent of volunteering. And even then caution is required. The search that provided the data produced here, while extensive, was far from exhaustive. A lifetime's study of every possible source would probably be necessary to produce a full picture. So it can safely be assumed that this more limited exercise has missed some of the volunteer corps of the period.

An indication of the geographical basis of volunteering in England, Wales, and Scotland during the American Revolution can be obtained from map 6.1, which is based on an analysis of the very varied sources just described. But this needs to be supplemented by a chronology that conveys the timing of the creation of the various volunteer formations. The first British volunteer corps of this period emerged in 1778. Aberdeen, having seen its offer to raise a regular army regiment refused, started to recruit a body of men in volunteer companies that May. Two more Scottish urban centers, Campbeltown and Ayr on the west coast, made some progress at this time in establishing "a very respectable force" from among their inhabitants.[7] This was merely a foretaste of what was to come, however; far more volunteer units were formed in the summer and autumn of the following year. In July 1779, a meeting in London agreed to raise twenty-four companies in Middlesex and Westminster, each of more than seventy officers and men.[8] In an apparently unconnected initiative, the officers and artificers of the Board of Works decided to create four companies, with a combined strength of 300 men.[9] In August a county meeting at Lewes, following the lead of the metropolis, pledged to raise twenty-four companies in Sussex.[10] Devon's freeholders, assembling a few days before the Lewes meeting, also fixed on twenty-four companies as appropriate for their county, while the governor of Dartmouth Castle, apparently acting on his own authority, organized 200 of the townsmen into a volunteer body.[11] By October, according to an officer in the Devon militia, there was "scarce a Town or Village in this County" that had not formed a company.[12] Neighboring Cornwall was hardly less active. Two companies were raised in Falmouth, three in Penryn, and one each in Helston, Marazion, and St. Austell. It was confidently predicted that the county would "furnish 3000d Men" by the next spring.[13] Elsewhere in the west country there was similar enthusiasm: at Lyme Regis in Dorset, 130 inhabitants "form'd themselves into a Corps"; at Bath in Somerset, a volunteer unit was created that August; and Bristol had its own independent corps by September.[14] Further east, some 240 men were drilled and organized into companies in Shrivenham Hundred in Berkshire.[15] On the coast of Kent, meanwhile, more than 300 of Dover's townsmen agreed to associate in a volunteer corps.[16] Nor was the north of England far behind. Military associations were formed at Stockton, County Durham, and at Bradford, Scarborough, Kirkby Moorside, and Whitby in Yorkshire.[17] In Scotland, a meeting at Dumfries offered to raise volunteer companies, as did similar meetings in Cardigan, Anglesey, and Pembrokeshire in Wales.[18]

If 1779 was perhaps the peak year so far as the formation of British volunteer corps was concerned, additional units emerged in 1780, 1781,

Map 6.1. Volunteer Corps in Britain, 1778–1783.

and particularly in 1782. In June 1780 there was further activity in the metropolis, where various corps emerged at this time, including the Light Horse Volunteers and the London Foot Association.[19] The same year saw Grampound in Cornwall form its own company, and that November the parish of Phillack, in St. Ives bay, undertook to raise a volunteer unit.[20] By this stage, there was also a volunteer artillery force at King's Lynn in Norfolk.[21] In 1781 the male inhabitants of Great Yarmouth formed several independent companies; while in Aberdeen, where the corps established in

1778 had been disbanded, another military association was created.[22] Edinburgh produced its own Defensive Band in the same year, following this up with the Caledonian Band in 1782.[23] There was a significant surge in the formation of units in this year; indeed, 1782 seems to have been not far behind 1779 in terms of the emergence of volunteer corps. By May 1782 Swansea and Neath already had two companies and planned to raise a third,[24] while the male inhabitants of Lewes agreed to form another three companies on top of the two they had brought into being in 1779.[25] Corps were established in Leeds and Sheffield; Liverpool pledged to raise ten companies and York five;[26] and military associations appeared in Birmingham, Chester, Manchester, and Shrewsbury.[27] Hull seems also to have raised its own volunteer unit at this time.[28] In Norfolk a cavalry corps, the Norfolk Rangers, was formed, and probably a number of other volunteer units, too, as the county's squires were reported to have "all turned military."[29]

II

After having established, in a necessarily impressionistic way, that there was something of a vogue for creating volunteer associations, attention must be turned to explaining this blossoming of the amateur military spirit. The most obvious answer is that volunteering was a response to external threats. The initial spur to the formation of the Scottish volunteer corps in 1778 was the predatory raids of the American privateer John Paul Jones. In April 1778, Jones attacked Whitehaven in Cumberland, putting a landing party ashore and burning a collier in the harbor.[30] He then sailed across the Solway Firth with the intention of kidnapping the Earl of Selkirk. Jones was unable to seize the earl, and he had to settle for stealing some silver, but his audacious attempt to bring the war to Britain itself sent shock waves through exposed coastal communities. As Henry Dundas, the lord advocate, explained in defense of the actions taken by Aberdeen, Campbeltown, and Ayr: "The apprehension thereby created gave rise to the idea amongst several of the Sea Port Towns of Scotland to put a body of their Inhabitants under Training . . . for the defence of the Shipping and other property belonging to these Towns."[31] Fear of Jones likewise led Hull's deputy town clerk in September 1779 to ask government for "a Speedy Supply of Artillery and Small Arms" and permission to appoint officers and form the inhabitants into a defensive force to protect the town.[32] It would seem that Jones's presence in the North Sea off the coast of Yorkshire was also the inspiration for the Scarborough and the Whitby volunteers, who came forward at the same time to defend their towns and shipping, for "the Inhabitants upon that coast" were said to be "greatly alarmd" by Jones's exploits.[33] By that stage, however, the main threat came from the French, who had entered the war in the summer of 1778, and their allies, the Spanish, who had become belligerents in June 1779.

Anxiety about the landing of regular enemy troops inspired the formation of many volunteer corps. The considerable bustle in the southwest, particularly in Devon and Cornwall, in the summer and autumn of 1779 was closely connected with the presence in the Channel off Plymouth of the combined Franco-Spanish fleet, which it was widely assumed was poised to put a considerable military force ashore.[34] Indeed, the geographical and chronological pattern of volunteer activity was clearly—and not surprisingly—linked with invasion fears. The decision of the Sussex county meeting to raise twenty-four volunteer companies is perfectly understandable when the county's vulnerability to attack is recognized. Likewise, the crop of volunteer corps formed in settlements along the east coast in 1781 and 1782 owed much to the Dutch joining the conflict at the very end of 1780; this seems to have been the stimulus to Great Yarmouth's creating several companies in March 1781, and it appears also to account for Aberdeen's second burst of enthusiasm. Norfolk's volunteer mania of the summer and autumn of 1782 can similarly be connected to apprehensions of a Dutch landing, as can Hull's raising a subscription to support its own volunteer force.[35]

Yet these military imperatives would surely have operated less strongly in many of the inland areas where volunteer bodies emerged, and even along the coast volunteer companies cannot be understood simply as responses to the danger of enemy incursions. At least some of the volunteer units were envisaged by those involved as helping to maintain order. The Berkshire volunteers organized by Lord Barrington, a former secretary at war, appear to have been inspired by a fear of popular disorder at a time when the county lacked any significant military presence. Barrington even claimed that it was his example that encouraged the formation of volunteer companies in Westminster and Middlesex, implying that these corps were intended to act as a local police force as much as to resist foreign invaders.[36] Many of the London associations did indeed carry out public order functions, especially during the Gordon Riots of June 1780—though, as will be seen, there was a major political row over whether they should be involved in the suppression of the disturbances.[37]

The subject of the relationship between the volunteers and the central agencies of the state has already been touched upon: some units sought and obtained official approval and the issue of government arms that went with such approval, while others remained determinedly "independent." But the relationship now needs to be considered more thoroughly. Did the state, by encouraging and fostering the formation of volunteer corps, play a significant part in the growth of volunteering? In 1782 volunteering was certainly regarded indulgently, even favorably, by the new Rockingham administration, and some of the expansion of volunteer activity in this year can surely be attributed to the encouraging attitude of the government. In opposition, Rockingham and his colleagues had supported popular arming as an antidote to what they saw as the dangerously authoritarian tendencies of government. In power, Rockingham's ministry proceeded to canvass views on a revised and "popular" militia, and even introduced legislation to promote the formation of volunteer corps.[38]

Volunteering was regarded with much trepidation, however, by Rockingham's predecessor, Lord North, whose administration presided over all but the closing stages of the American Revolution. North's ministry was not totally opposed in all circumstances to amateur military activity; at various times, both the king and North himself contemplated arming the people to oppose an invasion.[39] Indeed, there was an authoritarian argument in favor of volunteer corps—namely, that they habituated the people to military-style discipline and inculcated obedience—which was put vigorously by some government supporters.[40] Even so, the general tone of North's administration was far from encouraging. In part this was probably attributable to the advice that the government received from senior figures in the army, who were doubtful—to put it mildly—about the military utility of the volunteers. As one might expect of experienced professionals, they were convinced that poorly trained amateurs would be no match for the regular troops of an invading army.[41] There was also a worry that volunteer corps would compete with the army for recruits at the very time that it was seen as essential to enlist more men into the regular regiments.[42]

Yet these military considerations, important though they might have been, were probably eclipsed by political concerns. There was some anxiety that volunteer corps could serve as patronage vehicles for opponents of the government. The king was explicit about his fears that the Duke of Richmond, lord lieutenant of Sussex but a consistent enemy of the administration, would exploit the opportunity provided by the formation of volunteer corps to promote his political allies and so reinforce his local position.[43] There was also a less clearly articulated and more generalized anxiety about allowing armed bodies of men to operate beyond government control. In 1778, when Aberdeen began the vogue for forming volunteer companies, ministers stepped in to insist that the newly created corps be disbanded.

"However laudable may be the Motive of this Undertaking," wrote Lord Weymouth, one of the secretaries of state, "it is certainly contrary to Law."[44]

The sensitivity of the administration to the establishment of amateur military units seems to have increased, unsurprisingly, when the Irish volunteers assumed a clearly political character. Initially, the authorities at Dublin Castle looked upon the volunteers without any great hostility. The lord lieutenant even praised the efforts of the Belfast volunteers to put the town in a state of defense.[45] Given that Ireland's regular army garrison had been depleted by the demands of the war in America, and given the impossibility of reviving the Irish militia, it was almost inevitable that with the coming of a European conflict volunteer units would emerge to fill the military vacuum. So long as the volunteers were seen by the Irish and British governments primarily as military auxiliaries, who could provide valuable assistance to the army in the event of a Bourbon invasion, they continued to be viewed in a broadly positive manner. But once they started to ally with the parliamentary opposition in Dublin, and to press for changes in the Anglo-Irish relationship, official attitudes changed. In October 1779 the lord lieutenant became apprehensive, describing the volunteers as like an unchained lion: "tho' he wags his tail, his fangs may prove dangerous."[46] His anxiety was fully justified. That very month volunteers lined the streets when the Dublin Parliament met. An Irish volunteer officer rightly observed that such an intimidating display would "be the cause of some reflection on the other side of the water."[47] At the beginning of November, the volunteers in Dublin assembled in College Green to demand "Free Trade or Else," emphasizing their seriousness of purpose with a disciplined demonstration of musket-firing. Commercial concessions were soon forthcoming from the British government, but North was left fretting about "the danger of these irregular & independent Corps."[48]

Naturally enough, he was keen to avoid the same coercion being employed in Britain itself. This was less improbable than it might now seem. By the end of 1779 the American Revolution was causing considerable discontent. The rebellious colonists had not been subdued, yet the mounting costs of the war were pushing up domestic taxation. As the war dragged on without success, more and more Britons seemed to assume that the government's increased revenues were being squandered on buying support in the House of Commons. Mistakes were going unchecked, it was widely believed, because Parliament had lost its independence and become a mere rubber stamp for ministerial decisions. The entry of France and then Spain into the war had cut off or disrupted access to European markets, further increased taxes, diverted more money into public funds, and generally depressed economic activity. Even land values declined.[49] The final straw was the humiliating loss of control of the Channel in the summer of 1779. Sir William Meredith, an opposition MP, encapsulated the mood of dissatisfaction when he wrote of a "fatal torpor which hangs like the night-mare over all the powers of this Country."[50] So when members of the Yorkshire Association, founded in December 1779 to press for retrenchment in public expenditure and a reduction in the patronage powers of the crown, pointed approvingly to the role of the Irish volunteers in compelling redress of Irish grievances,[51] it was inevitable that ministers would feel nervous about the prospect of armed associations in Britain trying to force the government to adopt reforms.

Such fears were heightened by the Gordon Riots. For several days the capital was effectively at the mercy of a violent anti-Catholic frenzy. Once the riots were quelled, government supporters believed that a potential uprising, linked in some particularly imaginative minds with the parliamentary opposition,[52] had been narrowly averted. In this febrile atmosphere, friends to the administration were unsurprisingly anxious about the possession of arms by anyone that they thought might be unreliable. The government's view was that the suppression of the disturbances was the duty of the legally constituted military forces—the army and the established militia. There was much nervousness about the enthusiasm of the volunteers to play a key role in restoring order.[53] Hence Amherst's instructions during the riots that all volunteer corps formed without official sanction should be disbanded. It was surely no coincidence that when the principal inhabitants of Grampound, in faraway Cornwall, requested permission to form an independent company a few days after the riots had been suppressed, the government's initial response was to oppose the proposal. Not until a second application was made some time later did ministers temper their hostility and eventually acquiesce.[54]

If North's government offered little or no encouragement to volunteering, can it be said that much volunteer activity was directed *against* the government? There was certainly a political debate about the role of the volunteers, with the opposition to North's ministry, inside and outside Parliament, lionizing them as citizen soldiers who would resist the malign intentions of an authoritarian government as well as defend their communities from external attack. In this context, we should note that the parliamentary opposition made a considerable fuss when Amherst ordered the disarming of unauthorized volunteer corps during the Gordon Riots.[55] Beyond Parliament, Henry Wansey, a Wiltshire clothier of radical inclination, was delighted with the Bath volunteers, whom he saw as representative of a revived military spirit that might provide the basis for "the reformation of our Morals as well as our Constitution."[56] Richard Price, the well-known critic of the American aspect of the war and a consistent opponent of North's ministry, spoke in similarly idealistic language about the formation of volunteer companies at Great Yarmouth.[57] Resolutions passed by some of the county meetings in 1780 asserted the right to arm alongside calls for constitutional changes, and a subcommittee of the Westminster Committee of Association suggested that the large numbers of men under arms for the defense of the country was an argument in favor of extending the franchise.[58]

Whether the volunteers themselves thought in this way is, of course, another matter. At least some of them certainly seem to have envisaged themselves as providing a much-needed check to government power. The lawyer William Jones, for instance, who helped to organize a volunteer unit of barristers and students, was convinced that the greatest safeguard for the liberty of the subject was "a firelock in the hands of every gentleman."[59] But care should be taken not to exaggerate the oppositionist nature of volunteer activity. John Cartwright, the indefatigable radical pamphleteer, was pessimistic about the prospect of the British volunteers rendering "any essential service to the cause of freedom." In part this was because Cartwright believed that the British corps were not "sufficiently numerous" compared with their Irish counterparts, but the implication of his remarks was that the British volunteers also lacked political ambition.[60]

Political considerations of a rather different kind were of importance in explaining the involvement of some local figures and the successful creation of volunteer corps. One of the enduring legacies of the Namierite school has been a general recognition among historians that local struggles for power were often more important than national issues in eighteenth-century politics.[61] We need to appreciate how volunteering slotted into local tussles for control. In Cornwall, Francis Basset of Tehidy subscribed twenty guineas "& a Stand of Colours" for the companies being raised in Penryn. William Chaytor, one of the borough's sitting MPs, was informed by a local contact that Basset's "Generosity" "may possibly have political Motives." Basset, it was correctly surmised, was preparing for the forthcoming general election. To neutralize Basset's threat, Chaytor let it be known that he was giving sixty guineas to the subscription. It transpired, however, that this was insufficient. In the 1780 election, Basset, by now a baronet, was elected himself, and he secured the second Penryn seat for his running mate.[62] The details of this episode are accessible today thanks to the survival of Chaytor's papers on the management of Penryn. It seems unlikely that this was a unique situation. Political ambitions of a similar kind almost certainly influenced the support given to the volunteers in other local communities.

Even so, the social dimension of volunteering may well have been more important than the political. Here it is necessary to pause to consider the backgrounds of the volunteers. There were certainly humble volunteers who were men of little or no social standing. Some of those at Penryn were described as "poor Inhabitants & Labourers," clothed by a subscription raised in the town.[63] Likewise, one of the companies projected at York in May 1782 was to comprise "such as cannot afford to Arm, Cloth, & maintain themselves when employed on military duty."[64] At the other end of the spectrum, aristocratic or gentry officers were to be found in certain corps: the Earl of Buchan "and several other Gentlemen" were reported to have appeared in Edinburgh "in the uniform of the Caledonian Band."[65] But the middle-class character of volunteering cannot be denied. Contemporary cartoons depicted volunteers as tradesmen: "Taylors, Cobblers, bakers," the caption on one such cartoon proclaimed, "Always must Conquer; led by Engine Makers."[66] In the Great Yarmouth companies, both officers and rank-and-file volunteers seem to have been drawn from local "Merchants and Tradesmen."[67] The Scarborough volunteers, though including in their number a scattering of laborers, were mainly made up of local farmers, craftsmen, and shopkeepers.[68] In Leeds, the volunteers formed in 1782 were led by members of the town's mercantile community, but the ordinary volunteers were clearly also meant to be men of means. The rules of the corps specified that there was to be no pay and that each volunteer was expected to provide his own uniform.[69] The Birmingham volunteers were similarly to arm themselves at their own expense.[70] The Norfolk Rangers were said to be "a very respectable body of gentlemen, farmers and tradesmen"; while the Perth volunteers were sufficiently opulent to deter many young men "in decent stations" from enrolling "from a dread of its turning out an expensive business."[71] In London, lawyers formed a corps of their own, and bankers and merchants were prominent in other associations.[72] The Dover volunteers, led by merchants and shipowners, included in their ranks tailors, grocers, drapers, saddlers, and a wine merchant.[73]

This was a very different social profile to that in the regular army or the militia. True, the caricature of the eighteenth-century British army as manned by the very lowest elements of society in the ranks, led by an officer class drawn from the aristocracy and gentry, is now recognized to be inaccurate. There were far more officers from middling backgrounds, and far more rank-and-file soldiers who had been artisans, tradesmen, and sons of freeholders, than was once imagined.[74] Nevertheless, the middling element in the army's regiments, and in the militia, was much smaller than in the volunteers. Basic literacy levels, while not an exact indication of social standing, provide some interesting pointers. Of 102 men enrolled in the Essex militia from the Ilford subdivision between April 17, 1779, and February 16, 1780, only 11 could write their names.[75] Of the 316 volunteers listed in the projected Dover companies at about the same time, only 18 had to accede to the association by drawing a cross; the rest were able to provide a signature.[76]

Service in the volunteers had some obvious advantages over entry into the regular army or militia, especially for men from the "middling sort." A tract presuming to advise military associations on the general principles that ought to guide their organization and conduct argued that "to prevent the individuals of the Association from being injured in their *civil* capacity, care must be taken, that the times of *drilling and private exercise* be appointed both before and after the usual hours of labour."[77] This advice seems to have reflected common practice. Volunteer companies seem usually to have trained on weekday evenings and on Sundays, allowing their members to pursue their businesses without interruption. The Leeds volunteers, for instance, were expected to exercise on Monday, Wednesday and Friday between 6 and 8 p.m., while the Penryn companies met at 6 p.m. during the week and on Sunday mornings.[78]

Perhaps more importantly, the attractiveness of volunteer activity to the "middling sort" rested on its local nature. Volunteers nearly all seem to have seen themselves as performing a purely local defense function. Very few appear to have been willing to serve beyond their immediate environs. Arthur Holdsworth, governor of Dartmouth Castle, reported that the 200 volunteers raised in the town intended their service to be limited to its own defense. Similarly, the mayor of Great Yarmouth explained in 1781 that the "independent Companies" formed in his town were for its "internal Defence." The following year, his successor was more explicit: "their plan," he told Shelburne, "is confined to the local defence of the Town in Case of an attack by the Enemy."[79] By remaining within their own communities, the volunteers were able to assert their importance within those communities. Their parades and maneuvers were events that attracted much local interest.[80]

Conspicuous service, it can be speculated, was a means by which individual tradesmen and shopkeepers could seek to rise in the estimation of their peers and social superiors. Within the volunteers, or at least within some corps, an egalitarian tone was noticeable. The rules of association for a number of the volunteer companies made provision for the election of officers and the imposition of discipline by fines and expulsions rather than physical punishment.[81] While the military function of these associations was clear, it was equally evident that they envisaged themselves as societies in which the strict hierarchies of the regular army and militia were not to be replicated. All volunteers in such corps were eligible to be officers, and none could be treated in the same manner as lowly privates in the king's pay. In the Leeds volunteers, provision was even made for rotation of command, for no one was to be an officer for more than three months.[82]

All this suggests that the military associations can be viewed as a means by which individuals identified themselves as part of a respected and respectable segment of society. In this sense, volunteering was comparable to the other forms of associational activity at the time. A recent estimate points to the existence of some 12,000 clubs and societies established in English towns in the eighteenth century, with another 3,000 in Scottish towns and perhaps 750 in Welsh urban centers. These ranged from book societies and benefit societies, to debating and gambling clubs, philosophic and literary societies, and drinking and social clubs.[83] Forming and participating in these local clubs and societies, it has been argued, enabled the middle classes to build a collective identity.[84]

Volunteering might also have been a means by which communities as well as individuals and groups could achieve greater recognition. It has just been pointed out that associational activity generally was particularly notable in towns. The number of urban centers forming volunteer corps is surely also striking.[85] While county meetings could set in train local volunteering efforts, there was a significant urban dimension to volunteer activity. And several of the urban centers where volunteer corps were formed were a long way from exposed coasts (see map 6.1). Shrewsbury, York, Birmingham, Sheffield, Leeds, and Bradford were hardly in danger of attack from the enemy. At least some of these towns were "new" in the sense that they were rapidly growing commercial and manufacturing centers: the population of Leeds, which had stood at a mere 6,000 in 1700, was around 11,000 in 1750, and by 1801 had risen to 53,000; Sheffield's 12,000 inhabitants in 1750 had increased to 46,000 by 1801. Such dynamic expansion, and the importance of the manufacturing products of these towns in national, colonial, and international markets, no doubt imbued their leading lights with a sense of confidence. But we should not forget that the very "newness" of these towns could lead to a status anxiety among their elites. Successful though they were in their own terms, they remained conscious of their social inferiority to older, more established, landed elites in the rural areas that surrounded their towns. An indication of this, surely, is the keenness of Birmingham's leading inhabitants in the 1770s to enlist the patronage and approval of the Earl of Dartmouth, a government minister and a landowner in neighboring Staffordshire.[86] We can surmise that in places like Birmingham, Leeds, Sheffield, and Bradford, volunteering was influenced by what the business community saw as the need to demonstrate the importance of their towns to their wider localities. Birmingham's status in Warwickshire and the West Midlands generally had already been underlined in the 1774 general election, when its freeholders effectively chose one of Warwickshire's two MPs.[87] Nonetheless, continuing uncertainty about the town's standing might well have persuaded its chief manufacturers and businessmen to try to impress the neighboring gentry with their martial endeavors. A similar wish to further the claims of Sheffield, Leeds, and Bradford within Yorkshire perhaps influenced the formation of volunteer corps in these towns. Their volunteers certainly received publicity in newspapers read well beyond their boundaries. The *York Courant,* to give an example, informed its countywide readership of the virtuous behavior of "A Number of young Gentlemen and Tradesmen at Bradford," who had formed an association and "are now learning the Military Exercise, having provided themselves with Arms, a genteel Uniform, &c."[88]

The likely importance of local considerations should not lead to the conclusion that the volunteers were uninterested in the bigger picture. Local loyalties were not necessarily incompatible with national allegiance. Indeed, volunteering—for all its seemingly local inspiration and orientation— can even be seen as a manifestation of a growing popular identification with Britain.[89] Little is known about volunteer uniforms, but what is known might provide a few clues as to attitudes. Some corps had no uniforms as such: Barrington's Berkshire volunteers appear to have distinguished themselves merely by the wearing of a cockade in their hats.[90] But where uniforms existed, it seems that the wearing of red coats was popular. The corps formed from among the barristers and students of the Middle and Inner Temples, for instance, had scarlet coats with black facings, and the Royal Bath Volunteers were likewise dressed in red jackets.[91] Here, surely, is a sign of the desire of volunteers to link themselves—if only sartorially—with the army, a national institution.

Another indication of a national perspective might be the way in which county meetings decided upon the appropriate number of companies to be provided. We have seen that in July 1779 a meeting in the metropolis determined that Middlesex and Westminster should raise twenty-four, each of more than seventy officers and ordinary volunteers. Was it coincidental that

Devon's freeholders, meeting in August, also thought that *not less than* twenty-four companies was right for their county, or that Sussex's meeting a few days later decided on *at least* the same number?[92] It seems probable that both the Devonshire and Sussex meetings were unwilling to be outdone by the metropolis. Similarly, in the adjacent Welsh counties of Cardiganshire and Pembrokeshire, meetings of landowners that offered to raise volunteer companies in the summer of 1779 were no doubt influenced by a desire to be seen as comparing favorably with their neighbors. But if this competition and rivalry between counties and regions can be taken as a further sign of the pull of localism, it can also be interpreted as evidence of a desire to be regarded as making the proper contribution to a national effort against the country's enemies. Pride in local achievement needs to be put in a national context: counties and even smaller urban communities wanted to be perceived as pulling their own weight. Local and national agendas, in other words, were often not in conflict but, rather, complemented each other.

III

The Irish volunteers have already been mentioned as one of the reasons for the nervousness of Lord North's government about volunteering in Britain. The relationship between British and Irish volunteer corps now needs to be examined more closely, not so much in terms of the ways in which the Irish influenced the British, but more in comparative dimension. How similar was volunteering in Britain to volunteering in Ireland?

There were some obvious differences. Volunteering in Ireland was on a bigger scale. Estimates of volunteer strength need, of course, to be regarded with considerable caution. A great many Irish volunteer units emerged during the war, but not all of them existed at the same time; as will become apparent, companies were subsumed into battalions and battalions in regiments. The scope for double counting volunteers is therefore considerable. Contemporary claims of volunteer numbers varied greatly. In October 1779 a government-supporting Irish politician referred to "Twenty thousand men in arms," but this was almost certainly a figure plucked from the air for rhetorical effect. The following March, a British army officer wrote, with remarkable precision, that there were "about 43,000 of the Associated Volunteers" in Ireland. Two years later, the lord lieutenant, with rather less precision, conjured up the image of 30,000 volunteers "who would take the field tomorrow" if the British government failed to make the necessary concessions.[93] A recent calculation suggests that there were perhaps 40,000 by December 1779 and 60,000 by the middle of 1780. There might have been as many as 80,000 Irish volunteers at the end of 1781.[94] But whether we accept these figures or some of the more conservative guesses of the time, there can be little doubt that the number of volunteers in Ireland exceeded those in Britain.

As a result of its scale, volunteering captured the imagination of Protestant Ireland. The demand for uniforms, arms, and equipment generated much business for local producers, and volunteer dinners and balls became important social occasions.[95] In Ulster, particularly, volunteer events defined the social calendar and artifacts depicting and celebrating the volunteers were produced in considerable numbers.[96] Elsewhere in Ireland, however, volunteering was also of considerable importance for the much smaller Protestant population: its ceremonial aspects, a recent study has suggested, helped to symbolize Protestant power at a time when there was much Protestant anxiety about Catholic intentions.[97] Volunteering, in other words, entered deep into the culture of Protestant Ireland. The same cannot truly be said for its place in the hearts and minds of the British public, despite the existence of printed satires and other indications of interest in volunteering as a spectacle.

The Irish volunteers, it should be added, were much more clearly national in outlook than their British counterparts. In June 1778, the volunteers of Limavady, County Londonderry, were said to be motivated by "a sincere love of their Country and its Service," a claim that suggests something more than a purely local perspective.[98] By 1781 there was in effect a volunteer army, which saw itself (and not the regular army in Ireland) as the nation's military force. As a Dublin newspaper explained, the volunteers were "the people's army."[99] Such a perception was possible not least because Irish volunteers were often willing to join with other corps to form militarily efficient units. The reluctance of British volunteer companies to serve outside their own areas has already been noted. This localism was less apparent across the Irish Sea. In October 1779, the Tyrone Ditches and Acton Volunteers passed a resolution stating their desire to incorporate with other neighboring companies to form a battalion. On their own, they argued, they could do little to contribute to the defense of their country.[100]

Most obviously, perhaps, the Irish volunteers were much more overtly political than were the British volunteers. Some of the British companies had a political side to them; indeed, they were fondly viewed as potential auxiliaries by enthusiasts for reform. But Major Cartwright recognized that the British volunteers were neither numerous enough nor, he seemed to suggest, sufficiently politicized to be able to equal the achievements of the

Irish. There can be no doubting, on the other hand, the political nature of at least some of the Irish corps. The First Newry Volunteers, in their original agreement of association drawn up in September 1778, were explicit about their objective: "to resist Usurpation and maintain the Constitution."[101] Likewise, the Strabane barony volunteers declared in March 1780 that "Long have the Inhabitants of this Island complained of political restrictions inconsistent with their natural rights and highly prejudicial to their happiness." They went on, moreover, to identify the present crisis as "a favourable period . . . when they have it in their power, in some measure to obtain deliverance from these Injuries."[102] And obtain deliverance they did, for there can be no denying that the volunteers played a crucial role in securing for Ireland first commercial and then constitutional concessions from the North and Rockingham governments.

These differences between the British and Irish volunteers need to be set against the similarities, which were greater than might be imagined. Given the political reputation acquired by the Irish volunteers, it no doubt seems odd to emphasize their military origins. But as Lord Hillsborough explained in September 1779, a distinction needed to be made between those corps that were republican and pro-American and the majority that were raised by country gentlemen for defensive purposes. Put simply, many of the Irish corps, like their British counterparts, were initially intended to protect the country, or their part of it, from enemy attack. In 1779 the lord lieutenant wrote, "Unpleasant as the Institution of those Corps may be in many respects, there can be no doubt, in case of a French Invasion, that most material utility might be deriv'd from them."[103] That July, the quartermaster-general of the army in Ireland, David Dundas, envisaged the volunteers acting as auxiliaries to the regular troops, harassing the enemy as they tried to advance inland from their disembarkation points.[104] At almost exactly the same time, Adam Ferguson, the Scottish academic and government supporter, argued that in Britain an armed people, organized along the lines of the volunteers, would be well suited to "firing & shooting" at the enemy "from every Hedge & Bush & never Suffering them to move or to forrage or to halt undisturbed nor to be quiet in Front Flank or Rear."[105]

The Irish volunteers, like the British volunteers, performed public-order and police functions. Lord Barrington envisaged his Berkshire companies as a check against local lawlessness, while in London some of the military associations formed in 1779–80 played a role in suppressing the Gordon Riots and continued to act as a sort of unofficial police force thereafter. In Ireland, the entry of the French into the war, followed by the Spanish, revived Protestant fears of a Catholic uprising, reminiscent of the great insurrection of 1641, and this, according to various sources, was one of the principal spurs to the forming of volunteer companies.[106] It should also be noted that the first Irish volunteer bodies of the American war period were formed not in 1778, when French invasion threatened, but in 1775 and 1776. Their aim was to combat the Whiteboy agrarian terrorists, whose activities were causing much alarm among Protestant landowners and farmers.[107] The transfer to North America at this time of a significant portion of the British army in Ireland, which before the war was deployed in support of the civil authorities, helps to explain such initiatives. The threat of French and then Franco-Spanish invasion led to a concentration of the remaining regular troops from the spring and summer of 1778 and so increased the perceived need for irregular replacements to carry out policing functions. As the volunteers proper came into being, then, it was generally assumed that they would perform a role in helping to maintain law and order. James Hamilton, the absentee Earl of Abercorn's agent in Strabane, County Tyrone, though by no means an enthusiast for the volunteers, readily acknowledged their usefulness in this regard: "It is certain," he told the earl, "that they have put an end in this Country very much to house brakers and robbers."[108] The Doneraile Rangers, a corps formed in County Cork, were similarly employed in capturing those involved in rescuing local felons from justice, while in Dublin the volunteers helped to quell rioting and patrolled the streets to deter crime and apprehend burglars.[109] At the end of the war, when the Irish volunteers addressed the king on parliamentary reform, they unsurprisingly chose to emphasize this role. Through their efforts, they claimed, "the Laws and Police of this Kingdom have been better executed than at any former period within the Memory of Man."[110]

Another obvious similarity between Irish and British volunteering was the social background of the volunteers themselves. It has been established that British volunteering was largely a middle-class affair; there were aristocratic and gentry officers, and some poorer men in the ranks, but the volunteers were essentially drawn from the "middling sort." In Ireland, volunteer officers in rural areas tended to be significant landowners. In Ulster, for instance, the Earl of Charlemont was colonel of the Armagh regiment, while the two MPs for the county were lieutenant colonels of the two battalions. But there were many nonelite officers, especially in the urban areas. One of the lieutenants in the Belfast volunteers was Waddell Cunningham, a merchant, and another was Robert Hyndman, a tobacconist. In Cork, one of the leading officers was a clothier.[111] Many of the ordinary volunteers appear to have been from the middle ranks also. True, as in Britain, there were subscriptions to allow the less well off to become volunteers, and sometimes noble patrons—such as the Marquis of Rockingham in County Wicklow—underwrote the expenses of particular companies, which had the same effect.[112] Even so, in July 1779, the lord lieutenant was sure that "most of the Private men" in the volunteers were "either tradesmen or Farmers." Scattered anecdotal evidence backs up this assertion. A volunteer of Cashel, County Tipperary, killed in a brawl with regular troops following a dispute about debts due to him from an army officer, is described as a shoemaker of the town. The volunteers of Limavady, County Londonderry, were said to be all freeholders, able to provide their own arms and uniform. The company raised at Rathfriland, County Down, was reported to be made up of "men in business"; while the Belfast volunteers, reviewed in 1782, were sufficiently affluent to have equipped themselves at considerable expense: about £20 for an infantry volunteer and nearly £80 for a cavalryman.[113]

There are also clear parallels in the ways in which the Irish and British volunteers intersected with local politics. As noted earlier, patronizing the largely middle-class and enfranchised volunteers was believed to be vital to success in the electoral politics of Penryn in Cornwall. Much the same process is evident in Ireland. Was it purely coincidental that the lieutenant colonels of the Armagh volunteers were the MPs for the shire? They might have been elected to their paramilitary posts in deference to their local influence and political opinions, but it seems likely that they were alive to the political advantages of cultivating a connection with the volunteers. In County Tyrone, James Stewart of Killymoon, one of the sitting MPs, donated 100 guineas and promised to provide colors and even two field pieces to the local corps. There can be little doubt that he was actuated, in part at least, by the same electoral considerations that operated with the rival candidates in Penryn. A timely donation was intended to secure the support of the volunteers—many of whom were voters in his constituency—at the next general election. More immediately, it ensured that Stewart became the colonel of the Strabane barony battalion—a blow to his political opponent, the Earl of Abercorn, whose nephew and heir was expected to be given the command in recognition of the earl's dominant interest in Strabane itself.[114]

Finally, consideration must be given to the internal organization of the corps in Britain and Ireland. In this regard, as in so many others, experience on both sides of the Irish Sea was remarkably similar. In Ireland, as in Britain, volunteer corps elected their own officers, regulated admissions, and administered discipline through fines and expulsions rather than corporal punishment.[115] There was, of course, a political, or rather ideological, side to this egalitarianism; it was intended to demonstrate that volunteers were very different from professional soldiers. But there was also a class element. Volunteering, in Britain and Ireland, was a form of associational activity that centered on military events such as reviews, training, and parades but also included an important social dimension, especially in the form of regular dinners. A resolution of a County Sligo corps, meeting at Tobercurry in 1782, nicely captures this aspect of volunteering: "We do Sollemnly pledge ourselves to one a nother . . . in unfeigned friendship . . . & in the Mutual Support of each other, with our persons & lives."[116] In Ireland, as in Britain, volunteering provided an opportunity for members of the middle ranks of society to assert their own claims to recognition by their peers and by the wider community, while enabling the middle classes collectively to promote and protect themselves.

IV

There are important differences between the British and Irish experience. The more obvious national political agenda of some of the Irish corps needs especially to be borne in mind. But it would be wrong to assume from this that the British and Irish volunteers were separate and distinct entities. In the summer of 1775, as the American Revolution began in earnest, an Irish MP compared the Irish Protestants and their grievances with the rebellious colonists and theirs: "We are," he wrote, "in water colour what they are in fresco."[117] Perhaps the same could be said of the relationship between the British volunteer corps and their Irish counterparts.

Notes

Stephen Conway is a professor of history at University College London. He should like to thank the owners and custodians of the manuscript collections that he cites or from which he quotes. Parts of this essay are expanded and revised versions of material first published in his book on *The British Isles and the War of American Independence* (Oxford, 2000), and he is grateful to Oxford University Press for permission to present them here in a new form.

1. See, e.g., Ian J. F. Beckett, *The Amateur Military Tradition, 1558–1945* (Manchester, 1991); Glenn A. Steppler, *Britons to Arms! The Story of the British Volunteer Soldier* (Stoud, 1992). See also H. Cunningham, *The Volunteer Force: A Social and Political History, 1859–1908* (London, 1975) and, for older studies, R. P. Berry, *A History of the Formation and Development of the Volunteer Infantry* (London, 1903), and C. Sebag-Montefiore, *A History of the Volunteer Forces* (London, 1908).

2. Linda Colley, *Britons: Forging the Nation, 1707–1837* (New Haven, Conn., 1992), especially chap. 7 and appendices 1–3, and "The Reach of the State, the Appeal of the Nation," in Lawrence Stone, ed., *An Imperial State at War: Britain*

from 1689 to 1815 (London, 1994), 165–84; J. E. Cookson, "The English Volunteer Movement of the French Wars, 1793–1815: Some Contexts," *Historical Journal* 32 (1989): 867–91; Cookson, "The Rise and Fall of the Sutton Volunteers, 1803–4," *Historical Research* 64 (1991): 47–53; Cookson, "Patriotism and Social Structure: The Ely Volunteers, 1798–1808," *Journal of the Society for Army Historical Research* 71 (1993): 160–79; and Cookson, *The British Armed Nation, 1793–1815* (Oxford, 1997), especially chap. 3. See also Philip Woodfine, "'Unjustifiable and Illiberal': Military Patriotism and Civilian Values in the 1790s," in Bertrand Taithe and Tim Thornton, eds., *War: Identities in Conflict, 1300–2000* (Stroud, 1998), especially 85–86; Kevin Linch, "A Geography of Loyalism? The Local Military Forces of the West Riding of Yorkshire, 1794–1814," *War and Society* 19 (2001): 1–21.

3. See, e.g., T.G.F. Patterson, "The Volunteer Companies of Ulster, 1778–1793," *Irish Sword* 7 (1965–66): 91–116, 204–30, 308–12, and 8 (1967–68): 23–32, 92–97, 210–17; Maurice R. O'Connell, *Irish Politics and Social Conflict in the Age of the American Revolution* (Philadelphia, 1965), especially chap. 4; the essays in *Irish Sword* 13 (1977–79); Peter Smyth, "The Volunteers and Parliament," in Thomas Bartlett and D. W. Hayton, eds., *Penal Era and Golden Age: Essays in Irish History, 1690–1800* (Belfast, 1979), 113–36; R. B. McDowell, *Ireland in the Age of Imperialism and Revolution, 1760–1801* (Oxford, 1979), chap. 5; A.T.Q. Stewart, *A Deeper Silence: The Hidden Origins of the United Irishmen* (London, 1993), especially chaps. 1–2, 4–7; I. R. McBride, *Scripture Politics: Ulster Presbyterians and Irish Radicalism in the Late Eighteenth Century* (Oxford, 1998), especially 123–33.

4. Dr. Williams's Library, Wodrow-Kenrick Correspondence, MS 24.157(74).

5. Herbert Butterfield, *George III, Lord North, and the People* (London, 1949), 55.

6. For the direct relationship between the crown's commissioning officers in the corps and issuing arms, see Cornwall Record Office (Cornwall RO), Rogers of Penrose Papers, DD RP43.

7. Public Record Office (PRO), State Papers Scotland, SP 54/47, fos. 76, 77, 135, 306–7.

8. Ibid., War Office Papers, WO 34/116, fos. 20–21.

9. Ibid., WO 34/154, fos. 540, 548–49.

10. Ibid., Home Office Papers, HO 42/205, fo. 156.

11. Ibid., State Papers Military, SP 41/33, fos. 31, 39.

12. Wiltshire RO, Savernake MS 9, Lt. Matthew Bentham to Lord Ailesbury, October 10, 1779.

13. PRO, SP 41/33, fos. 53, 78, 89–90, 92, 101, 153, 157; Cornwall RO, Tremayne of Heligan Papers, DDT 1892/1; North Yorkshire RO, Chaytor Papers, ZQH 11/2/158 and 159.

14. PRO, HO 42/205, fo. 186; *Bath Chronicle*, August 19, 1779.

15. PRO, HO 42/205, fos. 136–37.

16. Ibid., WO 34/116, fos. 1–2.

17. *York Courant,* August 24 and 31, October 5, 1779; PRO, SP 41/33, fo. 179; PRO, HO 42/205, fo. 93.

18. PRO, WO 34/155, fo. 15; *Journals of the House of Commons* 37: 514–15.

19. *London Chronicle,* June 13–15, 17–20, 1780.

20. PRO, SP 41/33, fos. 266, 273, 277.

21. *Ipswich Journal,* July 22, 1780.

22. PRO, SP 41/33, fo. 301; PRO, HO 42/205, fo. 132; Norfolk RO, Great Yarmouth Corporation Records, Y/TC/36/20/10; SP 54/48, fos. 103, 105, 107, 125, 127.

23. John Robertson, *The Scottish Enlightenment and the Militia Issue* (Edinburgh, 1985), 137–38.

24. PRO, HO 42/205, fo. 159.

25. Ibid., fos. 152–54; British Library (BL), Pelham Papers, Add[itional] MS. 33128, fo. 79; V. Smith, ed., *The Town Book of Lewes, 1702–1837* (Sussex Record Society, 69, Lewes, 1973), 68–69.

26. *Leeds Intelligencer,* December 21 and 31, 1782; PRO, HO 42/205, fos. 111 and 113; York City Archives, Acc. 163, Diary of Dr. William White, May 14, 16, and 21, 1782.

27. *Aris's Birmingham Gazette,* June 3, August 12, September 23, 1782.

28. Hull RO, WM/7/6.

29. Beckett, *Amateur Military Tradition,* 70; *Mary Hardy's Diary,* ed. Basil Cozens-Hardy (Norfolk Record Society, 37, Norwich, 1968), 43; Leeds Archives, Ramsden Papers, Rockingham Letters, vol. 3b, Rev. William Palgrave to William Weddell, September 2 [1782].

30. For a contemporary account, see *The Diary of Isaac Fletcher of Underwood, Cumberland, 1756–1781,* ed. Angus J. L. Winchester (Cumberland & Westmorland Antiquarian and Archaeological Society, Extra Series, 27, Kendal, 1994), 351–52.

31. PRO, SP 54/47, fos. 306–7.

32. Ibid., SP 41/33, fo. 111. For the response, see Hull RO, Borough Records, BRL 1386/4.

33. BL, Leeds Papers, Add. MS 27918, fo. 11.

34. For the panic at this time see, e.g., Devon RO, Drake of Buckland Abbey Papers, 346/F23; Cornwall RO, Tremayne of Heligan Papers, DDT 2126 and Rogers of Penrose Papers, DDRP 37. For the background, see A. Temple Patterson, *The Other Amada: The Franco-Spanish Attempt to Invade Britain in 1779* (Manchester, 1960).

35. For reports of the Dutch fleet having left the Texel, see Historical Manuscripts Commission (HMC), *Dartmouth MSS,* 3 vols. (London, 1887–96), 3:258; Hull RO, Borough Records, BRL 1386/154.

36. National Library of Ireland (NLI), Heron Papers, MS 13038, Barrington to the Earl of Buckinghamshire, August 29, 1779. For the background to Barrington's association, see Tony Hayter, *The Army and the Crowd in Mid-Georgian England* (London, 1978), 73–74.

37. Nicholas Rogers, "Crowd and People in the Gordon Riots," in Eckhart Hellmuth, ed., *The Transformation of Political Culture: England and Germany in the Late Eighteenth Century* (Oxford, 1990), 53.

38. 22 Geo. III, ca. 79. For an example of the consultation, see Leicestershire RO, Lieutenancy Papers, LM 8/8/3; and for the background to the new ministry's thinking on militia reform, J. R. Western, *The English Militia in the Eighteenth Century* (London, 1965), 217–19; John Norris, *Shelburne and Reform* (London, 1963), 162–63; Stephen Conway, *The British Isles and the War of American Independence* (Oxford, 2000), chap. 4.

39. See, e.g., Kent Archives Office, Amherst Papers, U 1350 074/38, 39, 41.

40. See, e.g., Dr. Williams's Library, Wodrow-Kenrick Correspondence, MS 24.157(74).

41. See, e.g., PRO, WO 34/116, fo. 196.

42. See *The Pembroke Papers*, 2 vols., ed. Lord Herbert (London, 1939–50), 2:159; and the comments of Lord Poulett in PRO, SP 41/33, fo. 72.

43. *The Correspondence of King George III*, 6 vols., ed. Sir John Fortescue (London, 1927–28), 4:418.

44. PRO, SP 54/47, fo. 137. In the case of the Scottish associations, it should be added, English anxiety about arming the Scots might also have been a factor. For contemporary criticism of proposals for a Scottish militia, see the speech of John Sawbridge, in *The Parliamentary History of England*, 36 vols., ed. William Cobbett and J. Wright (London, 1806–20), 18:1236. For more on this subject generally, see Robertson, *Scottish Enlightenment and the Militia Issue*, chaps. 5 and 6.

45. Public Record Office of Northern Ireland (PRONI), Downshire Papers, D 607/B/29.

46. Hull University Library, Hotham Papers, DD HO 4/20, Earl of Buckinghamshire to Sir Charles Thompson, October 12, 1779.

47. HMC, *Charlemont MSS*, 2 vols. (London, 1891–93), 1:359.

48. NLI, Heron Papers, MS 13039, North to the Earl of Buckinghamshire, January 16, 1780.

49. For the economic dislocations caused by the war, see Conway, *British Isles and the War of American Independence*, chap. 2. For the political crisis of 1779–80, see Butterfield, *George III, Lord North and the People;* Ian R. Christie, *Wilkes, Wyvill, and Reform* (London, 1962), chap. 3 ; Eugene Charlton Black, *The Association: British Extraparliamentary Organization, 1769–1793* (Cambridge, Mass., 1963), chap. 2; Philip Harling, *The Waning of "Old Corruption": The Politics of Economical Reform, 1779–1846* (Oxford, 1996), 32–42; Conway, *British Isles and the War of American Independence*, chap. 6.

50. BL, Miscellaneous Papers, Add. MS 46473, fo. 87.

51. Christopher Wyvill, *Political Papers*, 6 vols. (York, 1794–1802), 1:12. See also Dr. Williams's Library, Wodrow-Kenrick Correspondence, MS 24.157(69).

52. See, e.g., Surrey RO (Guildford Muniment Room), Onslow MSS, 173/2/1/193.

53. See, e.g., BL, Liverpool Papers, Add. MS 38214, fo. 39.

54. PRO, SP 41/33, fos. 266, 273.

55. *Parliamentary History of England,* ed. Cobbett and Wright, 21:728, 733.

56. Wiltshire RO, Wansey Papers, 3/4/4/2.

57. *The Correspondence of Richard Price,* 3 vols., ed. W. Bernard Peach and D. O. Thomas (Durham, N.C., and Cardiff, 1983–94), 2:125.

58. Wyvill, *Political Papers,* 1:254–55; BL, Westminster Committee Papers, Add. MS 38593, fo. 41.

59. *The Letters of Sir William Jones,* 2 vols., ed. Garland Cannon (Oxford, 1970) 1:408.

60. NLI, Dobbs Papers, MS 2251, Cartwright to Francis Dobbs, January 12, 1780.

61. See., e.g., Sir Lewis Namier and John Brooke, *The History of Parliament: The House of Commons, 1754–1790,* 3 vols. (London, 1964), 1:57–96, for an analysis of general elections.

62. North Yorkshire RO, Chaytor Papers, ZQH 11/2/158, 159, 162.

63. Ibid., Z2H 11/2/58.

64. York City Archives, Dr. William White's Diary, May 14, 1782.

65. National Archives of Scotland, Logan Home of Edrom Muniments, GD 1/384/7/19.

66. British Museum, Department of Prints and Drawings, BM 5552, "The Terror of France, or the Westminster Volunteers," August 26, 1779. This is sometimes seen as a satire on the Eighty-fifth Foot, raised at about this time; but it could more appropriately be regarded as alluding to the volunteer companies formed in Middlesex and Westminster in July 1779. See also BM 5783, "He Wou'd a Soldier be, &c," August 1, 1780; BM 5784, "The Soldier Tired of Wars Alarms," September 6, 1780; BM 5785, "He Leads the—Van—Again," August 26, 1780; BM 5786, "The Cheseld Soldier, return'd to Business, or the Newgate Str——t Butcher," October 5, 1780.

67. PRO, HO 42/205, fo. 132.

68. North Yorkshire RO, Scarborough Corporation Records, DC/SCB, Return of volunteer companies, 1781.

69. Emily Hargrave, "The Early Leeds Volunteers," *Thoresby Society Publications* 28 (1923–27): 262; *Leeds Mercury,* June 25, 1782.

70. *Aris's Birmingham Gazette,* August 12, 1782.

71. *Norfolk Mercury,* September 14, 1782, cited in Beckett, *Amateur Military Tradition,* 70; HMC, *Laing MSS,* 2 vols. (London, 1914–25), 2:512.

72. *London Chronicle,* June 13–15, 17–20, 1780.

73. PRO, WO 34/116, fo. 1–2. I have assumed that for occupations *Bailey's British Directory . . . for the Year 1784,* 4 vols. (London, 1784), 3:343, though compiled a few years later, is probably a reasonable guide.

74. See, e.g., Arthur N. Gilbert, "An Analysis of Some Eighteenth-Century Army Recruiting Records," *Journal of the Society for Army Historical Research 54*

(1976): 38–47; Sylvia Frey, *The British Soldier in America: A Social History of Military Life in the Revolutionary Period* (Austin, Tex., 1981), chap. 1; Stephen Conway, "British Mobilization in the War of American Independence," *Historical Research* 72 (1999): 66–71, and *British Isles and the War of American Independence,* 31–35, 100–101; Peter Way, "Rebellion of the Regulars: Working Soldiers and the Mutiny of 1763–1764," *William and Mary Quarterly,* 3rd ser., 57 (2000): 768–69 and table 1; Stephen Brumwell, *Redcoats: The British Soldier and War in the Americas, 1755–1763* (Cambridge, 2002), 320 (table 8).

75. Essex RO, D/DHt T145/4.

76. PRO, WO 34/116, fos. 1–2.

77. *Hints of Some General Principles which may be Useful to Military Associations,* in *Tracts, Concerning the Ancient and Only True Legal Means of National Defence, by a Free Militia* (London, 1781), 77.

78. *Leeds Mercury,* June 25, 1782; PRO, SP 41/33, fos. 89–90.

79. PRO, SP 41/33, fos. 31, 301; PRO, HO 42/205, fo. 132.

80. See, e.g., *Mary Hardy's Diary,* 43.

81. See, e.g., *Aris's Birmingham Gazette,* August 12, 1782.

82. *Leeds Mercury,* June 25, 1782.

83. Peter Clark and R. A. Houston, "Culture and Leisure, 1700–1840," in Peter Clark, ed., *The Cambridge Urban History of Britain,* vol. 2, *1540–1840* (Cambridge, 2000), 587–88.

84. See particularly Jonathan Barry, "Bourgeois Collectivism? Urban Association and the Middling Sort," in Jonathan Barry and Christopher Brooks, eds., *The Middling Sort of People: Culture, Society, and Politics in England, 1550–1800* (London, 1994), 84–112. See also R. J. Morris, "Voluntary Societies and British Urban Elites, 1780–1850: An Analysis," *Historical Journal* 26 (1983): 95–118; "Clubs, Societies and Associations," in F. M. L. Thompson, ed., *Cambridge Social History of Britain, 1750–1850,* 3 vols. (Cambridge, 1990), 3:395–443. Middle-class associational activity is a running theme in Paul Langford, *Public Life and the Propertied Englishman, 1689–1798* (Oxford, 1991).

85. This was also to be the case in the next war (see, e.g., Linch, "A Geography of Loyalism?" esp. 11), as it had been on previous occasions when volunteer corps had been formed, such as in the '45 rebellion (see Colley, *Britons,* esp. 81–82 and appendix 1).

86. See, e.g., HMC, *Dartmouth MSS,* 3:198–99, 213–14, 232–37.

87. Namier and Brooke, *House of Commons, 1754–1790,* 1:399–400. See also John Money, *Experience and Identity: Birmingham and the West Midlands, 1760–1800* (Manchester, 1977), esp. chap. 7.

88. *York Courant,* August 31, 1779.

89. There is now a considerable body of literature on this subject, much of it inspired by Linda Colley's *Britons.* For Britishness during the American Revolution, see Conway, *British Isles and the War of American Independence,* chap. 5.

90. PRO, HO 42/205, fos. 136–37.

91. *London Chronicle,* June 13–15, 1780; C. C. P. Lawson, *A History of the Uniforms of the British Army,* 5 vols. (London, 1940–67), 3:159–62.

92. PRO, SP 41/33, fo. 39; PRO, HO 42/205, fo. 156.

93. *The Correspondence of the Right Hon. John Beresford,* ed. William Beresford, 2 vols. (London, 1854), 1:58; HMC, *Pembroke MSS* (London, 1884), 383; PRO, Granville Papers, 30/29/1, Earl of Carlisle to Lord Gower, March 23, 1782.

94. Peter Smyth, "'Our Cloud-Cap't Grenadiers': The Volunteers as a Military Force," *Irish Sword* 13 (1977–79): 185–207; David Dickson, *New Foundations: Ireland, 1660–1800,* 2nd ed. (Dublin, 2000), 165, 169.

95. See, e.g., the adverts inserted by Samuel Barr, of North Street, Belfast, in the *Belfast News-letter,* June 22–25, 1779, and by Denis Murphy, a Limerick innkeeper, in *Ferrar's Limerick Chronicle,* September 28, 1780.

96. McBride, *Scripture Politics,* 124–33.

97. David W. Miller, "Non-Professional Soldiery, ca. 1600–1800," in Thomas Bartlett and Keith Jeffery, eds., *A Military History of Ireland* (Cambridge, 1996), 328. For Protestant worries see, e.g., W. H. Crawford, ed., *Letters from an Ulster Land Agent, 1774–1785* (Belfast, 1976), 5; Thomas Campbell, *A Philosophical Survey of the South of Ireland* (London, 1777), 254, 299, 301–2; HMC, *Dartmouth MSS,* 3:240.

98. Trinity College Dublin (TCD), Conolly Papers, MS 3976/523.

99. *General Evening Post,* January 3, 1782.

100. HMC, *Charlemont MSS,* 1:360.

101. PRONI, T 3202/1A, Minute-book of the First Newry Volunteers.

102. Ibid., Stewart of Killymoon Papers, D/3167/2/25.

103. Ibid., Downshire Papers, D/607/B/86.

104. NLI, MS 14306, "Memorandum," July 1, 1779.

105. *The Correspondence of Adam Ferguson,* ed. Vincenzo Merolle, 2 vols. (London, 1995), 1:218. See also the plan for southern England, dated July 1779, in Amherst's papers: PRO, WO 34/153, fo. 514.

106. See NLI, Heron Papers, MS 13038, Earl of Shannon to the lord lieutenant, August 15, 1779; NLI, MS 14306, "Irish Military Associations," another paper by David Dundas, February 2, 1780.

107. *The Harcourt Papers,* ed. E. W. Harcourt (14 vols., Oxford, 1880–1905), 10:197; Maurice J. Bric, "The Whiteboy Movement in Tipperary, 1760–80," in William Nolan and Thomas G. McGrath, eds., *Tipperary: History and Society* (Dublin, 1985), 166.

108. PRONI, Abercorn Papers, D/623/A/44/29.

109. NLI, MS 12155, Minutes of the Doneraile Rangers, January 1, 1780; HMC, *Stopford Sackville MSS,* 2 vols. (London, 1904–10), 1:256; *General Evening Post,* January 22, February 16, March 12, 1782. The public-order side of the Dublin volunteers is also discussed in Brian Henry, *Dublin Hanged: Crime, Law Enforcement, and Punishment in Late Eighteenth-Century Dublin* (Dublin, 1994), esp. 17.

See also the comments in O'Connell, *Irish Politics and Social Conflict,* 83; Miller, "Non-Professional Soldiery," 327–28; and Dickson, *New Foundations,* 169.

110. BL, Hardwicke Papers, Add. MS 35621, fo. 281.

111. Eileen Black, "Volunteer Portraits in the Ulster Museum, Belfast," *Irish Sword* 13 (1977–79): 181–84; Richard Caulfield, ed., *The Council Book of the Corporation of the City of Cork* (Guildford, 1876), 932.

112. PRONI, Abercorn Papers, D/623/A/44/10; Sheffield Archives, Rockingham MSS, R1/1854a.

113. NLI, Heron Papers, MS 13038, Buckinghamshire to Sir Richard Heron, July 9, 1779; PRO, State Papers Ireland, SP 63/471, fo. 240, report of Major Alexander Ross, Eighty-first Foot, October 24, 1780; TCD, Conolly Papers, MS 39676/523; PRONI, Downshire Papers, D/607/B/91; *Pembroke Papers,* 2:206. See also O'Connell, *Irish Politics and Social Conflict,* esp. 88–91.

114. PRONI, Abercorn Papers, D/623/A/44/22. See also PRONI, Stewart of Killymoon Papers, D/3167/2/25, and A. P. W. Malcomson, "The Politics of 'Natural Right': The Abercorn Family and Strabane Borough, 1692–1800," *Historical Studies* 10 (1976): 43–90.

115. See, e.g., NLI, MS 838, Minutes of the Ennis Volunteers, February 15, June 21, 1779; NLI, MS 12155, Minutes of the Doneraile Rangers, July 12, August 16, 1779; PRONI, T 3202/1A, Minute-book of the First Newry Volunteers, August 1, 1780, September 29, October 28, 1783.

116. NLI, O'Hara Papers, MS 20282, minutes and resolutions of the Lyney corps, June 28, 1782.

117. Cited in McDowell, *Ireland in the Age of Imperialism and Revolution,* 241.

III

The War of 1812

7

A "Species of Milito-Nautico-Guerilla-Plundering Warfare"

Admiral Alexander Cochrane's Naval Campaign
against the United States, 1814–1815

C. J. Bartlett and Gene A. Smith

The Anglo-American War of 1812 served as an embarrassing and unwelcome diversion for a British government struggling for survival against Revolutionary France and Napoleon. The ongoing contest on the European continent, which had time and again stretched Britain's resources to the limit, during the summer of 1812 expanded into a troublesome conflict against the United States that left British policymakers facing a serious dilemma. Britain would have to continue operations against France, as well as defend Canada, protect British shipping from American warships and privateers, blockade the American coast to destroy commerce and hinder American naval operations, and aggressively take the transatlantic war to the shores of the upstart republic. These strategic objectives would tax a nation already reeling from the continued war with France and ultimately force military and naval officers to use innovative and aggressive unlimited warfare, or what Americans would term extreme and barbaric warfare, to achieve their objectives. And not surprisingly, both sides would vividly remember for years to come the "horrible species of warfare" that had been perpetrated during the conflict.[1]

Admiral Alexander Cochrane's role in the second war against America, not only his campaign but also the reasons behind his appointment as naval commander in chief, encapsulates the attitude of Britain as it went to war against the American Republic. Although Cochrane has sometimes been characterized in dismissive terms as an admiral whose first concern was prize money, his leading role in the conduct of the war deserves more serious consideration. His open contempt for the new nation, his conviction that its people lacked patriotism and its authority was fatally weak, chimed in with the views of many in London and inspired Cochrane to adopt a strategy of unconventional war designed to break the American will to fight. Even after Wellington ruled out the practicability of a conventional war in America in early 1814, Cochrane and others remained confident that nontraditional offensive action—incitement of slave uprisings, Indian alliances in the west, naval blockades, small-scale attacks on the American coast, as well as initiatives in Louisiana and the exploitation of New England disaffection—could all combine to bring the Americans to heel, perhaps even topple their republican experiment. Cochrane's tactics to some extent reflected British involvement in the violent and destructive wars sparked by the French Revolution, but echoes of the American War of Independence remained obvious as well. The Americans were believed still to be a people with little collective sense of their national interest, and whose immature government need not be taken seriously.

Although the war with the United States would always be a secondary theater of operations, once it began British policymakers and naval and military officers focused on how they could force the Americans into submission while protecting their colonial holdings in the Western Hemisphere. In fact, it quickly became apparent that Canada would serve an important role in British operations, as several commanders offered strategic assessments of the colony's role. In November 1812, only five months after the United States had declared war, Sir John Borlase Warren, then British commander of the North American Squadron, proposed an operation against New Orleans to divert the American attack against Canada. He insisted that such a diversion would close the Mississippi River as well as "cut off the resources of the American Southern States, . . . who are now actively employed against the Canadas." The following year Warren again called for his country to strike against the South and to bring "forward the Indians and Spanyards [sic] . . . and a division of black troops to cut off the resources of the Mississippi." This proposal represented one of the first suggestions about the forthcoming nature of the conflict.[2]

In 1813, other naval officers made similar suggestions for a British victory. Captain James Stirling sent a detailed memorandum on the geography of the Gulf of Mexico region to the First Lord of the Admiralty, Viscount Melville. According to Stirling, the conquest of Louisiana by British forces supported by Indians, blacks, and "displeased" Spaniards would place the states of Kentucky, Ohio, Tennessee, and Virginia "at the mercy of Great Britain." Likewise Admiral Henry Hotham, then the commanding officer at

Bermuda, suggested that "the place where Americans [were] most vulnerable is New Orleans and . . . [its capture] will be the severest blow America can meet with." Hotham also implied that an attack in the Gulf region would "check [the Americans'] operations against Canada."[3]

Each of these suggestions proposed bold action that the authors insisted would pay great dividends with little expense because they also employed the threat of servile rebellion, Indian uprisings, and the exploitation of discontented French and Spanish populations in the south. All of these options seemed expedient considering the limited resources available for the American war and the events that occurred during 1813. The fortunes of war in North America had worsened for Britain as army and naval forces suffered losses to Oliver Hazard Perry on Lake Erie and to William Henry Harrison at the Battle of the Thames. Moreover, British naval supremacy on Lake Ontario seemed to be threatened. Fortunately, the disintegration of Napoleon's European empire soon freed seasoned, battle-trained troops for North American service and permitted the government to refocus offensive operations against the United States. But until the revised strategy could be put into effect, the Royal Navy had instructions "to institute a strict and rigorous blockade of [American] ports and harbours . . . and of the River Mississippi."[4]

The secretary of state for war and colonies, Lord Bathurst, wrote anxiously to the Duke of Wellington in late January 1814, requesting suggestions as to how Britain might strike some decisive blow and bring a speedy end to the war. Wellington's discouraging reply maintained that even under the most favorable conditions, little could be achieved by a British offensive in North America. Apparently Wellington had been unimpressed by the naval raids undertaken by small forces of British marines and soldiers along the East Coast of the United States during 1813. Even so, the cabinet clung to the hope that boldly aggressive nontraditional offensive action might cause panic, demoralization, and physical damage among a people who were disparagingly dismissed by the prime minister, Lord Liverpool, as hopelessly divided and low-minded. Liverpool, unlike Wellington, had been greatly emboldened by reports of the material and moral effects of the coastal raids of 1813 in and around Chesapeake Bay under the energetic leadership of Rear Admiral George Cockburn. He and other cabinet colleagues, believing that small-scale operations might achieve disproportionate results, committed few naval and military forces to this strategy, even before Wellington replied. Limited, small-scale operations would not require large numbers of troops, ships, or resources.[5]

Bold and aggressive small-scale offensive operations against the Ameri-

can coast did require more vigorous leadership than had so far been provided by Admiral Warren, the senior officer in American waters. Despite a
good record as a young officer, some now described him as too secretive
and, even worse, too cautious. Besides, he did not seem wholeheartedly
committed to the American war. His successor, fifty-six-year-old Vice Admiral Sir Alexander F. I. Cochrane came to American waters with considerable small-boat experience in the Mediterranean. The uncle of the better-
known Captain Thomas Cochrane—the frigate captain with the "Nelson
touch"—appeared younger, more energetic, and very successful, having
been knighted for his participation in the 1806 Battle of Santo Domingo.[6]

Cochrane possessed another quality that made him appealing to the British government. He absolutely and unquestionably hated the United States;
this enmity stemmed from his brother's death at American hands during the
1781 siege of Yorktown. Yet Cochrane's prejudices mirrored more deeply
the prevalent and bitter anti-American attitudes displayed by so many Britons who were directly or indirectly engaged in the war. Americans—whom
writers in the press or speakers in Parliament variously described as irre-
sponsible, dishonest, and puffed-up democrats—represented, in short, a
menace to their own countrymen as well as to British interests. Most officers and government officials believed that they should not be accorded the
"civilities of war" as practiced by the European powers. Captain David
Milne, one of Cochrane's subordinates, believed the Americans "a sad despicable set," totally governed by "self-interest." Cochrane called them a
corrupt, cowardly, "whining, canting race" who lived in a ramshackle and
easily disrupted federal republic about to fall apart. Almost as soon as taking command, he increased the intensity of the war by instructing his officers to "act with the utmost hostility against the shores of the United
States." Subordinate Admiral Edward Codrington reinforced Cochrane's
decision, suggesting that taking violence and suffering to the doors of the
Americans would be the best way to win the war. Cochrane encouraged his
officers to show the Americans that they were "at the mercy of an invading
force" who could reduce American seaports to ashes and waste the surrounding countryside. This would provide some "retaliation for their savage conduct in Canada."[7]

As the naval commander in chief at the critical stage of the war, Cochrane
communicated with all major British figures involved in the fighting in
North America, including the commanders of naval and military forces in
Canada. He held responsibility for the disposition and use of a sizable
North American fleet during the 1814–15 campaigns. He also communi-
cated with London on questions of strategy, supplies, and reinforcements.

Figure 7.1. "Bird's-Eye View of the Battle of New Orleans, January 8, 1815. From a sketch by Latour, Jackson's Chief Engineer." Taken from Benson J. Lossing, *The Pictorial Field-Book of the War of 1812* (New York: Harper & Brothers, 1869), 1047. Reproduced with the permission of the Newberry Library.

Cochrane took a hands-on approach to the conflict in North America, unlike his predecessors. He had organized and directed the 1801 British amphibious landings at Aboukir Bay, sent to dispose of the French army deserted by Napoleon in 1799. During the following months his naval force had also kept the invading British army supplied; this has been described as one "of the classic instances of a well-planned, well-conducted, and completely successful conjoint operations." Afterward Cochrane played an active role during the capture of the French West Indian islands of Guadeloupe and Martinique, using his contacts with free blacks and slaves as well as with other disaffected peoples to isolate the dominant white French elite and so hasten the fall of the islands. No one could question his active managerial style or his attention to the smallest organizational detail.[8]

Although the Admiralty office considered Cochrane the right man for the job, not all agreed. His subordinate, Rear Admiral George Cockburn, who overshadowed Cochrane during the 1814 operations in the Chesapeake and most notably during the assault on Washington, perceived his commander's talents to be administrative rather than operational. Cochrane has also fared poorly in most histories of the Chesapeake campaign and the ill-fated attack on New Orleans, either being accorded a minor role

or accused of excessive interest in prize money and loot. Admiral Codrington emphatically proclaimed in October 1814 that prize money was
Cochrane's "last consideration." As such Cochrane deserves more serious
consideration because an examination of his role, in British operations
along the coast of the United States during 1814–15, in short, provides
insights into the cultural as well as the political, logistic, and military dimensions of the war and helps define the parameters of warfare during the War
of 1812.[9]

During the spring of 1814, Cochrane critically examined the resources at
his disposal. The well-placed naval station of Bermuda, some 640 miles to
the east, lay within reach of the Chesapeake and other objectives. It had a
better climate—an important attribute given the high death rate in the Caribbean—than the West Indies, and did not lie on the main hurricane routes.
One government spokesman reported to Parliament in March 1816 that
Bermuda "formed the great security of Canada, and was a point from which
a British fleet might sweep the whole extent of the coast of North America."
While Cochrane might have agreed with this assessment in terms of its
potential value, the reality he found in Bermuda during the spring of 1814
appeared somewhat different.[10]

Bermuda actually consisted of low-lying islands separated by a maze of
straits with many treacherous shallows. A brig, HMS *Carnation,* had fallen
victim to these in 1810, and navigation proved even more difficult for large
ships. Cochrane initiated an extensive dredging program to clear the approaches, but soon found that easier access to St. George's only highlighted
the harbor's inadequate fortifications—an enterprising enemy could easily
take advantage of the deepened channels with little fear of shore bombard-
ments. Additionally, the little town with its white houses seemed aestheti-
cally pleasing but offered naval personnel scant entertainment. Prices were
also high, and food was often in short supply because the islands relied on
easily interrupted provisions from the West Indies. In fact, the United States
had been an important source of supplies before the war. Cochrane soon
found that the increased number of ships taxed the island's supplies too
greatly, forcing him to send HMS *Bulwark* to the coast of New London,
Connecticut, in the hope that money-grabbing Americans would sell fresh
food for cash. Although he laid out $2,000 for this purpose, he found it
necessary to advertise in Bermuda for additional money to supplement the
monotonous salt meat and biscuit diet of his crews with fresh provisions.
Then an unexpected drought exposed the inadequacy of the existing storage
water tanks. Similar difficulties occurred in October and November 1814
when Cochrane temporarily used Jamaica as a staging base for the New

Orleans campaign. Fortunately, a timely convoy arrived with much needed provisions, little of which could be procured locally.[11]

The dockyard in Bermuda also proved to be perpetually short of labor and full of defects. Cochrane had to redirect several ships to Halifax, only to find that it, too, could not meet the needs of the ships on the station. In fact, the shortage of British or Canadian skilled labor forced the shipyard to employ American carpenters and coopers. Cochrane's efforts to improve the Bermuda yard proved equally difficult. During the fall of 1814 he found only eight shipwrights to assist in the refitting of his flagship and the other ships needing attention. He had to acknowledge that the station had inadequate facilities, as most of the stores of masts and timber remained exposed without cover as late as 1815. The sick and wounded also had to be housed in temporary accommodations whose lease would expire in September 1814. Although a permanent building had been authorized, its design did not suit the local conditions or building skills, forcing Cochrane to build three traditional wooden Bermuda "pavilions" with proper ventilation.[12]

Desertion proved another pressing problem with Cochrane soon complaining that seaman disappeared at a truly alarming rate. He blamed the merchants in St. George's, with their offers of better wages, and enlisted the military garrison to try to recover the men. Not surprisingly, desertion proved even more problematic in Halifax, as many men soon found their way to the United States. Even Admiral Cockburn, who supposedly had won the loyalty of his marines, found a slight desertion problem. He believed desertions could be eliminated by enlisting former American slaves as marines as they, at least, would not desert. David Milne, describing his ship as one of the more fortunate ones, complained he had an inadequate multinational crew—British, European, and American—that included ex-clerks, grooms, watchmakers, and grocers. He dismissed the marines as "positively the refuse of the corps." Even the Americans noted Cochrane's problems. On March 3, 1813, the *Norfolk Herald* reported nine cases of desertion within three days, including one seaman who supposedly had been continuously at sea for fourteen years.[13]

Cochrane sent several desperate appeals to London, pleading for more men to offset the losses from desertion, injury, and illness. He also confronted numerous requests from the naval commander on the Great Lakes to help man a new squadron to challenge the American flotilla in those waters. In fact, Cochrane had to send most of the 1st Marine battalion to Canada even though he initially planned for these men to be used in raids against Georgia and South Carolina at the end of 1814. Nor did matters improve with the termination of the European war. First Lord of the Admiralty Melville regretfully explained in October 1814 that he could not send additional marines to North America because he feared discontent would erupt into violence among the many sailors impatient for their postwar discharges, especially following their discharges after the first overthrow of Napoleon.[14]

Like his predecessor, Admiral Warren, Cochrane also complained that he did not have enough ships to meet his needs. Warren, who had more than ninety warships available to him during the spring of 1813, begrudgingly acknowledged that half of his fleet had to remain in the Caribbean to confront the French threat, while many of the remainder had to serve on convoy duty to protect against American privateers. The American fleet also posed an immediate threat, especially after the five impressive victories scored in single-ship actions against supposedly comparable British warships early in the war. These American victories, according to George Canning, broke "the sacred spell of the invincibility of the British navy." Furthermore, the fourteen American warships, manned by excellent captains and crews, were fast, well constructed, and heavily armed vessels that had to be contained, if for no other reason than to revive British morale. Warren and Cochrane both successfully concentrated their complement of British warships off the U.S. coast to reduce the naval threat, but in doing so enterprising American privateers—putting to sea from virtually any port, harbor, or inlet—eluded the blockade and wreaked havoc among British merchantmen. Warren had constantly warned the British government "of the impossibility of our trade navigating these seas [between the St Lawrence and the West Indies] unless a very extensive squadron is employed to scour the vicinity." But the Admiralty was unwilling to send Warren enough warships to blockade adequately the almost 2,000 miles of American coastline. In fact, Admiralty reports constantly reiterated that Warren had an overwhelming numerical superiority in ships, as well as several powerful ships-of-the-line, of which the Americans had none. Warren simply lacked enough vessels to institute an effective blockade of the United States, and as a result privateers drove up insurance rates to a level twice that during the recent wars with France.[15]

Cochrane, too, pleaded to the Admiralty for more ships, especially if they expected him to maintain the blockade and undertake serious attacks on the American coasts. The naval blockade restricted forays by the larger American warships, but the elusive privateers continued to harass British shipping. Even so, the blockade disrupted the commerce and economy of the Atlantic states, increasing the prices for scarce foreign goods and greatly reducing government revenues. And while the blockade's extension to New

England during the spring of 1814 increased the demands on the British fleet, Cochrane believed that the region's lack of enthusiasm for the war could be used to his advantage. Perhaps the blockade, if judiciously exercised, could cause enough material loss and emotional aggravation to intensify New England aloofness from the more belligerent states to the south and west. On the other hand, Cochrane faced pressure from Nova Scotia merchants to protect their highly profitable New England trade. They had built up large stocks of goods in expectation of its continuance. In this instance, the government gave Cochrane discretion to proceed as he thought best, and he chose to permit safe passage to some American skippers in return for information on hostile military deployments or for fresh food for his crews. Unfortunately, British privateers ignored the safe passage arrangements and seized American merchant ships, thus alienating the Americans and reducing the possibility of encouraging New England neutrality, ultimately forcing Cochrane to discontinue the use of passes.[16]

These difficulties underscored the problems encountered by Cochrane as he tried to organize adequate and effective naval operations for the Chesapeake Bay during the summer of 1814 and for later attacks against New Orleans, Georgia, and South Carolina. Facing such circumstances, Cochrane and other British officers worked diligently to restore their own reputations and that of their service. They willingly used all means at their disposal to secure speedy and dramatic victories, which unlike the war in Europe gave an extra edge to fighting in North America. The officers of the fleet also drew encouragement from Cockburn's 1813 operations in the Chesapeake. The Bay, a virtual inland sea that stretched north for some 200 miles from its narrow Atlantic inlet, offered the British easy access to the coasts of Virginia and Maryland and to the cities of Baltimore, Annapolis, and Washington, while also providing an ideal base of operations for demoralizing and humiliating the American war effort.

The goal of breaking the American will to fight inevitably provoked charges and countercharges of unnecessary violence and incendiarism from British participants in the campaign as well as from critics in London. British conduct in North American during the War of 1812, however, differed very little from the unlimited warfare that had been practiced in Europe since August 1793. The French Revolution had introduced new levels of destruction and violence that by the beginning of the nineteenth century had surpassed that imposed on the small-scale armies of the eighteenth century. Americans claimed that this new destructive intensity violated customary or legal warfare and contrasted sharply from traditional forms of war practiced by civilized nations. Yet British officers felt they were following European standards of warfare based on the desired objectives of the campaign. In some instances excessive violence and lack of discipline provided a means to an end, while in others strict discipline and control were directed only against targets of genuine military importance. Throughout, Cochrane and other British officers insisted that their illegitimate or "unsporting" acts of war simply represented a response to similar American actions. Americans had looted and burned the Canadian town of York, reportedly set booby-traps including drifting mines or torpedoes, poisoned food and water, and used individuals posing as civilians to fire random shots at British units. This unlimited form of American warfare forced the British to respond appropriately, climaxing with the temporary August 1814 occupation of Washington—with the controversial incidents of arson that accompanied it—and the unsuccessful attempt to do the same at Baltimore and New Orleans.[17]

British accounts of events sometimes offered the reasoning, prejudices, and emotions that led to specific acts of vengeance. *The Annual Register* of 1814 announced that it was "not to be expected that the war between America and Britain would be carried on in the most humane and honourable mode, especially by the Americans." It added that British "gentlemen" viewed the American "democrats" as their social inferiors, while many Americans vividly remembered the British use of Indians and Lord Dunmore's November 1775 pledge to free all slaves who would take up arms for King George III during the War for Independence. That conflict had also provided plenty of other precedents. Disillusioned Tory captain William Lovell, a naval officer whose father and uncle had both fought in the War for Independence, recalled his War of 1812 service in a caustic 1839 memoir. Writing of his disgust at American conduct during the War of 1812, he maintained that plundering by British forces had been forbidden. Any unconventional British acts of violence, he retorted, came only in re-sponse to the April 1813 American burning of the Canadian town of York, which had not deserved such harsh treatment. Lovell's anti-American feel-ings had become even more incensed because of the American use of "tor-pedoes," explosive devices used by Americans to blow holes in the hulls of British ships below the waterline. In late June 1813 Captain Thomas Hardy of HMS *Ramillies* had encountered an abandoned merchant ship off New London, Connecticut; when Hardy sent a party to board the schooner, the vessel suddenly exploded, killing Lieutenant John Geddes and ten seamen. Lovell insisted that he, too, had encountered concealed explosives on small coasting vessel with lines rigged to detonate the craft when boarded by

British forces. British officers thought that such use of "Infernal Machines" was absolutely despicable.[18]

During the mid-1830s Lieutenant James Scott produced a three-volume account of his naval career, in which he narrated at some length his experiences in the Chesapeake during 1813–14. He reported that Cockburn, whom he greatly admired, never faltered in his generosity to the weak and helpless. When a British raiding party unjustly despoiled an American's property, Scott maintained that the admiral reimbursed him. The pro-Federalist *Connecticut Mirror* reported that during the attack on Portsmouth, Virginia, British forces seized cattle and sheep but that Cockburn paid for the livestock, and he even paid a Mrs. Wallace a doubloon for each day that he stayed in her house. On another occasion, when the British seamen intercepted a stagecoach traveling from Philadelphia to Baltimore, Cockburn intervened on behalf of a milliner who had been robbed of her purse. In still another instance, Scott related how Cockburn paroled an American militia officer of genuine breeding—supposedly a real and rare gentleman—and returned his splendid horse. Yet Scott fully approved when Cockburn punished the enemy, such as when he ordered that livestock be taken without payment because Americans had fired on his troops while trying to purchase them. When the Americans resisted, Cockburn instructed his men to kill the cattle not needed by his army and burn their carcasses.[19]

Scott also derided Americans as being too ready to make a few dollars by trading with the British "whenever their own interest intervened between them and the public weal." He even mockingly described a group of American officers who visited his ship under a flag of truce in June 1813. "They were in regimentals, but certainly the fashion and cut of them rendered their exact rank and calling somewhat dubious." Moreover, the three officers' "sported red coats, silver epaulettes, and silver mounted side-arms, white linen waist-coats, and trousers of the same material" appeared ill-fitting and slovenly. Unshined Hessian boots and "old-fashioned French cocked-hats, with feathers, that might, from their towering height, have served for sky-scrapers, completed their attire." The appearance of the American officers combined with "the stiff unbending formality . . . , their starch-upright figures, placed in contact with the easy demeanour of the gentlemen they accosted, rendered the scene truly ridiculous" and, according to Scott, made it difficult for the British officers to keep a straight face.[20]

Scott also recalled another meeting under a flag of truce with one particularly uncouth American officer who chided him about recent British surprise night attacks to try to capture American six-pounder field pieces.

The American boldly challenged Scott to steal one from a fort that he commanded, adding, "But tarnation seize me in the bramble-bush if I don't blow you to hell within a mile of my command. . . . I would give you such a whipping as would cure you from rambling a-night, like a particular G--d----d tom-cat." Scott remembered that he used a former slave as a guide, led a party of seamen to the fort, and took it by surprise. After only a few shots the Americans fled, their commander in his shorts. Scott later gave the American officer's clothes and regimental colors to a sergeant in the newly formed British black "Colonial Marines." The fort commander, outraged and insulted that his clothes were being worn by a "G-- d----d black nigger," declared that this represented "the unkindest cut of all." Although the story may be apocryphal, Scott's account is instructive nonetheless because it sheds light on the attitudes of some British officers toward their American opponent even years after the events had taken place.[21]

Not all British participants agreed with Scott. Naval officer Frederic Chamier wondered in evident disgust whether "some savages, and perhaps men dressed one degree better than savages, commence a system of barbarity and desolation in the north; [that] we, pretending to be the most civilised nation on the face of the earth, must imitate their ravages in the south." Chamier had seen British units burning American property without cause or on the feeblest of excuses, namely, that all men of a certain age, whatever their dress, were likely militiamen. Chamier also recalled how raiding parties experimented to find the quickest way to burn a building, soon deciding that a fire to leeward was the most effective because this type of fire drew in air in such a way as to fan the flames into the heart of the house. The June 1813 sacking of Hampton, Virginia—when an Independent company of French Chasseurs, or "desperate Banditti," as one British office referred to them, raped innocent women, pillaged the town, and murdered in cold blood an American militia officer who had surrendered—represented the type of heinous barbaric type of warfare that Chamier so despised.[22]

Chamier also questioned the inconsistencies in British behavior. Apparently the approved practice, although not necessarily always observed, was for British forces to purchase food and live cattle even if below market value, whereas they were instructed to burn American houses. Yet at sea, everything seemed to be fair game as far as the American war was concerned. Chamier instead took a very different position on the conflict: "It has been held by many very good and clever men that, during war, private property should be respected: this is a very great mistake. Every man during war pays something towards the support of it: if this man is ruined he ceases to contribute, and thus the exchequer is impoverished: ergo, the more you ruin in a war, the more you hurt the nation at large." Adam Smith had written some years earlier that those who supported war from the safety of their homes should have to shoulder more of the expense. If confronted with such a burden, they might be more inclined to peace. Youthful subaltern George R. Gleig, who fought in both the Peninsular War and in North America, suggested that noncombatants be respected in wars between monarchies, but he also vowed that in wars against democracies the voters should experience "the real handicaps and miseries of warfare": "Burn their houses, plunder their property, block up their harbors, and destroy their shipping in a few places; and before you have time to proceed to the rest, you will be stopped by entreaties for peace." In addition, electorates would soon reject their war-making leaders.[23]

Cochrane wanted to take the war to the Americans in precisely this heavy-handed, destructive way. Captain Milne and Admiral Codrington were equally committed to Cochrane's plans. Admiral Cockburn's actions in 1813 also spoke far louder than any words. During the spring and early summer, his forces sacked Hampton, burned an important flour depot on the Elk River, and destroyed the Cecil or Principic cannon foundry on the Susquehanna River, all of which had important military value. Cochrane had also instructed his troops to burn several private homes and farms in Havre de Grace and along the Sassafras River (both in Maryland), from which Americans had fired against his troops. If American citizens continued to resist, they would have to suffer the consequences of war.[24]

Many senior British army officers expressed reservations about the way the war had been conducted. Colonel Sir Thomas Sydney Beckwith and General Robert Ross, each with only a few thousand soldiers at their disposal, could not be easily persuaded to embark on a destructive offensive operation into the heart of enemy territory without substantial intelligence of enemy strengths and deployments. While both officers worried about their lines of communication and logistics, Cockburn seemingly conducted haphazard raids that lacked discipline, order, and the most obvious military precautions. Cockburn's unorthodox campaign relied on speed, surprise, accurate information secured from locals and slaves, as well as the expectation that the American militias would offer little, if any, serious resistance. Regardless of his preparation and planning, Cockburn's tactics against civilian targets shocked some army officers. General Sir Henry Smith, taken aback by the occupation of Washington, surmised that Cockburn would have burned the entire city if possible. Writing of the dismay expressed by many of his fellow officers, he compared the Duke of Wellington's "humane warfare in the south of France" and the incendiary Chesapeake warfare of the "Red Savage of the woods." Colonel Arthur Brooke rejoined that torching the city was a justified act of war, resulting from the civilian attacks against British troops; Lord Bathurst defended the burning of the city because the Americans had attempted to assassinate General Ross. He insisted that the whole affair "was as fine a thing as done [during] this war and a rub to the Americans that can never be forgotten."[25]

These predatory British operations in the Chesapeake ignited hostile American feelings that would not be soon forgotten. As early as the spring of 1813, the American newspaper *Niles' Weekly Register* had labeled Admiral Warren as the "spoiler in the Chesapeake," whereas Cockburn would soon be demonized as "Go-burn." The paper likened Cockburn to "Satan in his cloud, when he saw the blood of man from murdered Abel first crimson the earth, exulting at the damning deed, and treating the suppliant females with the rudest curses and most vile appellations." A naturalized Irishman, supposedly a James O'Boyle from Virginia, even offered $1,000 for the head of "the notorious incendiary and infamous scoundrel, . . . British Admiral Cockburn, or 500 dollars for each of his ears on delivery." Yet Cockburn felt it necessary to take extreme actions against a populace who would go to any length to harass his forces. The American militia he faced had fired on his troops, then melted away into the countryside and posed as civilian noncombatants. The British therefore relied on extreme, unorthodox tactics aimed at intimidating and overawing the American people with deliberate acts of "frightfulness" and destroying the material things that Americans needed to fight. As a result, the war devolved into "a vicious little war," with both sides perpetrating numerous outrages.[26]

The war in North America became even more vicious during the spring and summer of 1814. Long before assuming command, Cochrane had drafted a strategic plan and discussed it at length with the Admiralty Office. He suggested that New Orleans and Virginia were the two most vulnerable places in America and that both could be taken. New Orleans and the Mississippi River watershed served as the outlet for western American commerce, and Cochrane thought that seizing the port and river would weaken the United States so as to divide the Atlantic from the trans-Appalachian states. The resulting internal pressure would bring down the American government. In Virginia he proposed two targets: the state's few cities and the black slave population. Cochrane had reported, and Cockburn had proven, that most Virginia cities could be assaulted easily with small mobile forces because of the abundance of navigable rivers. These attacks would throw the Virginia countryside into disarray. He also asserted that the slave population, who were "British in their hearts, . . . might be of great use if war should be prosecuted with vigor." Slave labor girded the southern economy and provided the underpinning and structure of society, and Cochrane understood that any disruptions would leave Virginians in a state of panic.[27]

During the spring of 1813 Admiral Warren had acknowledged the potential importance of a servile insurrection. He had reported that "the Black population of the countries evince . . . the strongest predilection for the cause of Great Britain" and that "the White inhabitants have suffered great alarm from the discovery of parties of Negroes . . . exercising with arms in the Night." Moreover, the presence of British warships in American waters had emboldened slaves, who deserted in increasing numbers. Warren learned that the slaves made valuable local guides and, not surprisingly, that the "Blacks of Virginia and Maryland would cheerfully take up Arms and join us against the Americans."[28]

The possibility of interjecting a racial component that would unquestionably escalate the war in North America may have appealed to military commanders in hostile territory running short of men and supplies, but it did not appeal to the Ministry. Lord Bathurst had included guidelines for dealing with American slaves in his secret March 1813 orders to Colonel Beckwith, and these instructions firmly ruled out inciting slave revolts. Bathurst's directive did permit individual slaves who became involved in British operations to be removed from the United States for their own safety and to be given protection and granted freedom. The secretary clearly hoped that the numbers would be small, since "the Public became bound to maintain them." Yet these orders proved inadequate because they underestimated the considerable number of slaves that would escape their bondage. In fact, the Bermudan Legislative Council pleaded as early as mid-August 1813 that no more refugees be sent to the island, since the growing number might undermine the social and economic stability of the island community.[29]

Bathurst revised his opinion in January 1814 when he advised the Admiralty to assist all slaves wishing to leave the United States. Possible recruits for the West India regiments—perhaps as many as 5,000—from Georgia and South Carolina should be sent to Bermuda. By August 1814, both Bathurst and Melville had again reconsidered, now warning Cochrane against encouraging slave uprisings for fear of atrocities. Indeed, Melville feared a corps of slaves might prove as dangerous or injurious to British as to American interests. Bathurst still believed that only those fearing for their safety or wishing to enter British colonial regiments should be accepted, and that number would be manageable. Cochrane, himself a slave owner in Trinidad, cherished hopes of recruiting slaves from the southern plantations to bolster his West Indian regiments, although he later reported that they would not "volunteer their services to the West India Regiments." Even so, Cochrane believed that using slave combatants would be "more terrible to the Americans than any troops that could be brought forward."[30]

Cochrane possessed several pieces of information that helped form his judgment, but one of the most important may have been a November 1813 letter sent from Captain Robert Barrie to his predecessor. Barrie reported that he had some 120 slaves from Virginia and Maryland aboard HMS *Dragon* and that he was convinced even more would "cheerfully take up arms and join us against the Americans." Such optimism prompted Cochrane to issue a bold proclamation in early April 1814, offering freedom for any slave who would enter "into His Majesty's Service" or relocate "as Free Settlers into some of His Majesty's Colonies." They and their families would be received in British posts or warships, and all who enlisted in military or dockyard service would receive a bounty of twenty dollars, as well as the same pay and clothing allowance as the marines. Since Cochrane did not need additional seamen, those who enlisted for naval service received a bounty of only ten dollars. This promise of freedom and employment—much like Lord Dunmore's during the American War for Independence—lured an untold number of southern slaves from their American bondage, with some 600 signing up as "Colonial Marines" and many others taking passage to Bermuda, Nova Scotia, Trinidad, and other British colonies.[31]

Cockburn, in contrast, initially expressed doubts, thinking it necessary for the British to establish themselves in force on the mainland before slaves would rise in any considerable numbers. But once Cochrane issued his proclamation, Cockburn immediately had to find a suitable island in the Chesapeake that could serve as a British base of operations and as an accessible receiving station for runaway slaves. By mid-May, Cockburn had occupied Tangier Island, begun constructing a fort and barracks, and sent slaves to the mainland to report on British activities. Within days, slaves began arriving at the island, and by September some 300 had agreed to join the Colonial Marines. Trained and commanded by Sergeant William Hammond, the former slaves participated in British operations from May 1814 onward, even marching on Washington with Ross's army in late August. Although Cockburn initially thought that these new soldiers were "naturally neither very valorous nor very active," he soon admitted that he had underestimated their qualities and potential. They had responded so well to British training that he now preferred them to his own marines. Sergeant Hammond, acknowledging their "steadiness," reported that they would soon "equal their brother soldiers in the performance of every part of their duty." Cockburn quickly realized that they were fitter and stronger; in operations ashore they committed no outrages; accustomed to hot weather, they withstood long marches and arduous labor better than the average marine. Captain Charles B. H. Ross reported that during one operation the Colonial Marines had performed well, "their conduct marked by great spirit and vivacity, and perfect obedience." Lieutenant Scott also welcomed their knowledge of local terrain, claiming that they made excellent scouts and reliable guides. Admirable in nighttime operations, their knowledge and experience made it easier for small raiding parties to elude or surprise American forces.[32]

If in the end fewer slaves arrived than Cochrane expected, the British nonetheless had acquired a very tough and loyal auxiliary force, and this army of runaway slaves made an indelible mark on the psyche of American planters. It apparently "caused a most general and undisguised alarm" or a fear that bordered on panic and paranoia. Cockburn declared that the Americans "expect Blacky will have no mercy on them and they know that he understands bush fighting and the locality of the *woods* as well as themselves and can perhaps play at hide and seek in them even better." The mere presence of the British fleet off the coast created a double-edged problem for American planters. It emboldened slaves to flee while also making the countryside virtually indefensible. Should the militia be called out to confront a British threat, then slaves would have free rein to flee or rise against their masters. The British benefited in either case, and Cockburn took great pride in noting the degree of alarm among the planters as revealed in the local press.[33]

The Colonial Marines saw their first action on the morning of May 30, 1814, when Cockburn sent a small force under Captain Charles Ross to take an American battery on Pangoteake (Pungoteague, Virginia) Creek, opposite Tangier Island. During the assault, "though one of them [Colonial Marines] was shot and died instantly in front of the others at Pangoteake, it did not daunt or check the others, but on the contrary animated them to seek revenge." In short order, the British burned three barracks and captured a small-caliber field gun that later would be awarded to the Colonial Marines for their service. In fact, Cockburn praised "the Colonial Marines, who were for the *first* time, employed in Arms against their old Masters, and behaved to the admiration of every Body." The former slaves participated in a number of other operations throughout the summer, including a series of June attacks in which a group of thirty burned more than 2,500 hogsheads of tobacco in Benedict and Marlborough, Maryland. Again, they reportedly "conducted themselves with the utmost order, forbearance, and regularity" even though they "might expect to meet their former masters." In early August, Cockburn himself led a force of some 500 men, including 120 now-experienced members of the Colonial Marines, into Virginia where they encountered an American militia force on the Kinsale Heights near the mouth of the Potomac. Cockburn achieved another quick and speedy victory with few losses, but he acknowledged it could have been far different because his army ventured through well-wooded country, ideal for an enemy ambush. But no such ambush or attack occurred, convincing him that a march on the American capital was eminently feasible given the limited capabilities of the local militias.[34]

The Colonial Marines—or "platoons of uniformed negroes" as they were derisively called—had excited great angst in the southern American states. Cochrane's decision to mobilize them had exposed a tremendous American weakness, which Cockburn exploited. Throughout the summer of 1814 local, state, and federal leaders grappled with the possibility that Cochrane and Cockburn would foment a full-scale slave insurrection, and this preoccupation opened the door for Cockburn to ravage the Virginia and Maryland coastline while encountering virtually no opposition. By August Cockburn had become convinced that with anticipated reinforcements—as many as 30,000 supposedly coming from Gibraltar, Sicily, Bordeaux, England, and Ireland—they could easily seize major targets such as Washington and Baltimore. Even though Cochrane surmised that the "desertion of the black population . . . backed with 20,000 British troops," would hurl Madison from his presidential throne, he suggested the first major attack be directed at Baltimore, followed up with assaults against Philadelphia, Annapolis, and Washington. Cockburn explored the approaches to each city, before concluding that Washington offered the most advantages and the easiest accessibility. In late July and early August Cockburn made nine diversionary raids in Virginia and Maryland, distracting Americans and greatly damaging their war-making ability. These types of tactics played well into Cochrane's overall objectives, for he had ordered his commanders "to destroy and lay waste" to all towns within their reach. Cockburn was doing exactly as instructed.[35]

The most difficult objective that Cockburn had was convincing Cochrane and General Robert Ross that the city of Washington should be their primary objective. Cochrane still believed that capturing one of the major seaports would be far more destructive to American morale. General Ross, meanwhile, was extremely reluctant to place his 4,000 men in the middle of hostile territory with a long supply line. Cockburn described the success of previous naval raids and even offered to let Ross participate in a planned raid against an American factory on St. George's Island in the Potomac. During the August 16 assault, British forces destroyed the facility and returned without encountering opposition, vividly demonstrating to Ross what could be achieved with limited resources and risk. Ross became convinced that an attack against Washington could be carried off successfully.[36]

The late August 1814 campaign against Washington, spanning thirteen days and involving only 4,500 men, was an unqualified British success that represented the high-water mark of the war. British forces easily invaded and captured the American capital, burned public buildings including the capitol and president's house, and returned to the safety of British warships while suffering very few casualties. Cochrane and his naval forces had brought the war to the United States as effectively as the war had been taken to Napoleon. In doing so, Cochrane had given Cockburn's marines and Ross's soldiers the chance for glory and success. Aside from Commodore Joshua Barney's men, who had destroyed their gunboats and retreated to Bladensburg where they put up a spirited defense, British forces encountered no serious resistance. Despite the ease of the Washington campaign, Cockburn encountered further objections before Cochrane and Ross agreed to attack Baltimore—in this instance their reservations were justified, as the Americans had the fortifications and men to offer a stiffer resistance, ultimately forcing a British retreat.[37]

Cochrane exercised great caution before and during each operation because he had learned that, even though the war had ended in Europe, he would receive very few reinforcements. Also, he had far larger concerns as commander of the North American station than simply the operational details of the Chesapeake campaign. He had to deal with the daily responsibilities of manning and provisioning a sizable squadron on a distant station with few bases of supply. He held responsibility for tightening the blockade of the American coastline, seizing shipping, and destroying the enemy's economy. Throughout, he remained committed to harassing the coast of New England, the Carolinas and Georgia, as well as the Chesapeake Bay. In fact, Cochrane was still convinced that his plan to strike, destroy, and ransom would break the American will to fight. Yet he also had strategic responsibility for the entire North American war, and by the late summer of 1814, his thoughts had turned to the next theater of operations—an attack on New Orleans and increased raids along the coasts of Georgia and South Carolina. And while some writers have suggested that Cochrane's interest in booty and prize money motivated his attack on New Orleans, his correspondence reveals serious hopes of wresting the city and the mouth of the Mississippi permanently from American control, which in the end would severely damage the American war effort.[38]

Soon after his appointment, Cochrane had boasted that with "15,000 of Lord Wellington's Army all the country south west of the Chesapeake might be restored to the dominion of Great Britain." He also boldly proposed that a small force—of regulars, Indians, black slaves, Baratarian pirates, and disaffected citizens—could "take possession of N. Orleans by which we should have considerably weakened the [American] efforts against Canada." Cochrane's ambitious plan, virtually the same as Warren's the year before, resonated strongly with the Lords of the Admiralty, especially after the summer 1814 reports of victorious raids against the American coast. In late July, Viscount Melville requested a confidential opinion from Admiral Sir William Domett about a possible Louisiana campaign, and the officer suggested an operation with troops assembling during the fall of 1814 at Negril Point in Jamaica and departing no later than December. With that endorsement, the Admiralty in early August 1814 approved Cochrane's plan for an attack, although he would have to wait until later in the year, pending the availability of Wellington's Peninsular veterans. In the meantime, Cochrane was allotted twenty shallow-draft vessels and additional arms for his anticipated Indian allies.[39]

Cochrane had learned during the spring of 1814 that the southern Indians were also fighting against the United States, but he lacked accurate and timely information. For example, he did not know that one tribe, the Creeks, had been fighting a civil war in which one faction remained loyal to the United States and that the other had suffered a devastating defeat against Andrew Jackson in the Battle of Horseshoe Bend on March 27, 1814. Unaware of the fate of the Creeks, Cochrane signed a proclamation to assist the southern Indians the day following the battle at Horseshoe Bend. Cochrane also did not realize that the other major southern tribes— the Cherokees and Choctaws—had sided completely with the Americans. Knowing only that a sizable number of Indians were still fighting a common foe, Cochrane had sent Captain Hugh Pigot and a small complement of men to the Gulf with arms and supplies for the Indians. Brevet Captain George Woodbine stayed among the southern Indians throughout the summer and fall of 1814, training and drilling, supplying and feeding, as well as trying to recruit additional warriors. Throughout, Woodbine reported to Cochrane that the Indians were potentially powerful allies who could be counted on during the Louisiana campaign. Cochrane learned in early December that the southern Indians hostile to the United States could actually contribute very little to British operations.[40]

During the Chesapeake campaign Cochrane had experienced considerable success encouraging slaves to run away and arming many against their former masters. Cochrane had become convinced that "thousands [of slaves] will join upon their masters['] horses" simply because of "their hatred to the citizens of the United States." He had found so little difficulty recruiting and employing slaves that he anticipated similar results along the slaveholding Gulf. Besides, reports from Florida and Louisiana already indicated that there was "a strong and irresistible party in the free people of colour, and the slaves who to a man will join" the British. True, slaves fled from Georgia and the Mississippi Territory to the British base on the Apalachicola River in Spanish Florida, but never in enough numbers to undermine American morale or alter the outcome of the Louisiana campaign. More important, very few of the Louisiana slaves that Cochrane anticipated would don red coats actually assisted the British, and fewer still participated in the Louisiana campaign. Instead, Andrew Jackson guaranteed "a full and entire pardon" to slaves who helped defend the city and promised a monetary and land bounty to those "sons of freedom"—or free blacks—who agreed to support the American cause. Jackson's proclamations ultimately denied to Cochrane another important source of much-needed manpower.[41]

Jean Lafitte and his Baratarian associates represented a third potential source of manpower that Cochrane wanted to employ during the Louisiana campaign. Based on the Island of Barataria to the south and west of New Orleans, this lawless group supplied slaves and other contraband goods to the settlers of Louisiana. They blatantly plundered foreign merchant ships, disregarded international neutrality laws, and violated American revenue laws. The U.S. government could do little to suppress their lawless activities. Cochrane seized on the idea that the Baratarians could provide assistance either by joining the British expedition or by remaining neutral, and in early September 1814 he sent Captain Nicholas Lockyer to meet with Jean Lafitte. For two days the two men discussed the prospects of an alliance in which the Baratarians would provide their assistance and knowledge, and in return the British would offer to protect and aid Lafitte and his associates in their struggle against the United States. Lafitte ultimately refused the British offer and instead chose to join the Americans, depriving Cochrane of an important source of manpower as well as vital information regarding the geography of the region.[42]

Unsuccessful in recruiting the Baratarians, Indians, or runaway slaves, Cochrane turned to the disaffected populations of Louisiana and Spanish Florida, whom he mistakenly thought were "very anxious to get rid of the

Americans." He had been led to believe that the disposition of the region's inhabitants toward Great Britain was "as various and as motley as" the population itself. He had been informed that the Spaniards supported their country and the French theirs, but both groups would work against the Americans. This suggestion convinced Cochrane that the expeditionary force might "find in the inhabitants a general and decided disposition to withdraw from their recent connexion [sic] with the United States." If he, indeed, found this attitude, Cochrane had instructions to secure both "their favour and co-operation," which would provide the British "the whole Province of Louisiana from the United States."[43]

Cochrane again encountered difficulty, as he did not find a population eager to assist his force. The September 1814 British and Indian invasion of Pensacola, Florida, provided a more realistic indication of what Cochrane might find in Louisiana. British commanders believed that the Spanish in Florida would appreciate and readily accept military support. Instead, they found that officials and citizens refused to cooperate or assist with preparations to defend the town. British forces responded by dealing harshly with merchants, citizens, and officials. They threatened to destroy the city, and they took with them slaves and the Spanish garrison without permission in November 1814 as they evacuated the city, which angered and alienated the people of Pensacola. When the Americans entered the city, Andrew Jackson made sure that Spanish citizens were treated fairly, which both surprised and pleased them. News of the American and British occupations and of the treatment of Spanish citizens, not surprisingly, found its way across the Gulf to New Orleans and helped create enmity and suspicion, driving Louisianans firmly into the American fold and again depriving Cochrane of another important source of support.[44]

Cochrane failed to gain the support he anticipated from the Indians, slaves, Baratarians, and discontented population, and without this help, he had to modify his operational plans. Initially, he had wanted to land troops at Pensacola or Mobile and proceed overland against New Orleans. But the failed September 1814 attack against Fort Bowyer (at the entrance of Mobile Bay) and loss of the frigate *Hermes,* combined with the November evacuation of Pensacola, left Cochrane with reduced options. British activities along the Gulf—especially Major Edward Nicolls's recruiting of slaves and Indians and fortification of Prospect Bluff on the Apalachicola River—had also frightened Americans in the region into acting. Cochrane's inability to secure the necessary small boats that he needed for the shallow waters of the Gulf of Mexico created still another problem. He had known for some time that he could not reduce New Orleans without shallow-draft vessels, and throughout the summer he had instructed his officers to collect all the small craft that they could; the Admiralty had also ordered twenty shallow-draft vessels be made available for the Louisiana expedition. But by December Cochrane admitted that he was still "deficient in Flat Boats or the means of transporting Troops into shallow water." Regardless of the setbacks, British operatives along the Gulf continued to offer rosy forecasts for the campaign, promising Cochrane "jam tomorrow, but never jam today."[45]

Cochrane had a personal interest in the southern campaign, but he also had to focus on the larger strategic picture. The conquest of New Orleans would relieve American pressure from Canada and also foment division within the United States. He had also outlined his plans to the Admiralty for the early months of 1815. Confident that New Orleans and the Gulf region would be subdued before the end of the year or shortly thereafter, Cochrane suggested in early October 1814 that some 6,000 troops should descend on the coast of Georgia and South Carolina. "Satisfied that these two states will be at our Mercy," he maintained that he could raise additional companies of Colonial Marines during the winter and by April "recommence our operations in the Chesapeake." He sent Admiral Cockburn to seize Cumberland Island off the south Georgia coast, harass coastal towns, and recruit slaves and Indians into his ranks. Cockburn's aggressive strike-and-retreat warfare—nothing more than a diversionary attack along the coast of Georgia and South Carolina—would stimulate and support Cochrane's operations in the Gulf while also satisfying his larger strategic objectives, ultimately permitting him to expand the swath of destruction that would bring the Americans to their knees.[46]

Some accounts of the disastrous New Orleans campaign hint that the operation represented an end in itself rather than the means to an end. But that was not the case. Throughout the fall of 1814, Cochrane had continued operations along the Atlantic, intensified the blockade of New England, and expanded the war to Georgia and South Carolina. The New Orleans campaign, which would relieve the pressure on Canada, represented but one more operation within his broader strategy of harassing the Americans until they begged for peace. In this instance New Orleans also offered important material and territorial possibilities. Regardless, the campaign against New Orleans failed for a variety of reasons, including the limitations of using Jamaica as a base, the nonarrival of the shallow-draft vessels needed to move and supply the army, the inability to recruit additional troops along the Gulf, as well as the loss of speed and surprise as Jackson received sufficient warning to halt a British land advance beside the Mississippi on January 8, 1815.[47]

The disillusionment shared by many of Cochrane's military counterparts did not seem to faze him. He encouraged General John Lambert, who assumed command of British forces after Pakenham's death, to renew the attack, and later sent a squadron of ships up the Mississippi River to bombard Fort St. Philip, hoping that its capitulation would open a water route to the city's doorstep. Neither succeeded. Doubtless Cochrane felt he had done his duty. His seamen had made extraordinary efforts to ensure that the army was placed on the east bank of the Mississippi River and to provide it with reinforcements, supplies, and artillery. At this point, the task of capturing the city rested solely with the soldiers, and they had failed—or so it must have seemed to Cochrane, who remained some distance from the problems of facing an army on a narrow front and strongly fortified with superior artillery. After the failed January 8, 1815, attack on the Plains of Chalmette and subsequent attack against Fort St. Philip, Cochrane focused on other operations in the Gulf, as well as off the coast of Georgia, South Carolina, and New England. In early February 1815, British forces captured Fort Bowyer at the entrance to Mobile Bay, which offered a foothold along the Gulf Coast from which the army could march overland against New Orleans. Before British forces could secure the city of Mobile, news arrived indicating that the British and American governments had concluded the Treaty of Ghent on December 24, 1814, and that the two governments had ratified the agreement.[48]

Cochrane's operations in the Gulf had yielded poor results, while those in New England paid considerable dividends. After intensifying the northeastern blockade in April 1814, Cochrane learned that Federalist leaders of the region were not committed to the war. Most had anticipated that the war would end shortly after the fall of Napoleon and liberation of France, and the European peace would permit them to continue their profitable trade with Nova Scotia. Instead, Cochrane tightened the blockade, instructing his commanders to exert just enough economic pressure to encourage New England neutrality, if not separatism. He also encouraged his officers to reach mutually advantageous understandings with local merchants and shipowners and to continue monitoring New England attitudes concerning the war. Meanwhile, Admiral Edward Griffith led a joint army-navy attack against Eastport and Castine, Maine, giving the British control of 100 miles of coastline as well as several coastal islands. The occupation of Maine also brought the offensive war of the Chesapeake north, prompting many to believe that the district would serve as a base of operations for continued coastal attacks throughout the region, which heightened American fears and fueled rumors of New England separation. Admirals Hotham and Griffith reported mixed signals from Rhode Island, plus confidential oral proposals—supposedly from Massachusetts—for a separate peace or at least for a discontinuance of hostilities. Those rumors gained credence between December 15, 1814 and January 5, 1815, when Federalist leaders convened in Hartford, Connecticut.[49]

Cochrane indicated on January 5, 1815, that he was willing to lift the blockade against all states that would separate themselves from the Union. He also hinted that he might relax the blockade if states simply withdrew from the conflict. Yet the results of the Hartford Convention did not meet Cochrane's expectations. The Convention had made no "irrevocable" step leading to disunion or separation, instead only listing their grievances and calling for a second meeting before June 1815. Those grievances would never be presented to President Madison or the federal government, and the Hartford Convention, unlike the victory at New Orleans, would quickly be overshadowed by news of the Treaty of Ghent. Cochrane had reason to feel that he had been robbed of another opportunity to weaken the United States. In fact, Codrington, who regretted the discreditable war and Britain's failure to give the Americans a drubbing "in the open," reported that Cochrane was "most amazingly cast down by this peace."[50]

The War of 1812 revived intense passions first generated during the American War of Independence, and echoed the overt anti-American passions of some British officers and politicians. Despite great animosity on both sides, the conclusion of the war settled none of the main differences between the two peoples, leaving many to believe that another conflict loomed on the horizon. David Milne, a strong critic of most things American, posited in May 1815 that, although peace with the United States was desirable, he believed that American naval power should be "nipt in the bud" or none of the British West Indies would be safe. Furthermore, if Cuba fell under American influence or control, he insisted that the United States would become a great naval power. Other British officers and politicians believed it inevitable that the United States would grow in overall strength. As early as the 1820s, Foreign Secretary George Canning was using U.S. mercantile and naval potential to persuade his reluctant colleagues to recognize the new Latin American republics and to secure British interests in the southern continent.[51]

The Admiralty, sufficiently impressed by the American naval threat, favored and at times even roughly achieved a three-power navy. And as in the days preceding the War of 1812, politicians, and naval and military officers contemplated the character of a forthcoming war with the United States. One of Lord Palmerston's responses at the time of a war scare with the United States in 1854 could have been lifted straight from Cochrane's papers forty years earlier. If the Americans resorted to privateering, he angrily remarked, Britain should "retaliate by burning all their Sea Coast Towns." The following year he argued even more vehemently that Americans were highly vulnerable in "their Slave States, and a British Force landed in the southern part of the Union, proclaiming freedom to the Blacks, would shake many of the stars from their banner." Admittedly, Palmerston often blustered but even the more tactful Foreign Secretary Lord Clarendon in 1856 referred to Americans as "that nation of pirates" who should be made to observe "the usages of civilised nations." Americans, too, also feared British naval raids for years to come. In the aftermath of the war, Congress appropriated money for a series of fortifications to be built along the Atlantic and across the Gulf of Mexico to prevent the depredations of the coast as had occurred during the War of 1812. As late as 1837, Secretary of War Joel R. Poinsett reported to the Senate the need for coastal defense, urging additional appropriations lest the United States again suffer from invasions and the uncivilized warfare perpetrated during the second war with Britain.[52]

The War of 1812 had been fought from different perspectives. The Americans had harkened back to the eighteenth century and based much of their expectations on lessons learned from their victory over the British during the War for Independence. American ideas, goals, and even weapons were, in fact, modeled on the anachronistic eighteenth century. Since the American War for Independence, the British had fought in the Netherlands, West Indies, India, Egypt, Portugal, and Spain, and by 1812 had incorporated new forms of unlimited warfare. They learned guerilla-style fighting from the Spanish, economic warfare and how to live off the land from the French, and even the destructive capabilities of a full-scale slave insurrection from events in Santo Domingo. During the North American war, they employed Indian allies who in instances showed Americans no quarter, even burning and killing those who surrendered to British officers. Moreover, Cochrane's forces along the Atlantic coast and in the Gulf of Mexico tried to break the Americans' will to fight by burning public and private property, looting, requisitioning livestock, and at Hampton, Virginia, even committing unauthorized rape and murder. This "species of milito-nautico-guerilla-plundering warfare," as Sir Harry Smith described the War of 1812 and Cochrane's campaign in North America, left an indelible mark on both sides of the Atlantic that would be remembered for years to come.[53]

Despite the losses and the accusations, the war changed British attitudes about their former colonies very little, as many Britons still viewed Americans as ungrateful degenerates who should be chastised and punished for their pretensions in any way possible. Not for them the ill-grounded euphoria and refurbishment of national character that caught hold in America. But British administrators thereafter admitted that in dealing with even the ramshackle American Republic, "half-measures would not succeed."[54] Although perceptions would change very slowly, never again would Britain so underestimate its overgrown offspring as to think it could be militarily subdued or politically overthrown by a mere campaign of terror and harassment.

Notes

1. Christopher D. Hall, *British Strategy in the Napoleonic War, 1803–1815* (Manchester, 1992), 196–97; Donald R. Hickey, *The War of 1812: A Forgotten Conflict* (Urbana, 1989), 304–5.

2. John Borlase Warren to Lord Melville, November 18, 1812, November 16, 1813, Warren Papers, National Maritime Museum, Greenwich.

3. James Stirling to Viscount Melville, March 17, 1813, James Stirling Memorandum, The Historic New Orleans Collection (hereinafter cited as THNOC); Henry Hotham Book of Remarks, 1813, Hotham Collection, DDHO 7/99, Brynmor Jones Library, University of Hull.

4. Brian Jenkins, *Henry Goulburn, 1784–1856: A Political Biography* (Montreal, 1996), 79–80; James Pack, *The Man Who Burned the White House: Admiral Sir George Cockburn, 1772–1853* (Emsworth, Hants, England, 1987), 171; Lord Bathurst to Lords Commissioners of the Admiralty, March 25, 1813, British Public Records Office, Admiralty Office Papers(hereinafter cited as PRO, ADM), 1/4223, Kew, England; Viscount Melville to Admiral Hope, November 13, 1812, Robert Saunders-Dundas Papers, National Maritime Museum, Greenwich.

5. Bathurst to Wellington, January 28, 1814, 2nd Duke of Wellington, *Supplementary Dispatches and Memoranda of the Duke of Wellington* (London, 1858–72), 8:547; John Gurwood, ed., *Dispatches of the Duke of Wellington: During His Various Campaigns in India, Denmark, Portugal, Spain, the Low Countries, and France, from 1799 to 1818* (London, 1835–38), 11:526; Jenkins, *Henry Goulburn*, 77–81.

6. For a brief overview of the naval war, see chapter 16 of G. J. Marcus, *The Age of Nelson: The Royal Navy, 1793–1815* (New York, 1971) or chapters 5–7 of Wade G. Dudley, *Splintering the Wooden Wall: The British Blockade of the United States, 1812–1815* (Annapolis, 2003). The Alexander F. I. Cochrane Papers (hereinafter cited as CP), National Library of Scotland, Edinburgh, include copies of Admiralty letters to Warren with implicit and explicit criticism of his conduct; MS 2340, fos.

37–42, 46, 75–76. For the navy and the war in 1813, see William S. Dudley, *The Naval War of 1812: A Documentary History,* vol. 2 (Washington, D.C., 1992).

7. Cochrane to Cockburn, April 24, 28, 1814, and Cochrane to Melville, March 10, 1814, CP; Pack, *The Man Who Burned the White House,* 166–67; Historical Manuscripts Commission (hereinafter cited as HMC), *Report on the Manuscripts of Col. David Milne Home* (London, 1902), 160–61; Lady Bourchier, ed., *Memoir of the Life of Admiral Sir Edward Codrington* (London, 1875), 1:310–13. Note General Sir Henry Smith's comment that the Americans, with some notable exceptions, were "not accustomed to the civility of war, like our old associates, the French." See G. C. Moore Smith, ed., *The Autobiography of Lieutenant-General Sir Henry Smith* (London, 1901), 240.

8. Marcus, *Age of Nelson,* 203. See CP, MS 2316, fos. 180–84, 187–90; MS 2318, fos. 43–44; MS 2572, fos. 155–56.

9. Pack, *The Man Who Burned the White House,* 166; Bourchier, *Memoir of Edward Codrington,* 1:321, 333.

10. Kenneth Bourne, *Britain and the Balance of Power in North America, 1815–1908* (London, 1967), 48.

11. See correspondence in CP, MS 2348, fos. 7–9; MS 2330, fos. 21–26, 32.

12. See 1814 correspondence of the admiral in Halifax, CP, MS 2327, fos. 11, 42, 68, and CP, MS 2348, fos. 7–8.

13. Pack, *The Man Who Burned the White House,* chaps. 11–14; Cockburn to Cochrane, June 25, 1814, CP; HMC, *Milne Home MSS,* 61–63.

14. For correspondence, see CP, MS 2326, fos. 188, 270–71; Melville to Cochrane, October 14, 1814, CP.

15. For more detail, see Marcus, *Age of Nelson,* 456–59, and Dudley, *Splintering the Wooden Walls,* 81–85.

16. See CP, MS 2345, fos. 2–5, 10; MS 2326 fos. 106–7, 180–81; MS 2348, fos. 89–91; MS 2349, fos. 185–86; MS 2574, fos. 89–90, 101–2; see also Reginald Horsman, *The War of 1812* (London, 1969), 144–45.

17. Robin F. A. Fabel, "The Laws of War in the 1812 Conflict," *Journal of American Studies* 14 (1980): 199–200; Hickey, *The War of 1812,* 129–30; J.C.A. Stagg, *Mr. Madison's War: Politics, Diplomacy, and Warfare in the Early American Republic, 1783–1830* (Princeton, 1983), 407–8.

18. C. J. Bartlett, "Gentlemen versus Democrats: Cultural Prejudice and Military Strategy in Britain in the War of 1812," *War in History* 1 (1994): 143–50, 153–54; Proclamation of the Earl of Dunmore, November 7, 1775, Tracy W. McGregor Library, Albert and Shirley Small Special Collections Library, University of Virginia Library; *Annual Register 1814,* 318; William Lovell, *Personal Narrative of Events, 1799–1815* (London, 1979), 167–71, 190; Thomas M. Hardy to John Borlase Warren, June 26, 1813, PRO, ADM 1/504, 51–53, and Warren to John W. Croker, July 22, 1813, PRO ADM 1/504, 49, both copies are in Dudley, *Naval War of 1812: A Documentary History,* 2:162–63.

19. James Scott, *Recollections of a Naval Life* (London, 1834), 3:122 ff., 158–60; *Connecticut Mirror,* August 9, 1813.

20. Scott, 3:122–23.

21. Ibid., 3:129–36.

22. Frederic Chamier, *The Life of a Sailor* (London, 1833), 2:110–11, 114–22; Alistair J. Nichols, "'Desperate Banditti'? The Independent Companies of Foreigners," *Journal of the Society for Army Historical Research* 79 (2001): 283–84; Sydney Beckwith to John Borlase Warren, July 5, 1813, ADM 1/504, 45–46.

23. Chamier, 2:112–15; Adam Smith, *The Wealth of Nations* (London, 1966), 872, 878; George R. Gleig, *An Officer: A Narrative of the Campaigns of the British Army at Washington and New Orleans* (London, 1821), 374–77. Note also Gleig Papers, National Library of Scotland, Edinburgh, with letters recording his experiences in the war in America, MS 3869.

24. Cochrane to Melville, March 10, 1814, CP, MS 2345, fo. 1 ff.; Cochrane to Cockburn, April 28, 1814, CP, MS 2349, fo. 30; HMC, *Milne Home MSS,* 165; Bourchier, *Memoir of Codrington,* 1:313; Roger Morriss, *Cockburn and the British Navy in Transition: Admiral Sir George Cockburn, 1772–1853* (Columbia, S.C., 1997), 91–93.

25. Moore Smith, ed., *Autobiography of Smith,* 201–2; Colonel Arthur Brooke American War Journal, 1814–15, August 30, 1814, Brookenborough Papers, D/3004/D/2, Ulster American Folk Park, Omagh, Northern Ireland; Fabel, "The Laws of War in the 1812 Conflict," 210.

26. *Niles' Weekly Register,* May 15, 1813, 182; 4:5, January 8, 1814, 5:312; June 25, 1814, 6:279; May 22, 1813, 4:196; Pack, *The Man Who Burned the White House,* 155; Marcus, *Age of Nelson,* 42; Geoffrey Francis Andrew Best, *Humanity in Warfare* (London, 1980), 111–12.

27. Draft by Cochrane, ca. April 27–28, 1812, CP, 2574, fo. 3; Cochrane to Melville, July 17, 1814, CP 2345, fo. 13; Dudley, *Splintering the Wooden Wall,* 118–19; Morriss, *Cockburn and the British Navy in Transition,* 96–99.

28. Warren to John W. Coker, May 28, 1813, PRO ADM 1/503, 278–80; Robert Barrie to Warren, November 14, 1813, PRO ADM 1/505, 66–67; Cochrane's Proclamation, April 2, 1814, PRO ADM 1/508, 579; Alexander Cochrane, *The Fighting Cochranes: A Scottish Clan over Six Hundred Years of Naval and Military History* (London, 1983), 255; Cochrane to Cockburn, April 29, 1814, CP, MS 2349, fo. 29.

29. Earl Bathurst to Sydney Beckwith, March 20, 1813, CP, MS 2326, fos. 3–10; copy in CP, MS 2326, fo. 233, and Dudley, *Naval War of 1812,* 2:325–26; Frank A. Cassell, "Slaves of the Chesapeake Bay Area and the War of 1812," *Journal of Negro History* 57 (1972): 145.

30. Goulburn to Crocker, January 19, 1814, copy in CP, MS 2342, fos. 63–66; Melville to Cochrane, August 10, 1814, CP, MS 2574, fos. 169–70; Bathurst to Cochrane, October 26, 1814, CP, MS 2327, fo. 260; Cochrane to Bathurst, July 14, 1814, PRO WO 1/141.

31. Robert Barrie to Warren, November 14, 1813, PRO ADM 1/505, 66–67; Cochrane's Proclamation, April 2, 1814, PRO ADM 1/508, 579; Cochrane to Cockburn, April 29, 1814, CP, MS 2349, fo. 29.

32. Cockburn wrote a series of letters to Cochrane between April 2 and June 25, 1814, CP, MS 2574, fos. 99–139; MS 2333, fos. 18–138; Morriss, *Cockburn and the British Navy in Transition*, 98–99; RM 7/7/13 Order Book, October 25, 1814, Royal Engineers Museum, Swansea; Charles B. H. Ross to Cockburn, May 29, 1814, PRO ADM 1/507, 68–70; Scott, *Recollections*, 3:115, 120–21.

33. Cockburn to Cochrane, May 10, 1814, CP, MS 2574, fo. 103; Cassell, "Slaves in the War of 1812," 153; Sally Hadden, *Slave Patrols: Law and Violence in Virginia and the Carolinas* (Cambridge, Mass., 2001), 162–63. Cockburn wrote a series of letters to Cochrane between April 2 and June 25, 1814, CP, MS 2574, fos. 99–139; MS 2333, fos. 18–138.

34. Robert Barrie to Cockburn, June 19, 1814, PRO ADM 1/507, 81–86; Cockburn to Cochrane, May 10, 1814, CP, MS 2574, fo. 103; Cockburn to Cochrane, June 25, 1814, CP, MS 2574, fo. 135; Scott, *Recollections*, 3:253–64; Christopher T. George, *Terror on the Chesapeake: The War of 1812 on the Bay* (Shippensburg, Pa., 2000), 80.

35. John P. Hungerford to James Barbour, August 5, 1814, *Calendar Virginia State Papers and Other Manuscripts from January 1, 1808 to December 1, 1835; Preserved in the Capital, at Richmond* (Richmond, 1892) 10:367; Cochrane to Cockburn, July 1, 1814, CP, MS 2346; Cockburn to Cochrane, June 25, 1814, CP, MS 2574, fo. 135; Cockburn to Robert Barrie, June 26, 1814, Barrie Papers, William L. Clements Library, Ann Arbor, Michigan; Morriss, *Cockburn and the British Navy in Transition*, 100–102; Keith S. Dent, *The British Navy and the Anglo-American War of 1812 to 1815* (M.A. thesis, University of Leeds, 1949), 326.

36. Morriss, *Cockburn and the British Navy in Transition*, 100–102; George, *Terror on the Chesapeake*, 81; Gleig, *Narrative of the Campaigns of the British Army at Washington and New Orleans*, 148.

37. Contemporary critics of the British burning of Washington included some of the service personnel who took part as well as a number of members of Parliament: See T. C. Hansard, ed., *Parliamentary Debates from the Year 1803 to the Present Time*, vol. 29, November 8, 1813, columns 16–18, 34–40, 70–73, 75. Whitbread, the most outspoken critic of the American war, railed that the conflict was "abhorrent to every principle of legitimate warfare." He also condemned the burning of Washington, remarking, "We had done what the Goths refused to do at Rome." The best accounts of the Chesapeake campaign are George, *Terror on the Chesapeake;* Anthony S. Pitch, *The Burning of Washington: The British Invasion of 1814* (Annapolis, Md., 1998); and Joseph A. Whitehorne, *The Battle for Baltimore, 1814* (Baltimore, 1997). For an abbreviated account of the campaign, see Mahon, *War of 1812*, 289–316, and Hickey, *War of 1812*, 195–204.

38. Melville to Cochrane, May 22, 1814, CP, MS 2574, fos. 130–31; Dudley, *Splintering the Wooden Wall*, 115–19.

39. Cochrane to Melville, March 10, 1814, CP, MS 2345, fos. 1–5; Cochrane's Observations to Lord Melville Relative to America, 1814, War of 1812 MSS, Lilly Library, Indiana University, Bloomington; Lord Melville to William Domett, July 23, 1814, and Domett to Melville, July 26, 1814, both in Melville Castle Muniments, GD 51/2/523/1–2, National Archives of Scotland, Edinburgh; John Wilson Croker to Alexander Cochrane, August 10, 1814, PRO, WO 1/141, 15–24.

40. John K. Mahon, "British Strategy and Southern Indians: War of 1812," *Florida Historical Quarterly* 44 (April 1966): 287–98; John Sugden, "The Southern Indians in the War of 1812: The Closing Phase," *Florida Historical Quarterly* 60 (1982): 273 ff.; George Woodbine to Cochrane, July 25, 1814, CP, MSS 2328. The British support for and attempt to recruit southern Indian during the conflict is recounted in Frank L. Owsley Jr., *Struggle for the Gulf Borderland: The Creek War and the Battle of New Orleans, 1812–1815* (Gainesville, 1981)—pages 98–102 detail Cochrane's plans to use Indians during the New Orleans campaign—and in Claudio Saunt, *A New Order of Things: Property, Power, and the Transformation of the Creek Indians, 1733–1816* (Cambridge, 1999), 273–90.

41. Cochrane to Bathurst, July 14, 1814, PRO, WO 1/141; George Woodbine to Hugh Pigot, May 25, 28, 1814, and Edward Nicolls to Cochrane, August 12, 1814, CP, MS 2328; Arsène Lacarrière Latour, *Historical Memoir of the War in West and Louisiana in 1814–15, with an Atlas,* ed. Gene A. Smith (1816; reprint, Gainesville, 1999), 149, 205–6.

42. Jane Lucas DeGrummond, *The Baratarians and the Battle of New Orleans* (Baton Rouge: Louisiana State University Press, 1961), 37–48; Nicolls to Cochrane, July 27, 1814, CP, MS 2328; Arthur P. Hayne to Inspector General Office, Seventh Military District, September 17, 1814, Butler Family Papers, HNOC; Owsley, *Struggle for the Gulf,* 109–12; Edward Nicolls to Monsieur Lafitte, August 31, 1814, and William H. Percy to Monsieur Lafitte, September 1, 1814, both in the Edward Nicolls and William H. Percy Letters, THNOC; Latour, *Historical Memoir,* 25–29.

43. Edward Nicolls to Cochrane, July 27, August 12, 1814, CP, MS 2328; Bathurst to Robert Ross, September 6, 1814, PRO, WO 6/2, 9–13; Benson J. Lossing, *Pictorial Field-Book of the War of 1812* (New York, 1869), 1026.

44. John Innerarity to James Innerarity, November 7, 1814, "Letters of John Innerarity," *Florida Historical Quarterly* 9 (1931): 127–30; Vincente de Ordozgoitti to Juan Ruiz Apodaca, September 21, 1814, Archivo General de Indies, Cuba, legajo 1856; James Gordon to Cochrane, November 18, 1814, PRO, ADM 1/505; Frank L. Owsley Jr., "British and Indian Activities in Spanish West Florida during the War of 1812," *Florida Historical Quarterly* 46 (1967): 119–20.

45. Nicolls to Cochrane, August 12, 1814, CP, MS 2328; Cochrane to Hugh Pigot, June 9, 1814, Cochrane Papers, MS 2346; Edward Codrington to Mrs. Edward Codrington, June 7, 1814, Sir Edward Codrington Papers, COD/7/1, National Maritime Museum, Greenwich; Cochrane to Admiralty, October 3, 1814, CP, MS 2348, fos. 86–87.

46. Cochrane to Admiralty, October 3, 1814, CP, MS 2348, fos. 86–87; Cochrane to Nicolls, December 3, 1814, CP, MS 2346, fos. 16–17; see also MS 2349, fos. 214–16, 252–53; Cochrane to Cockburn, January 5, 1815, CP, MS 2349, fo. 234.

47. Owsley, *Struggle for the Gulf Borderlands*, 96–101; Robin Reilly, *The British at the Gates: The New Orleans Campaign in the War of 1812* (New York, 1974), 161–64; Hickey, *The War of 1812*, 204–5.

48. J. Leitch Wright Jr., *Britain and the American Frontier, 1783–1815* (Athens, Ga., 1975), 179–81; Hickey, *The War of 1812*, 212–13.

49. Robert Aitchison Memoir, 56–58, HNOC; Stagg, *Mr. Madison's War*, 469–80; Cochrane to the Judge of the Vice-Admiralty Court, October 3, 1814, CP, MS 2349, fos. 185–86; MS 2332, fos. 88–97 and Griffith to Cochrane, November 10, 1814, CP, MS 2574, fos. 148–51.

50. Cochrane to Griffith, January 5, 1815, CP, MS 2346, fos. 19–20; Bourchier, *Memoir of Codrington*, 1:340.

51. HMC, *Milne Home MSS*, 168; C. J. Bartlett, *Great Britain and Sea Power, 1815–53* (Oxford, 1963), 70–71; Wendy Hinde, *George Canning* (London, 1973), 352–53.

52. Bartlett, *Great Britain and Sea Power*, 71, 125, 214–15, 274–76; Martin Papers, British Library, London, Additional MS 41410, fos. 50–124; W. N. Medlicott, Kenneth Bourne, and Donald Cameron Watt, eds., *Studies in International History* (London, 1967), 150, 155, 166.

53. Fabel, "The Laws of War in the 1812 Conflict," 217–18; Moore Smith, ed., *Autobiography of Smith*, 200–201.

54. Bradford Perkins, *The Creation of an American Republic, 1776–1865*, vol. 1 of *The Cambridge History of American Foreign Relations* (Cambridge, 1993), 146.

8

Experiencing the War of 1812

Michael A. Bellesiles

The War of 1812 holds a special place in American history. Some of the nation's most powerful national icons emerged from this conflict: the national anthem and the glorification of "Old Glory," Jackson at New Orleans and Perry at Lake Erie. The war created a generation of national leaders: Andrew Jackson, William Henry Harrison, Richard M. Johnson, and Winfield Scott. Yet the war itself is rarely discussed, except within terms of these national symbols. Almost completely forgotten is the humiliation of the burning of the nation's capital and the generally abysmal performance of U.S. forces against smaller British contingents. To avoid explaining the disasters, historians often focus on the same set of iconic stories. Even defeats, such as the militia's refusal to cross over into Canada to aid American troops pinned down by British regulars, are translated into principled actions in defense of Constitutional interpretation. Public memories become an invented tradition of heroism, while source documents from the war evidence a very different set of experiences.

The veterans of the War of 1812 found little worth reporting or remembering.[1] Where those who had served in the American Revolution, no matter how briefly, could always find meaning in their service,[2] the experience of war in the years 1811–14 seemed meaningless and boring. This variation in the structure of the experience of warfare does not mean that the War of 1812 was in some way even more pointless and dull than other wars; rather, it is to suggest that those who served during the War of 1812 seldom succeeded in placing that conflict in any sort of coherent narrative. The vast majority of those who served in the War of 1812 had no idea why the United States was at war with England or what the goal of their service in that war might have been, nor could they make much sense of their sacrifices. In this regard, it was a war like no other in American history, a war without meaning or even usable rhetoric.

It is easy to understand how common soldiers could not quite grasp the meaning of the war they were fighting, for few contemporaries did. President James Madison attempted to explain the war to the American people in his war message. But it was a confusing statement, mixing together the impressment of sailors, the violation of neutral rights, and affronts to national honor. Madison referred to "the complicated and transcendent injustice" of British policy and the "crying enormity" of impressment, under which "thousands of American citizens . . . have been torn from their country and from everything dear to them."[3] Yet it has often been pointed out that those areas most directly touched by the impressment crisis, the eastern seaports, were least supportive of the war.[4] And since Britain's legal backing for impressment, the notorious Orders in Council, had been revoked in response to American diplomatic efforts prior to the declaration of war, many Americans must have been sincerely puzzled by Madison's retaining this justification for war.

Madison had not yet learned of the revocation of the Orders in Council when he called on Congress to declare war, but the news reached the United States soon enough for Congress to have saved everyone a lot of embarrassment and trouble by not voting for war or by proclaiming a bloodless victory and declaring peace. Yet congressional Republicans quickly squashed Federalist proposals in favor of peace and did their best to justify the war on other grounds, confusing both their constituents and later historians.[5] Among the reasons coherently presented by congressional supporters for the declaration of war were the impressment of sailors, the Orders of Council disrupting the American economy, British interference with American commerce, British affronts to American national honor, the arming and inciting of the western Indians, the assumption that Britain sought to reclaim the United States for its empire, the certain conquest of Canada by the Americans in the event of war, the promotion of American economic development, national unity, and the chance to match the accomplishments of "The Fathers."[6]

The alternative causalities often contradicted one another, especially when the conquest of Canada was given as or denied as a goal of the war. John Randolph, an arch opponent of the war, dismissed it from the start as "a war of conquest, a war for the acquisition of territory" unsuited to a republican government.[7] William R. King of North Carolina denied that "this will be a war of aggrandizement, a war of conquest. I am as little disposed to extend the territory [of the United States] as any other individual in this House." However, "I trust if our differences with Great Britain are not speedily adjusted, (of which, indeed, I have no expectation,) we shall take Canada. Yes, sir, by force."[8] Having denied an intention to conquer Canada, King and his fellow Republicans gloried in the certainty of it. Ronald L. Hatzenbuehler and Robert L. Ivie have argued that the declaration of war was delayed because the Republicans could not figure out how to justify it.[9] Put another way, the Republicans knew that they wanted a war with Britain, but they were just not sure why.

Further muddying the patriotic waters was the fact that thousands of Americans opposed the war from its start. This confusion over causality and loyal dissent from the war became evident when President Madison called for a day of prayer. Many ministers, including those who reluctantly supported the war effort once it was declared, thought that the nation's sins had brought on the conflict and that the only resulting good would be a realization of that fallen state.[10] Even several of those speaking in support of the war, such as Hosea Ballou in Portsmouth, New Hampshire, maintained that the war had resulted from the sins of both the United States and Great Britain.[11] Some ministers remained bluntly opposed to the war even after battle was joined with the British. In the second year of the war, Benjamin Bell called it "unnecessary, impolitic and unjust" and prayed for an end to this "murderous war."[12] The Reverend Jacob Catlin reminded his congregation that those who live by the sword shall die by the sword—hardly words tending to encourage enlistments.[13] On occasion, ministers delivered antiwar sermons to the troops. The Reverend James Flint called on the Massachusetts troops to give thanks that they were not being led by "some cowardly minion of President Madison, into the wilds of Canada, there to perish by disease, or to whiten the plains of battle with your bones."[14]

In addition to sermons, there were dozens of political speeches and pamphlets attacking the war. The most common charge was that Madison declared a war without cause for political purposes. John Lowell accused Madison of intending to use the war to establish "an Immense Standing Army."[15] For others, it was obvious that the war's true purpose was either the conquest of Canada for the benefit of western land speculators or an effort to fix the Republicans firmly in power.[16] Many Republicans and Federalists joined together in 1812 to support the antiwar candidacy of DeWitt Clinton. As a meeting of the York County Republicans stated, "Because [President Madison] has precepitately [sic] and rashly urged Congress to declare war at a time when the country was unprepared with the means of carrying it to success," and as "the inauspicious circumstances under which the war was commenced and the weakness with which it has thus far been conducted furnish no flattering pre-sage that the same councils will bring it to a speedy and honorable termination," they felt that Madison should be replaced as president. Several politicians who had supported the war, such as Representative Joseph Lefever of Pennsylvania, came out in opposition to Madison by late summer.[17] Madison's reelection victory in 1812 was narrow enough—128 electoral votes to 89 for Clinton—that if Pennsylvania had gone the other way, Clinton would have been elected.[18] From its first few months, then, the War of 1812 was broadly opposed and bitterly resented.

Given this lack of unity and a cohesive sense of purpose, it is little wonder that soldiers then and later had difficulty structuring their experiences. Soldiers in the American Revolution had consistently framed their war as a battle for independence or freedom, or seen it as a struggle against a tyrant intent on enslaving them. In the War of 1812, few common soldiers recorded any reason for the war; they served from a sense of duty or for the money.

What makes this lack of a coherent vision for the war most mysterious is the long certainty that there would be a war. Most political leaders, even those living in the far west, saw war with Britain as probable for at least five years prior to its declaration. In 1807 Governor William Hull of Michigan Territory wrote Secretary of War Henry Dearborn that "differences with England will not be settled, . . . [and] war will be the consequence."[19] Similar sentiments were expressed regularly until 1812.[20] As early as 1807, President Thomas Jefferson suggested that Governor Hull begin planning an invasion of Canada.[21]

Yet the U.S. government made almost no preparation for this widely expected war.[22] Many contemporaries saw this flaw clearly, but their objections were ignored for ideological reasons. In the current popular imagination, early America enjoyed the protection of a vigilant militia that rushed forth to defend the nation's liberty at a moment's notice. In the last twenty years, historians of the American Revolution have debated and largely derided that model.[23] Yet little attention has been paid to the new nation's first sustained military conflict, the War of 1812, which shows beyond doubt the fallacy of this ideological reliance.[24] It was an article of faith among most Jeffersonian Republicans in the years leading up to the war with Britain that the American militia would just spring into martial glory as if by magic, defeat the Indians and British, and conquer Canada. Thus when President Jefferson suggested that Governor Hull prepare for the invasion of Canada, he spoke entirely in terms of the local militia.[25]

Jefferson's government had made one concession toward preparing the militia for battle. In 1808 Congress passed an act to arm the militia, making the largest single appropriation of the government, $200,000 per year to buy arms for the militia. However, it took decades for this program to become fully operational, by which time all but a few states had accepted the lesson of the War of 1812 and abandoned their militia. Nonetheless, the federal government was able to provide a few thousand firearms to the state militia by 1812, but little else, and many of those most knowledgeable of the militia warned that the nation's defense leaned on a weak staff.[26] Once the war started, Britain fielded a small but professional army, while the United States relied on amateurs. Within a few weeks of the war's official beginning, it was evident to anyone with military experience that the United States had made an enormous error in putting all its eggs into a basket borne by militia.[27]

Those living on the most exposed frontiers of Ohio and the territories of Indiana and Michigan knew that the militia offered thin defensive cover and absolutely no offensive capacity at all. Ohio's two senators, Thomas Worthington and Alexander Campbell, both opposed the war (though Campbell missed the vote), largely because they thought their region defenseless and warned that Britain could conquer the Ohio River valley.[28] As word of Tecumseh's organization of the region's Indians reached Governor Hull of Michigan Territory in 1810, he wrote the War Department that Michigan was defenseless. Even after the victory at Tippecanoe, Acting Governor Reuben Attwater told the War Department that the Territory would fall to the Indians without the aid of federal troops.[29] In December 1811 the Detroit Committee of Public Safety begged for federal troops.[30] By March 1812 Hull was warning the government that not only could they not expect the western militia to launch any offensive operations but that the British could easily conquer Michigan in the event of war.[31] With only 119 federal troops in the territory, Hull had no doubt but that the British would crush them; this longtime Jeffersonian abandoned his faith in the militia at the first occasion of its use.[32] This was a definite case of cognitive dissonance; even while the country moved inexorably toward a war to be fought by militia, the federal government was receiving assurances that defensive operations would end in disaster without regulars. Instead of acting, the War Department reassured Attwater with a peculiar double negative: the defense of the frontier "has not been unattended to."[33]

The United States behaved like a somnolent warrior, unwilling to move. Secretary of War William Eustis's first letter to General Hull on June 18, 1812, which was sent by special messenger, did not mention the recent declaration of war; a second letter, informing the commanding general in the west that the country was at war, was sent through the regular mail. The British thus learned of the war eight days sooner than did Hull.[34] General

Dearborn began his invasion of Canada from Lake Champlain with an army of 7,000. But despite his orders "not to lose a moment in attacking the British posts in his front,"[35] he procrastinated for months, losing 2,000 militia as their enlistments ran out. When he finally moved on November 16, he surrounded a British blockhouse, allowing the enemy to escape by not posting adequate guards and then "enjoyed a brief half-hour's contest with some New York militia, coming from another direction, before finding out the mistake."[36] After this action against his own forces, and faced with the refusal of most of his militia to enter Canada, Dearborn abandoned the campaign and retreated to winter quarters.[37] It is little wonder that so many soldiers wrote of those in charge with contempt.

By the end of 1812, most rational observers agreed with the editor of the *National Intelligencer:* "Every day's experience tends to force on our minds a conviction that we are unwilling to receive, that the volunteer militia are not precisely the species of force on which to rely for carrying on war, however competent they may be to repel invasion."[38] Some members of the militia attempted to defend their performance—after the war. But even then, most would not bother. The militia and regular troops agreed on many particulars, including the inability of their officers. But what stands out most in all their personal accounts is the tedium of their experience.

As far as the average soldier is concerned, most wars consist of the same basic components of boredom and repetitious dull routine. But compared with the American Revolution or the Mexican War or the Civil War, the War of 1812 took on an almost deadly ennui because few common soldiers could put these experiences into any larger context. Based primarily on sources from the northern part of the United States, it appears that the common soldier could not make the routine take on some sort of transcendent meaning. Memoirs of the American Revolution, even by privates, spoke of "services faithfully and truly performed in his country's defense in the war of Revolution,"[39] of spirited pursuits of the enemy who "charged upon us, and we repulsed them and continued our attack" even though "the British light horse charged upon us twice more,"[40] and vivid memories of dramatic moments, as when one "heard the voice of Colonel Warner, like thunder, 'Fix bayonets. Charge.'"[41] Most of the diaries and memoirs from the War of 1812 can be summarized as marching, mud, and, in the words of Captain Daniel Cushing, "This day nothing new."[42]

For those involved, even the more heroic moments of the war rarely rise above the mundane. The successful defense of Fort Meigs is especially significant in this regard because of the large number of diaries, letters, and memoirs associated with this action. A major concern of those stationed at Fort Meigs, as elsewhere, was filth. Most of the militia and volunteers had no experience of camp life, of living with large numbers of men. After repeated exhortations to cleanliness had been ignored, General William Henry Harrison found it necessary to order, "Anyone found easing himself or emptying his filth in violation of these orders" had to clean up the camp's filth for a week.[43] Harrison also made each officer responsible for seeing "that his men are clean and properly dressed, . . . that his mens Quarters are clean, . . . [and] that all the men are at their Quarters at the beating of Tattoo."[44]

Alternating with boredom were periods of heightened tension that often led nowhere. "Gen. Harrison gave notice this evening that he expected to be attacked every night," although days and then weeks passed without action. States of constant alert like this could make the men very nervous. On one occasion a group of sixteen men were sent out from Fort Meigs "to lie in ambush for Indians." Around 9 p.m., the officer in charge "ordered the men to fire in the bushes, saying, 'There are Indians, There are Indians,' and pointing to the place. The men obeyed. . . . The flash of the guns was seen and the reports heard in our camp, which caused alarm. Immediately the drums beat 'To arms' and every man who could lift his musket was on parade in ten minutes, although a greater part were in bunk [ill], but it soon proved to be a false alarm and all returned to bed."[45]

False alarms were a constant occurrence. A night's sleep could be interrupted by the troops rushing to arms after "One of the sentinels shot a horse last night supposing it to be an Indian."[46] In September 1812, Harrison's army was called to arms nearly every day by nervous sentinels firing their guns at what they took to be enemy troops as they edged their way toward the relief of Fort Wayne.[47] Only once was there an actual reason for an alarm: a single Indian was wounded by the sentinels, who "got his gun and blanket." When this relief party arrived at Fort Wayne, they learned that the captain had wanted to surrender, but was overruled by the lieutenant. The relief party could find no Indians, and the captain resigned in disgrace. And still the sentinels persisted in firing their guns in alarm. On one of these occasions, "we formed in order of battle for half an hour, during which time it rained very hard, and rendered many of our guns unfit to do execution, except the bayonets."[48] In General Edward Tupper's command, "One of the sentinels of the bullock guard discharged the contents of his gun at an Indian, as he thought, . . . deserted the bullocks, and retreated to camp. A party was immediately sent in pursuit of the Indians, and behold! they found Michael Paul cutting a bee tree."[49] These alarms, as one journal recorded, "seemed to shake the boasted valor of some of our bravest he-roes."[50] But the opposite case was potentially even more dangerous, taking the alarms for granted. "At dark we heard a gun fire at the general Camp but a thing so often Repeated could not alarm us anymore."[51]

Sometimes the alarm guns were real, though the ensuing actions could be less than epic. Fort Meigs was besieged three times in 1813. Participants recorded some rather unsatisfying battles. "This day employed in mounting one eighteen pounder and three twelve pounders. This evening we fired . . . a point blank shot; owing to the bad state the cannon was in and not having a full charge of powder for that distance, the ball fell short, striking the side of the hill, bounded, pitched into the house and stopped." Several of the soldiers were surprised at how little damage occurred during long ex-changes of fire in which "the bullets flew all around us." [52] Another soldier wrote that the fire from the enemy was "as thick as hail," yet by the end of the day "we sustained but little injury . . . having but one or two men killed, and five or six wounded."[53] At the third British attack on Fort Meigs, "They have been firing into our camp five days and have not killed one man yet."[54] The British left after seven days without having killed any Americans, ex-cept those in the initial ambush. It was safe inside the fort, so long as their commander did not foolishly surrender as Hull had at Detroit, leading to the only deaths in the campaign when Indians killed some of the prisoners.[55] Otherwise, it was a very boring business serving in the American army in the War of 1812.

Soldiers sought a number of entertainments to relieve the boredom of camp life. Most of these involved drinking. Officers and enlisted men alike got drunk regularly. The usual way of dealing with drunken soldiers was to throw them in the river. "Three men put into the river for getting drunk and fighting in their tents, took a bathing and returned to duty." Three days later, they "Put two men in the river for getting drunk." These regular dunkings worked fine until Christmas 1812 when "the devil got into the soldiers," and the sober officers could barely maintain control of the camp. Despite these problems, officers continued to supply alcohol to the rank and file, as there were few other positive incentives available. "The soldiers were indulged this day, having been very much fatigued the last three days. They took great liberties, visited the towns, got drunk, quarreled and fought. Two or three got whipped and complaint came to me."[56]

By November 1813, General Harrison was ordering that "If any man is discovered in a state of intoxication besides the proper punishment for his offence, the Commanding officer shall endeavor to discover the person who enabled him to become intoxicated and report his name . . . for his punishment." This effort to punish the supplier proved insufficient, leading Harrison to add, "The distillation of grain in the present state of the Country cannot be permitted." Despite these efforts to control the flow of alcohol, within a month an officer at Fort Meigs was complaining, "The relaxation of Military discipline and irregularity exhibited by the troops at this post must be ascribed to the unrestrained use of Spirituous liquors." Drunkenness among the ranks occasioned all sorts of misconduct and dangerous behavior, such as the unauthorized "discharge of firearms." As Harrison wrote in general orders for his army, "The General receives almost hourly complaints of the Depredation and improper conduct of the men." Lieutenant John Henderson became so drunk that he claimed command of the fort. Yet as long as no harm was done, such a miscreant could expect to be "released from arrest & resume his sword."[57] On another occasion a Lieutenant Jackson struck Lieutenant Jacob Smith with a stick. The court-martial found Jackson "guilty" but "acquitted [him] honourably." Harrison intervened, "believing that the acquittal and condemnation of a Prisoner in the same sentence is a novelty in the proceedings of a Courts Martial." He dissolved the court and ordered a new court-martial with officers who did not know Jackson.[58]

Such drinking fits in with an atmosphere of general boredom and fatigue. Occasionally the loneliness and homesickness could overwhelm a soldier. After not receiving a letter for weeks, one soldier caught in a particularly tedious camp wrote his wife, "i do some times think you have for got me or do not care any more about me."[59] Such anxieties were heightened by the constant uncertainty of the location of the British and Indians. Under some commanders, such as Harrison and Jackson, they spent a great deal of time marching about trying to find their enemy; under others, such as Dearborn and Winchester, they marched about trying to avoid them. Diaries elaborate on the theme of seemingly ceaseless marching: "[We] marched four miles, our two wagons . . . both got stuck in the mud and could not move any farther that night. Rained very hard, became very dark, no tent, no fire, nothing to make fire with, hemmed in with a very steep hill on one side and a very wet and muddy bottom on the other." Captain Cushing wondered if it could get worse; he discovered that it could. "It continued raining until about two o'clock that night, then began to snow very fast." The following day's march was limited to a quarter mile. Three weeks later the same units "moved on through the worst piece of road I ever traveled, up to our knees in mud and water almost every step." Settling down in one place did not improve matters: "Our camp is overwhelmed with mud and water; my eyes never saw such a place for mankind to live in."[60] As a private in the Kentucky volunteers put it, "It rained most of the time, which made it disagreeable travelling and encamping. These hardships tended a little to quench the excessive patriotic flame that had blazed so conspicuously at the different musters and barbecues."[61] An Indiana recruit's diary was dominated by bad weather: "it Began to Rain. we ware Dismisst it Rained hard till sunset. . . . it stopt Raining and Began to Snow and Blow hard. . . . it was the Disagreeablest night I ever saw."[62]

In such circumstances even the officers began to ignore their duty. "The Brigadier General has been astonished to learn from the report of a vigilant officer—That officers are in the habit of leaving their guards and of justifying such conduct by saying 'It had been the practice here.' If it has been the practice officers cannot too soon know that it must be discontinued."[63] Harrison repeatedly battled with the "evil" of his officers' "inattention . . . to their Duty to the law to Regulations and to all orders." Even during the Tippecanoe campaign, when an encounter with the Indians was daily expected, the officers failed to keep their companies in readiness. As one diary reported, "our Company not Parading as usuel the governor [Harrison] threatened to brake the officers."[64] Two years later Harrison complained before all his men, "An order is issued and not one officer in ten knows of its existence or attends to its details. The time of many is too often illy or idly spent and the important interest of the service [and] the imperious calls of duty are neglected or executed in such a way as to add little to the good of the service." Harrison found it necessary to state that he would "hereafter hold all officers responsible for the execution of every order. It is not enough for Gentlemen merely to execute the letter of their Duty and then to sit idly down ignorant of the present and careless of the future."[65]

But Harrison and the other senior officers were fighting an uphill battle. "The Officers of this post are called on for the last time to correct abuses of the most disgraceful kind to the American Arms. The Soldiers are permitted to roam abroad committing depredations of almost every kind on the peaceful and helpless citizens—Robberies are committed on private as well as public Property—Idleness[,] toleration [of] drunkenness, contempt and mutiny are rearing their ghastly forms in the very heart of our Camp."[66] Many of Harrison's officers undermined his efforts to keep his troops sober. One private recorded that "we mooved after Breckfast into town and our Capt treated and also a tavern keeper. . . . much whisky drunk which caused quarreling." Some of the diaries could have been written by a member of a modern fraternity, and for much the same reason. Most of the volunteers were young men who had never been away from home and had never been in the company of so many other young men. An Indiana militiaman recorded in his diary that his unit "overtook the army encampt at a branch which was the first time I ever saw gard set out." Within a few days, this private was drinking heavily. He was sent out as part of a company searching for signs of Indians, the captain first providing them with whiskey. "Stopt at tare holt found no indians went down to drink. . . . Lost our horses found them a mile down the river then went to Drink."[67]

It is worth remembering that alcohol was not only one of the few available painkillers but also a common medicinal treatment for a wide variety of ailments. As with most armies, the soldiers had more to fear from illness than from the enemy. Their camps were generally damp and unhealthy shambles. "Our situation is extremely unpleasant," wrote one private. "Four of this army have gone to the silent tomb to-day, never more to visit their friends in Kentucky; the fever is very prevalent in camp; nearly every day there is one or more buried."[68] The same soldier wrote later that year, "Our sufferings at this place have been greater than if we had been in a severe battle. More than one hundred lives have been lost, owing to our bad accommodations! . . . The camp has become a loathsome place."[69] Another soldier on the Niagara frontier wrote home, "we have a considerable [amount] of sickness in our fort—i saw as much as 50 that was buryed in a bout 6 weakes."[70] At Fort Meigs, according to one officer, "not more than one-third of the army [is] fit for duty."[71]

That troop morale was abysmally low is easily understood, for the shortage and poor quality of food alone kept most soldiers malnourished. The federal government had made no plans for provisioning its soldiers, assuming that local authorities would see to the feeding of the nation's forces. Those acting with such confidence in the support of state governments knew nothing of the American Revolution, when the states had risked the defeat of American independence rather than spend money on supplying the Continental army.[72] Yet even if the states had met these idealistic expectations, the United States army often operated on the nation's frontiers and over the border in Canada. As one private recorded in his journal in 1812, "There has been great murmuring in camp, on account of the scarcity of provisions, which threatened a dissolution of this army." Food shortages convinced many soldiers to return home. "We have drawn no flour since the 10th, in consequence of which there was a letter handed to the General last night secretly, which stated that the volunteers in two days, except flour came before that time, would start and go to it." The officers spoke of "mutiny," but could do little to resolve the situation. Finally, "A little flour came to camp once more; quarter-rations of that article were issued, which was welcomed by rejoicing throughout camp."[73] Colonel Winder, commander of Fort Niagara at the time, reported, "We are literally starving on this end of the line, for bread."[74]

Hunger and the stress of battle could lead to some counterproductive behavior. After the Battle of Tippecanoe, the dragoons set fire to Prophet's Town without collecting the food there, even though they had been several days without rations. "I arrived at the town when it was about half on fire," wrote one volunteer. "I found large quantities of corn, beans and peas. I filled my knapsack with these articles and carried them to the camp and divided them with the members of our mess, consisting of six men. Having these articles of food, we declined eating horse-flash, which was eaten by a large portion of our men."[75] A Pennsylvania regiment marching into Canada in 1814 drew "rations for three days, every pound of which had been left on the shore in consequence of the badness of its quality."[76] The bitterness is evident in a soldier's description of looting a deserted Indian village and being "better supplied with provisions than we have been since we embarked in the service."[77]

Clothing also presented a problem for the United States army, as neither the federal nor state governments had made provision for winter campaigns in 1812. By December many of the troops on the Canadian border were "dangerously frostbitten." "There are many who have not shoes and clothes sufficient to keep them from freezing." Soldiers mocked the failure of the government to properly equip their army: "After three months' preparation for this expedition, we commenced our march in great splendor." Elias Darnell sarcastically described the scene: "Our clothes and blankets looked as if they had never been acquainted with water, but intimately with dirt, smoke, and soot; in fact, we have become acquainted with one much despised in Kentucky, under whose government we are obliged to live, whose name is 'Poverty.'"[78] When uniforms were supplied the following spring, many soldiers turned right around and sold them, especially the cold weather clothes that they hoped not to need. Reports that the militia volunteers were selling their uniforms led Harrison to order that clothing be inspected every week.[79] The failure of military logistics did more to undermine the American war effort than did the small British armies operating in North America.

From the start of the war, money was foremost in the minds of many potential soldiers. Thousands of American men calculated that they had more to gain from staying home than from marching off to war, while those who volunteered hoped for a useful recompense for their time and service. In August 1812, the Kentucky volunteers commanded by General Payne refused to march to the aid of General Hull's army in Detroit until they received "two months' pay in advance." Payne was able to get these funds from the federal government, but did not issue ammunition until they were within range of the enemy for fear the troops would mutiny.[80] One private rejected the pleas of his wife that he come home, insisting that he was not going to leave until he received his back pay.[81] Whether in the militia or the regular army, most soldiers in the War of 1812 seemed always to be waiting for their pay and always ended up feeling that their country still owed them further recompense.

Dissatisfactions over pay and food occasionally reached the point of mutiny. In one of the most famous events of the war, Andrew Jackson twice threatened to fire on his starving volunteer infantry as they tried to head home.[82] Less well known are a number of other, often successful mutinies. In 1814 General George Izard reported to the secretary of war that the "crowds of disorganized, unarmed militia" posed a threat to his forces. He described the New York militia as "between four and six thousand, without guns, mutinous, and determined to move off (as they came,) *en masse*" if they did not receive their discharge pay in advance.[83] That same month, at least half the privates on duty with the Pennsylvania militia signed "a mutinous paper" stating "that they had determined not to march from camp, until they had received the amount of pay due them for their services, alleging as their apology, that many of them were much at a loss for shoes and other cloathing." The officers of the regiment did not know what to do and waited for several days for some assistance. When none was coming, they ordered the troops to assemble for the march. When most did not, the suspected "ringleader" was arrested. "The peaceable portion of the men immediately fell into rank, leaving a number strolling about, as if undecided what course to pursue." Warned that one of his men "in my rear was loading his gun to shoot me," Captain Samuel White "wheeled round, sprang upon him, wrested the gun from him, and despatched him also to the guard house." Major Marlin loaded the cannon "with grape and cannister" and pointed it at the troops. "The line was promptly formed, the order of march given, and the regiment moved off in perfect order."[84] It had been necessary to threaten their own troops with artillery to get them to march to Buffalo.

On November 1, 1812, "a daring mutiny broke out" in General Daniel Miller's brigade in Buffalo. One hundred militia stacked their arms and headed home; another 100 "stacked their arms and stood by them."[85] Miller allowed the 100 who left to continue homeward, promising better quarters to those who stayed. In writing of this event, Lieutenant Colonel J. W. Livingston described the brigade as "little better than an undisciplined rabble." He blamed the officers for the "spirit of mutiny . . . pervad[ing] the camp."[86] General Alexander Smyth ordered the trial of five of the militia for desertion, and they were found guilty and shot. Miller and several officers were dismissed for failing to prevent the mutiny, and the brigade was mixed in with other units.[87] There were several additional mutinies among the militia at Utica and Manlius and among volunteers and militia at Buffalo. The soldiers, or so General Smyth suspected, had also learned more subtle forms of refusing to serve, such as declaring themselves sick.[88]

There are indications in these sources that Smyth was correct in perceiving subtle forms of protest. The safest and most typical method was sluggish marching. Deliberately slowing to a stately crawl could drive the officers to give in to most demands.[89] There were occasional creative acts of resistance to military authority. Some of the soldiers in General Tupper's command fired their guns to celebrate Christmas Eve. The general ordered them to stop; a few minutes later there were more gunshots. "The whole army was ordered to parade in order of battle; strict orders were given to suppress the firing. About an hour before day the firing commenced again."[90] Using the militia required skill at negotiation. One member of the Indiana militia recorded that after marching around "till late" his company "mutinized with some of Capt heath's men." Assured they would return to camp, they "marched back at sunset and dismisst in order."[91] Some members of the militia, especially in New England, took their protest a step further and traded with the enemy. An English officer described how at dinner a visitor arrived. "His servant said he believed he must be a kind of Yankee gentleman, for he wore his hat in the parlor, and spit on the carpet." He was an American major of the Vermont militia with 100 head of cattle to sell; the British were buying. The American said, "They do say that it is wrong to supply an innimy, and I think so too; but I don't call that man my innimy who buys what I have to sell, and gives a genteel price for it."[92]

In such a war, the usual solace of religion and patriotism did not always come to reassure the men. Some soldiers, especially the Methodists, saw the military encampments as an opportunity to re-create a frontier revival. John Patterson, a private in the 22d Regiment of the U.S. Infantry, turned to religion. He wrote his "Dear and loving companion," Levina, in 1812 that "there is as much appearance of peace as war." In their camp on the Niagara frontier, "reading and writeing is my cheapest imployment—on Sunday we go to meating to any denomination as we think proper." Patterson was concerned about his neighbors' response to his enlistment: "i hope that you will pray for me—and i hope that the friends will not dispise you or me because i am a souldier."[93] Lacking a regular minister, Patterson began preaching himself: "i have took up the cross," he wrote his wife, "and do preach twice a weak to the souldiers."[94] More typically, soldiers attended services on Sunday but made little note of the text or experience. One Sunday Captain Cushing reported, "We had a sermon preached this evening by Mr. Baggin; he had a great deal to say about the river Jordan—a story that will not do for soldiers."[95]

The river Jordan for the majority of these soldiers was the one they had to cross on their journey back home. There is no evidence that this return trip was ever taken reluctantly. "Lieut. Meek obtained leave to go home today, as pleased as a child with a rattle." Less fortunate was a Lieutenant Larwill, who "returned this day; got defeated by the water that covers the whole face of the earth." Larwill became depressed over his failure to get home and tried again with a Quebecois guide. The most eloquent and extended passage in Cushing's diary is his description of his friend's adventure. Larwill made eight miles the first day and was just settling down for the night when he heard a noise. His guide proclaimed it an owl and went to shoot it.

> But O, the report of the gun very much alarmed the warrior [Larwill], he starts, he stops, he pants for breath, he hears the near approach of death, he does not stop to know the fate of his companion, nor to wait to know if it was the Frenchman's gun or Indian rifle that had won; but left his sword, his coat, his script [for pay], and through the swamp he nimbly skipped, until he arrived at Sandusky bank, the river wide, the current swift, and he himself without a skift. He looked about and saw his fate, that there was no other escape but for him to try his active limbs and see if he the gulf could swim, he plunges in and struggles hard, but could not reach the other shore; he turns and with his eyes, he sees the Frenchman to his great surprise.

The guide helped him out of the water and back to Fort Meigs.[96]

Many senior officers simply gave up. While the temporary commander of Fort Meigs, Colonel Leftwich assumed that his Virginia militia, who had only a few days of service left, would undertake no significant tasks. As he told one captain, "he couldn't make the militia do anything, and therefore they might as well be in their tents."[97] Not expecting to be around long, Leftwich stopped work on the stockade and even took down the fence already in place to use for fuel rather than send his forces out into the nearby woods. Captain Eleazer D. Wood, who had overseen the construction of these fortifications, was horrified when he returned to the fort, writing that Leftwich "was not even fit for a pack-horse master, much less to be entrusted with such an important command."[98] As it turned out, the Virginians had no intention of fighting the enemy: "For, on the 6th of April, finding that we were threatened with an immediate attack, . . . the Virginians to a man, and to their eternal disgrace, had gone home, their General [Leftwich] the first to set the example." However, 150 of the Pennsylvania troops did vote to stay on at the fort for another fifteen days, whereupon they also left.[99] The British attacked the following week.

Officers were fortunate in that they could resign their commissions and leave. "Our 2d Lieutenant Resigned and gone home," reads one diary. The common soldiers were not so fortunate. They had enlisted for specific periods and had to see that time through. The only alternative, and one that many took, was desertion. A few days after the lieutenant just mentioned left for home, the same diarist writes in passing, "6 men run away."[100] Even though Fort Meigs was a remote position hundreds of miles from the homes of most of the soldiers present, desertions remained a real problem, with courts-martial taking up a great deal of the officers' time.[101] One can hear the annoyance in a diary entry such as this: "Sunday, [February] 28th—I am sitting in a court martial; it commenced on the 26th."[102] General Adamson Tannehill reported that most of his army was "infected with the same dishonorable contagion—desertion. I am at a loss how to express my feelings on the present state of our little army."[103] It is likely that most dissatisfied soldiers just headed home, but occasionally one actually moved to betray his country. "This day a general court martial sentenced John T. Mosby, a private . . . for threatening to blow up the magazine and then to desert to the British." The most curious aspect of such desertions is the mildness of punishment; on one occasion General Harrison ordered a deserter whipped, but pardoned him just as the whip was about to be laid on.[104] Even Private Mosby received a humiliation punishment rather than being executed. The Americans just could not afford to lose many men, no matter how poorly trained or sullen in their duty.[105]

From the start of the war, some observers appreciated that the United States fooled only itself in believing that an unprepared army of volunteers and militia could defend the country, let alone launch offensive operations. In January 1813 General Harrison was supposed to defend the northwestern frontier and invade Upper Canada with 1,500 men, most of them militia from Virginia and Pennsylvania. Captain Eleazer Wood was astounded that anyone could believe that these goals "were to be attained with a force almost entirely composed of *raw militia*." Wood quoted a friend that most of his fellow officers were "incapable of learning" the necessary military skills while "the men [were] entirely unaccustomed" to military discipline.[106]

Just getting the soldiers to show up posed major hurdles. When the governor of Pennsylvania called for the state's volunteer troops to rendezvous at Gettysburg on February 28, 1814, to meet a possible British invasion, so few appeared that the courts-martial assessed $40,000 in delinquency fines. Of course collecting that money was another matter entirely.[107] When they showed up, the militia and volunteers could be astoundingly unorganized, marching off without some of their company, devoting time to cutting down "bee trees," chasing their horses when they were not properly staked, and getting lost regularly.[108] Those with some experience at smithing found themselves steadily employed repairing firearms. One member of the militia wrote often that he "staid all day in camp and cut out a gun," meaning to remove lead stuck in a rifle or musket barrel as a consequence of its being improperly loaded.[109]

Commanding officers could not avoid the embarrassment of reporting that their troops had run away. Outside of Baltimore on September 12, 1814, General John Stricker of the Maryland militia had placed his riflemen in "a thick low pine wood beyond the blacksmith's shop, with a large sedgefield in front," with the rest of his third brigade of 1,400 men in the open to receive the British attack. "Imagine my chagrin when I perceived the whole rifle corps falling back on my main position" at the first sighting of the British. They wanted to be with the crowd when the British attacked, rather than behind cover. Stricker put the riflemen with other troops. They opened fire when the enemy was at too great a distance, and Stricker ordered a cease-fire until the British were within range of his cannon. When he attempted to have one regiment wheel at a right angle, it produced "some confusion in that quarter." At this point, the Fifty-first Regiment "delivered one random fire and retreated precipitately, and in such confusion, as to render every effort to rally them ineffective."[110] He had no choice but to withdraw before "superior numbers." But the next day they felt "increased confidence"[111] and were ready for further duty. However, the British had also left. The Third Brigade lost twenty-four men in the battle, with fifty Americans taken prisoner.[112]

Flight or the refusal to participate in battle were the most common, and perhaps perfectly logical, response of the militia to the sight of warfare.[113] The most notorious example of the latter impulse came at the Battle of Queenston Heights, the culmination of a campaign that revealed abundantly the danger of the militia ideology. New York's militia quota under the April 10, 1812, federal militia act was 13,500. By July 4, 2,800 militia and 300 regulars were at Black Rock. When General Stephen Van Rensselaer asked for volunteers to attack a British schooner at Prescott, only sixty-six men were willing to serve, leading to the cancellation of that plan. Van Rensselaer informed General Dearborn that his troops were too ill armed for anything but defensive actions, if that.[114] "Alarm pervades the country, and distrust among the troops. They are incessantly pressing for furloughs under every possible pretence. Many are without shoes; all are clamorous for pay; many are sick. . . . While we are thus growing weaker our enemy is growing stronger. . . . They are fortifying almost every prominent point from Fort Erie to Fort George. . . . I have no reinforcements of men, no ordnance or munitions of war."[115] Nonetheless, Dearborn urged Van Rensselaer to seize the initiative before British reinforcements could arrive. The New York commander procrastinated as long as he could, finally leading his forces into the disastrous attack at Queenston Heights,[116] where the militia refused to cross over into Canada to rescue their fellow Americans, doing "no more fighting than spectators in a balloon might have claimed."[117] It is little wonder that Van Rensselaer's successor, General Alexander Smyth, wrote Secretary of War Eustis on October 20, 1812, "Place no confidence in detached militia, they have disgraced the nation."[118]

But then the new regular troops were little better; they were not yet trained and mostly poorly armed. Captain William King wrote that the Twelfth and Fourteenth Regiments lacked arms and other equipment, while those guns they had were in "infamously bad order" and the troops were "ignorant of their duty." And then, the worst insult, he compared them to militia: "They are mere militia, and, if possible, even worse; and if taken into action in their present state, will prove more dangerous to themselves than to their enemy."[119]

Their troops' inexperience proved a real detriment to the American war effort. Even officers could record, as did Captain Daniel Cushing at the second siege of Fort Meigs in 1813, "This is the first time I have discharged a piece at an enemy in 30 years."[120] Most of the men had little or no experience with firearms. "This day one of Capt. Bradford's corporals was accidentally shot by one of his men through the leg."[121] In 1812 one of the Kentucky volunteers "was accidentally shot through the head by one of the mounted riflemen," and a few days later another Kentuckian "wounded a man as he was feeding his horse, believing him to be an Indian." Such incidents happened far too often for the comfort of those practicing in the use of firearms.[122] And occasionally they shot themselves. As one private wrote his wife, "i receiveed an axident by my own guns going off" during a false alarm, tearing off part of his finger.[123]

Untrained soldiers could be trained, with sufficient time and effort, though the troops themselves generally hated it.[124] Unfortunately for the Americans, few commanding officers were willing to risk the resultant unpopularity of actually requiring regular drill. Winfield Scott, who would write the army's official training manual after the war, made the most concerted effort to train the troops under his command and with the most positive results. At the Battle of Chippewa, the U.S. forces behaved with greater coolness under fire than they had yet demonstrated. Major Thomas Jesup's forces "hotly pressed by the British right screened by a log fence, advanced upon its flank in face of a deadly fire, coolly marching with arms at a support, and then, charging with the bayonet, routed everything before him."[125] One of the British officers later stated, "It was clear enough that we had something besides militiamen to deal with."[126] Similarly, at the Battle of Niagara Falls, Colonel Miller and his Twenty-first Regiment attacked the British artillery position in classic European style: delivering a single volley and rushing in with their bayonets, capturing the British cannon. The British commander wrote in his official dispatch, "in so determined a manner was the American attack directed against our guns, that our artillerymen were bayoneted by them in the very act of loading."[127]

But other problems, particularly the lack of supplies, exceeded the abilities of even as formidable an officer as Winfield Scott to address. One of the most considerable difficulties was the shortage of firearms. Repeatedly volunteers would show up without arms and be left to stand around or even to roam about individually, often without ever taking part in the campaign or battle, yet still submitting claims on the state for their pay.[128] Pennsylvania exhausted its store of federal firearms received under the 1808 Militia Act in arming the volunteer militia in the war's first months. Governor Simon Snyder asked the secretary of war to send more arms so that other militia units could be armed, only to be informed that the federal government did not have a surplus. Pennsylvania's militia thus continued poorly armed throughout the war,[129] and yet Pennsylvania contributed more militia than any other state and received a larger reimbursement, $188,900.[130] As one historian has written, "These problems were not solved during the war and constantly hampered effective use of the militia."[131] When units had firearms, they often lacked the requisite ammunition. Diaries contain entries such as "We held a council, and concluded it was useless to alter our line of march, as we had no cartridges with us for the guns."[132]

Given these equipment shortages, the failure of many militia to enter battle may become easier to understand. Governor Snyder sent 2,000 of his poorly armed militia north to join General Smyth's forces at Buffalo with specific orders that they invade Canada: "otherwise they will render no service to their country."[133] Though there were 7,000 troops under Smyth's command, he could only convince 1,500 to join him in invading Canada. When the time came to cross, only 413 were willing to do so, inducing Smyth to twice embark and then disembark his troops.[134] There was little doubt that an American landing near Fort Erie would have met no resistance, for three American sailors landed and spent two hours looting and burning houses on the Canadian shore. They may have intended to mock or goad the militia, which had boarded their ships and refused to leave.[135] It is little wonder that Smyth bitterly called his forces a crowd "who go to the bank of the Niagara to look on a battle as on a theatrical exhibition," and if "disappointed of the sight break their muskets, or if they are without rations for a day desert."[136] When Smyth told the troops that "he could not depend on the militia and had not regular troops sufficient" for further operations, the militia "fired off all of their ammunition" and dissolved their companies. There were also reported cases of soldiers firing at Smyth with a $200 reward for the soldier who shot him.[137] His subordinate, General Peter B. Porter, accused Smyth of cowardice, which led to a duel in which neither man was hurt. Many of the soldiers hoped they would shoot one another.[138]

The Pennsylvania militia was willing to do occasional battle with one another and Federalist hotelkeepers. On November 25, 1812, some fifty militia stormed Pomeroy's hotel in Buffalo because the innkeeper opposed the war. The militia first wrecked and then set fire to the hotel. When locals attempted to put out the fire, they were three times driven back by militia armed with bayonets. When an artillery company was sent to restore order, the militia attacked them. Two people died in the riot, and General Smyth had to detach 300 of his regulars to protect Buffalo from the militia.[139] In the aftermath of this riot, all but 267 Pennsylvania militia went home. Smyth dismissed the officers and attempted to integrate the remaining Pennsylvania troops with other units, but they also left before the end of the month. None of the 2,000 militia Governor Snyder had sent north to invade Canada saw any action in the campaign of 1812, except against Pomeroy's hotel.[140] General Smyth retired shortly thereafter.[141]

The most famous failure of the U.S. Army and militia came in the defense of Washington, D.C. Incredibly, the government made no plans to protect the capital until six weeks before it fell. On July 1, 1814, the cabinet prepared "a programme of defense," which looked formidable on paper in imagining an army of some 100,000 militia. And then, as though to convince himself that the militia was sufficient, the secretary of war sent 500 regulars from Washington to the northern frontier, leaving just 330 for the capital's defense, along with, in reality, just 4,700 militia.[142] They faced a pathetic British army of 4,370 mixed troops that lacked cavalry and heavy artillery, came from spending months aboard ship, and faced a forty-mile march through August humidity.[143] As a later military scholar summarized the situation, "Our so-called army, except Barney's seamen and Peter's regulars, was a heterogeneous mass without order or discipline, and had scarcely one officer with the least knowledge of actual warfare."[144]

At the "disgraceful action" at Bladensburg on August 24, 1814, the American forces were drawn up in three straight lines without cover from the three British cannon. Two militia regiments fled at their first sight of the British rockets. Most of the remaining 12,000 Americans followed their example as Ross swept the field with only two of his brigades.[145] The troops at Fort Washington fled "on the discharge of the first shell of the enemy."[146] Dolly Madison stood on the roof of the White House "turning my spy-glass in every direction, and watching with unwearied anxiety," she wrote on August 23, 1813. "I can descry only groups of military, wandering in all directions, as if there was a lack of arms, or of spirit to fight for their own fireside."[147]

Fairly typical was the experience of John S. Gallagher, a private in the Virginia militia. The call to come to the defense of Washington reached Jefferson County, Virginia, on August 22, 1814. At a public meeting fifty militiamen vowed to set forth the next day. Before heading to the capital, "we marched to Harper's Ferry, eight miles distant, to procure arms." There fifty of the workers under the command of Superintendent Stubblefield joined them. Halfway to Washington, the superintendent and several workers decided "to return to carry on the manufacture of arms, a duty equally as important as fighting." The British already occupied the capital by the time Gallagher's company arrived, so they headed toward Baltimore. On the way, they were ordered back to Washington, which the British had abandoned. "Though there had been but little time for drill," his company "felt something more than the confidence of raw militiamen, and, I may say, were 'eager for the fray.'" So they fired their rifles from the bluffs at the British ships in the Potomac, while Commodore Porter directed the artillery. For two hours the militia fired "at the decks and rigging" while the British returned cannon fire, the first two shots disabling two American cannon and killing one of Gallagher's neighbors. Gallagher was certain that the

British lost more men than the Americans "notwithstanding our imperfect defences." Despite the overwhelming American defeat at Washington, Gallagher still praised the "gallant and efficient service" of the militia.[148]

The experience of battle certainly appears in many of these diaries and journals, but not very often. That paucity of attention accurately reflects the nature of this warfare. The War of 1812 had few land battles, and most of those were of short duration. The three sieges of Fort Meigs and the campaign for New Orleans stand out as sustained military encounters between hostile forces. Far more typical are the accounts of marches and countermarches ending in the dismissal of the militia. Even the aggressive generals like Harrison and Jackson spent far more time destroying Indian villages than actually coming into contact with the Indians. For instance, Elias Darnell, a private in Harrison's army, spent two weeks in the fall of 1812 burning the fields and houses of the Indians and eating their "good corn" without actually seeing any Indians.[149] Similarly, an American soldier involved in the invasion of Canada in early 1814 recorded that the British retreated before their advance: "The only hostile demonstration on our part was, the destruction of some mills employed in manufacturing flour for the army, together with some houses" at Dover, where "a few women . . . had white clothes hanging upon broomsticks suing for peace." He insisted, "Every possible respect was paid to the women and children, and the best part of the furniture in the houses which were destroyed, was even carried out by the troops previous to their being set on fire."[150]

Battles tended to be brief encounters, often terminated by a single volley or cannonade. Captain Samuel White of the Pennsylvania volunteers offered a concise summary of the Battle of Fort Erie in early July 1814. In White's telling, the Americans stumbled into battle after General Jacob Brown ordered some men to beat off the Indians hanging around their flanks. The Indians retreated after a brief exchange of fire and the Americans pursued, right into a trap. British Regulars opened up with artillery, staggering the Americans. General Brown responded by ordering his whole command to attack. Major Jesup advanced his troops across the open ground to "within twenty paces of the enemy's line," ordering them "to level and fire, causing such havoc in the enemy's line as forced them to retreat."[151] This single volley found support from the British magazine exploding, and the British retreated, taking many prisoners with them, including Captain White. It was a quick action with only a few casualties, and the Americans left in possession of the field and little else.[152] An even briefer encounter was Proctor's third attack on Fort Meigs in August 1813, which was halted by a single shot from Croghan's only cannon at point-blank range.[153]

Encounters with the enemy, even by small units, could completely demoralize American forces. Near Fort Defiance, some U.S. troops found a party of twenty or thirty Indians. "They took them to be those friendly Indians who were with us," but quickly discovered their error as "four or five of the Indians fired at the same time," killing one of the Americans. General Tupper's mounted Kentucky riflemen were nearby and gave pursuit "in scattered order," but "finding the enemy's force superior they had to retreat." The next day a majority of Tupper's force "refused to march," leaving the general no choice but to cancel his "contemplated expedition." The Kentuckians "returned home" even though their period of enlistment had not yet expired. Apparently just seeing hostile Indians was sufficient military experience for them.[154]

By the end of the war, honor seemed the only cause, and narrative, left. A Lieutenant Douglass wrote that his friend Eleazer Wood, killed at the Battle of Niagara, died for "the honor of her [United States] arms."[155] Writing in 1816, General Jacob Brown wrote that his soldiers' sacrifices were "for the honor of their country and the glory of her arms."[156]

That honor was only truly salvaged after the war had officially ended, with Andrew Jackson's stunning victory over the British at New Orleans. For nearly every American who wrote about the War of 1812 over the next century and a half, the Battle of New Orleans served as a giant sigh of relief. Finally they could record the type of American victory they had expected from the start. In many accounts it appears as though the War of 1812 was fought in order for Andrew Jackson to defeat the British at New Orleans, which is certainly the way it appeared to Jackson afterwards.

The Battle of New Orleans allowed onetime critics of the militia and volunteer troops to return to prewar rhetoric. Thus the Philadelphia *Aurora,* which had often made clear its disgust with the poor performance of untrained troops, now trumpeted the victory of "raw militia, hastily collected together from the adjoining country, and commanded by farmers and planters."[157] That the editor knew better was irrelevant; the rhetoric was not. Restoring a vision of a glorious militia saved face for the Jeffersonians and allowed them to prevent the expansion of the U.S. Army. Senator George M. Troup, who had called for a larger standing army during the war, set the tone with his praise for "the farmers of the country triumphantly victorious over the conquerors of Europe." Suffering from a convenient amnesia, he insisted that the war proved that militia could beat regulars and called for a standing army of just 10,000 men.[158] The Republicans were operating in a fantasy world; some members of the House reversed themselves. Thus Joseph Desha, who had declared the militia a waste of money, suddenly called for reducing the army to 6,000, declaring the militia "better security than ten, or even fifty thousand regulars. . . . We have boasted that a well organized militia was the bulwark of our liberty, and recent circumstances have proved it to be a fact."[159]

John C. Calhoun worked hardest to return Congress to reality, reminding them that "it is easier to keep soldiers than to get them."[160] Nonetheless, Desha's reduction won by a wide margin in the House, which eventually compromised with the Senate for an army of 10,000.[161] Yet, at the same time, the political leadership of the majority of the states allowed the militia system to die.[162] The result was a reduction in both the standing army and the near demise of the militia. Congress did, however, increase appropriations for West Point, and over the next thirty years created a very credible officer corps. The realities of the War of 1812 made it abundantly clear to those with any interest in the military that the United States would at the very least need a well trained pool of officers in case of future war. It was primarily West Point graduates who led the United States to victory in the Mexican War and who led the two sides in the Civil War.[163]

Congressional action replicated popular opinion. Some writers attempted to remind people that the whole war had not been a series of battles like that at New Orleans. "A Militia-Man" in the National Intelligencer had a simple counterargument to those who thought the United States could rely on the militia: "we will point to the ruins of the capitol."[164] Such opinions, while widely voiced, were in the minority. Thanks to the Battle of New Orleans, Americans could feel good about themselves and praise their own heroism. Amid the celebrations, Hezekiah Niles sounded a note of caution. He credited regulars and militia for the victories in the last year of the war and hoped that the nation would learn from the "experience derived in the war" by improving the military at every level.[165]

There was supposed to have been a narrative, that of the gallant militia rushing to the defense of the nation's liberty and crushing all foes. But that mythology, which flew in the face of the realities of the American Revolution, collapsed within a few months of Congress's declaration of war in 1812. The change can be clearly seen in the attitude of one member of Congress, John C. Calhoun of South Carolina. On December 11, 1811, Calhoun, speaking in favor of a larger standing army, assured the House that they need not fear a slave rebellion in the case of war, for "our militia

[is] best prepared." Nor need they fear a professional army, whether domestic or foreign. "Can 1,000,000 of militia be overpowered by 30,000 regulars? . . . Sir, I have no such contemptuous idea of our militia—their untaught bravery is sufficient to crush all foreign and internal attempts on their country's liberties."[166] One year later he was calling for the country to "no longer rely on the hazardous aid of volunteers and militia."[167] By the time the war ended, Calhoun was demanding the complete reform of the militia, aiming to make it more like a standing army or at least a useful supplement to one. "I would not only arm the militia, but I would extend their term of service and make them efficient."[168] As secretary of war, Calhoun would struggle to create the sort of selective militia that Washington, Knox, and Hamilton had dreamed of, and he would fail as completely as they had.

The Canadian perspective gives a good sense of the American narrative void. Canadian memoirs published from the war generally frame events within the defense of their homeland from American aggression. Thus the introduction to Dr. William Dunlop's memoir reads like a deliberate parody of American mythology. Here is a tale of "the desperate circumstances under which a mere handful of French Canadian and Loyalist colonists emerged from their primitive villages and log cabins and with Spartan courage and hardihood drove back the invader again and again and captured large areas of his territory."[169] Dunlop described the superiority of the Canadian militia when compared with the Americans: "They had all a serviceable effective appearance—had been pretty well drilled, and their arms being direct from the tower, were in perfectly good order." These French militia sang "their voyageur songs, . . . followed by a shout of *Vive le Roi.*" Throughout his account, Dunlop offers an exact reversal of American ideology. The Canadians were "fighting for their homes and friends, and almost in sight of their wives and children," and thus "have an additional incentive over those who fight for pay and glory." In contrast, the "American regulars, if equal, were not superior to our [militia] troops in drill and discipline, the great majority of them having been enlisted for a period too short to form a soldier, under the most favorable circumstances." The Americans "found themselves in a country so decidedly hostile, that their retreating ranks were thinned by the peasantry firing on them from behind fences and stumps; and it was evident that every man they met was an enemy."[170]

The American Revolution transformed its participants; the War of 1812 depressed most of those who played a part. Given the Revolution's historic outcome, stories told by veterans over the ensuing fifty years had a logical structure that easily lent itself to making even mundane experiences into adventure stories, the preferred style of storytelling.[171] As Alfred Young has written about a specific veteran, "His experiences [in the Revolution] transformed him, giving him a sense of citizenship and personal worth."[172] Those attempting to tell exciting stories about the War of 1812 were far less fortunate and often embarrassed by the whole sorry tale. As a consequence, memoirs of the War of 1812 often come off as an inverted saga, lacking heroes or heroic action, rich on flight and the avoidance of battle and responsibility, and producing little tangible good.

The war had begun with repeated assurances that an aroused people could never be defeated, that a democratic republic could not lose. The only way to make sense of the disasters of the War of 1812 was to construct a mythology around a few glorious deeds, such as Fort McHenry and the Battle of New Orleans, yanking them firmly out of their context and making them stand in isolation from other events. This was not partial history; this was not history at all. Rather, the United States needed fabulous fables that endorsed their self-perception of strength and virtue, demonstrating the superiority of their democracy and its right to possess the continent.[173] Memories of the war threatened the useful lies and found no celebration, further deepening the reluctance of veterans to speak of their experiences.

There is poignancy to the meeting of the veterans of the War of 1812 in Schuylerville, New York, in 1856. Instead of celebrating their own heroism, they marked the victory at Saratoga in 1777. But they did attempt to connect themselves to those heroes. The "old soldiers" of the War of 1812 "are the natural successors of the heroic men of the revolution." After all, they fought "against the same enemy [. . . and] in vindicating the same rights of commerce and national independence at the cannon's mouth."[174] This organization was the first of its kind in New York, organized in 1853. They had joined together after exhausting their patience over the failure of the New York legislature to act upon a resolution of April 21, 1818, that had called upon "the Commissary General to audit and settle the accounts properly chargeable to the state of New York, for the services and contingent expenses of the volunteers and militia of the state." The following year and every year thereafter, the legislature set aside all claims "on the ground that the act of 1818 *provided for their adjustment*," not their payment.[175] The legislature continued to ignore the veterans, only a handful of whom would ever receive a pension in the aftermath of the Civil War. But then the veterans of 1812 had lost their war.

Notes

1. The structure and historical uses of memory have become a significant issue for historians in the last fifteen years. See esp. David Thelen, ed., "Memory and American History," special issue of *Journal of American History* 75 (1989); Paul Connerton, *How Societies Remember* (Cambridge: Cambridge University Press, 1989); Michael Kammen, *Mystic Chords of Memory: The Transformation of Tradition in American Culture* (New York: Knopf, 1991); Daniel L. Schachter, *Searching for Memory: The Brain, the Mind, and the Past* (New York: Basic Books, 1996); Jay Winter, *Sites of Memory, Sites of Mourning: The Great War in European Cultural History* (Cambridge: Cambridge University Press, 1995); Jonathan F. Vance, *Death So Noble: Memory, Meaning, and the First World War* (Vancouver: University of British Columbia Press, 1997).

2. See John C. Dann, ed., *The Revolution Remembered: Eyewitness Accounts of the War for Independence* (Chicago: University of Chicago Press, 1980); Alfred F. Young, *The Shoemaker and the Tea Party: Memory and the American Revolution* (Boston: Beacon, 1999).

3. James D. Richardson, comp., *Messages and Papers of the Presidents, 1789–1907,* 20 vols. (New York: Bureau of National Literature and Art, 1897–1917), 1:499–505.

4. William Ray Barlow insisted that the far west was equally outraged over violations of maritime rights. "The Coming of the War of 1812 in Michigan Territory," *Michigan History* 53 (1969): 91–107.

5. The best work on the causes of the war remains Bradford Perkins, *Prologue to War: England and the United States, 1805–1812* (Berkeley: University of California Press, 1961). There has been surprisingly little work done on the historiography of the War of 1812. See Warren H. Goodman, "The Origins of the War of 1812: A Survey of Changing Interpretations," *Mississippi Valley Historical Review* 28 (1941): 171–86.

6. Report on the Causes and Reasons for War, June 3, 1812, *Annals of the Congress of the United States,* 12th Cong., 1st sess., pt. 1 (Washington: Gales and Seaton, 1853), 1546–54.

7. Ibid., 446.

8. Ibid., 518.

9. Ronald L. Hatzenbuehler and Robert L. Ivie, "Justifying the War of 1812: Toward a Model of Congressional Behavior in Early War Crises," *Social Science History* 4 (1980): 453–77. See also Leland R. Johnson, "The Suspense Was Hell: The Senate Vote for War in 1812," *Indiana Magazine of History* 65 (1969): 247–67.

10. See, e.g., Samuel Austin, *A Sermon, Preached in Worcester, Massachusetts, on the Occasion of the Special Fast* (Worcester, Mass.: Isaac Sturtevant, 1812); Francis Brown, *A Sermon, Delivered July 23, 1812, on Occasion of the State Fast* (Portland, Maine: Hyde, Lord, 1812); John Cleaveland, *A Discourse Delivered on the Day of National Humiliation and Prayer* (Boston: Samuel T. Armstrong, 1812);

Jacob Catlin, *Alarm to the Churches* (Stockbridge, Mass.: H. Willard, 1812); Reuben Holcomb, *A Discourse, in Two Parts, Delivered at Sterling, Massachusetts, Thursday, July 23, 1812, at the State Fast* (Worcester, Mass.: Isaac Sturtevant, 1812); Jedidiah Morse, *A Sermon, Delivered at Charlestown, July 23, 1812* (Charlestown, Mass.: Samuel Etheridge, 1812). For a later version of this argument, see Daniel A. Atkinson, *Independence Sermon, Delivered July 4, 1814 at Hanover, N. Jersey* (Newark, N.J.: John Tuttle, 1814).

11. Hosea Ballou, *A Sermon, Delivered at Portsmouth, N.H. Appropriate to the Occasion of a Day of Humiliation and Prayer* (Portsmouth, N.H.: W. Weeks, 1812). See also William Ellery Channing, *A Sermon, Preached in Boston July 23, 1812, the Day of the Publick Fast* (Boston: Greenough and Stebbins, 1812); Henry Colman, *A Sermon* (Boston: Joshua Belcher, 1812). For a later version of this argument that both sides were sinful, see Abraham Burnham, *Antichrist* (Concord, N.H.: George Hough, 1814).

12. Benjamin Bell, *A Sermon Preached at Steuben April 1813* (Sangerfield, N.Y.: J. Tenney, 1814).

13. Jacob Catlin, *The Horrors of War* (Stockbridge, Mass.: H. Willard, 1813). See also Kiah Bayley, *War a Calamity Greatly to be Dreaded* (Hallowell, Maine: N. Cheever, 1812); Nathan S. S. Beman, *A Sermon, Delivered at the Meeting House of the Second Parish in Portland, August 20, 1812* (Portland, Maine: Hyde, Lord, 1812); John S. J. Gardiner, *A Discourse, Delivered at Trinity Church, Boston, April 9, 1812, on the Day of Publick Fast* (Boston: Munroe and Francis, 1812); James Abercrombie, *Two Sermons* (Philadelphia: Moses Thomas, 1812); Lemuel Haynes, *Dissimulation Illustrated* (Rutland, Conn.: Washington Benevolent Society, 1814); John Lathrop, *A Discourse on the Law of Retaliation, Delivered in the New Brick Church, February 6, 1814* (Boston: James W. Burditt, 1814).

14. James Flint, *God a Refuge and an Habitation in Times of Calamity and Danger* (Boston: C. Stebbins, 1814).

15. [John Lowell], *Perpetual War, the Policy of Mr. Madison* (Boston: Chester Stebbins, 1812), title page.

16. See [John Lowell], *Mr. Madison's War* (Boston: Russell and Cutler, 1812); Samuel Austin, *The Apology of Patriots; or, The Heresy of the Friends of the Washington and Peace Policy Defended* (Worcester, Mass.: Isaac Sturtevant, 1812); Supplement to the Boston *Weekly Messenger* (Boston: John Eliot Jr., 1812); Thomas Andros, *The Grand Era of Ruin to Nations from Foreign Influence* (Boston: Samuel T. Armstrong, 1812); Lewis Bigelow, *An Oration, Pronounced at Templeton, July 5, 1813* (Worcester, Mass.: Isaac Sturtevant, 1813); Stephen Bemis, *The First of Patriots Gathered to His Grace in Peace; and the Evil Brought upon His Country* (Worcester, Mass.: William Manning, 1815).

17. Victor A. Sapio, *Pennsylvania and the War of 1812* (Lexington: University Press of Kentucky, 1970), 172–74; Pittsburgh *Gazette*, September 18, 1812; *Pennsylvania Farmer* (Lancaster), August 26, September 2, 1812.

18. Sapio, *Pennsylvania and the War of 1812*, 180–81.

19. Hull to Dearborn, December 11, 1807, *Michigan Pioneer Collections* 40 (1929): 228.

20. See, e.g., *Michigan Pioneer Collections* 8 (1886): 602; Clarence E. Carter, ed., *Territory of Michigan, 1805–1820,* vol. 10 of *Territorial Papers of the United States* (Washington: Government Printing Office, 1942), 303, 319.

21. Jefferson to Hull, March 21, 1807, *Michigan Pioneer Collections* 8 (1886): 583.

22. Lawrence Delbert Cress, *Citizens in Arms: The Army and the Militia in American Society to the War of 1812* (Chapel Hill: University of North Carolina Press, 1982), 150–71.

23. One of the more interesting early histories of the War of 1812 makes roughly this point, citing Washington and other Revolutionary leaders to reject a reliance on the militia and explain the utter necessity of trained troops and officers. George W. Cullum, *Campaigns of the War of 1812–15, Against Great Britain, Sketched and Criticized* (New York: James Miller, 1879), 9–35. For more recent examinations of the reliance on militia, see Cress, *Citizens in Arms;* Charles Royster, *A Revolutionary People at War: The Continental Army and American Character, 1775–1783* (Chapel Hill: University of North Carolina Press, 1979).

24. A notable exception is Carl Edward Skeen, *Citizen Soldiers in the War of 1812* (Lexington: University Press of Kentucky, 1999).

25. Jefferson to Hull, March 21, 1807, *Michigan Pioneer Collections* 8 (1886): 583.

26. William Henry Harrison, "Militia Discipline," *National Intelligencer* (Washington, D.C.), September 21 and October 1, 1810; Robert S. Lambert, ed., "The Conduct of the Militia at Tippecanoe: Elihu Stout's Controversy with Colonel John P. Boyd, January, 1812," *Indiana Magazine of History* 51 (1955): 237–50; Gale Thornborough and Dorothy Riker, eds., "Journals of the General Assembly of Indiana Territory, 1805–1815," *Indiana Historical Collections* 32 (1950): 2–17, 392–401, 409–16, 421, 426–33, 478; Michael A. Bellesiles, *Arming America: The Origins of a National Gun Culture* (New York: Knopf, 2000), 208–60.

27. Carl Edward Skeen summarizes the case well. "The militia, which was to be the primary force for waging the war, was simply not organized, trained, disciplined, equipped, armed, or ready. The failures of the first year, in fact, revealed that militias were unlikely to be useful at all for conducting any offensive operations—and only marginally useful for defensive purposes." Skeen, *Citizen Soldiers,* 105.

28. William Ray Barlow, "The Coming of the War of 1812 in Michigan Territory," *Michigan History* 53 (1969): 106; Worthington Papers, Ohio Historical Society, Columbus.

29. Carter, ed., *Territory of Michigan,* 314–20, 326, 376–77.

30. U.S. Congress, *American State Papers: Documents, Legislative and Executive, of the Congress of the United States,* Class II: *Indian Affairs,* 2 vols. (Washington, D.C.: Gales and Seaton, 1832–34), 1:780–82.

31. Hull to Dearborn(?), March 6, 1812, Richard C. Knopf, ed., *Document*

Transactions of the War of 1812 in the Northwest (Columbus: Ohio State Museum, 1947), 6, pt. 1: 80; William Hull, *Report of the Trial of Brigadier General William Hull* (New York: Eastburn, Kirk, 1814), 136–37; Glenn Tucker, *Poltroons and Patriots* (Indianapolis: Bobbs-Merrill, 1954), 1:148.

32. *Michigan Pioneer Collections* 40 (1929): 159, 171, 179–81, 214–16, 371, 445; Carter, ed., *Territory of Michigan*, 131, 134–36.

33. Clarence E. Carter, ed., *Territory of Michigan,* 379–80. More appeals for federal troops followed. Knopf, ed., *Document Transactions* 6, pt. 1: 47, 152.

34. Cullum, *Campaigns of the War of 1812–15,* 74–75.

35. Quoted, ibid., 70.

36. Ibid., 70.

37. Skeen, *Citizen Soldiers,* 105; Allan S. Everest, *The War of 1812 in the Champlain Valley* (Syracuse, N.Y.: Syracuse University Press, 1981), 91–92.

38. *National Intelligencer* (Washington, D.C.), December 22, 1812.

39. Richard Durfee in Dann, ed., *The Revolution Remembered,* 34.

40. Joseph Wood, ibid., 39

41. Thomas Wood, ibid., 90.

42. Diary of Captain Daniel Cushing in Harlow Lindley, ed., *Fort Meigs and the War of 1812* (Columbus, Ohio, 1975), 98. Samuel White wrote in his memoir of the weeks passing "without any occurrence of note taking place." Samuel White, *History of the American Troops, during the Late War, under the Command of Colonels Fenton and Campbell* (Baltimore: by the author, 1830), 6. Private John Patterson wrote, "There is nothing extraordinary happened lately." John to Levina Patterson, February 18, 1813, in Florence Howard and Mary Howard, eds., "The Letters of John Patterson, 1812–1813," *Western Pennsylvania Historical Magazine* 23 (1940): 106. The Canadian William Dunlop writes that most of his time in service "would be tiresome to detail, . . . one day being an exact counterpart of another." William Dunlop, *Recollections of the War of 1812* (Toronto: Historical, 1908), 94.

43. Orderly book of Cushing's Company, 2d U.S. Artillery, April 1813 to February 1814, in Lindley, ed., *Fort Meigs,* 55.

44. Ibid., 69.

45. Cushing diary, in Lindley, ed., *Fort Meigs,* 102, 107.

46. Ibid., 114.

47. Elias Darnell, *A Journal Containing an Accurate and Interesting Account of the Hardships, Sufferings, Battles, Defeat, and Captivity of Those Heroic Kentucky Volunteers and Regulars, Commanded by General Winchester* (Philadelphia: Lippincott, Grambo, 1854), 10.

48. Darnell, *Journal,* 12–17. See also ibid., 25, 29; Isaac Naylor, "The Battle of Tippecanoe: As Described by Judge Isaac Naylor, a Participant," *Indiana Magazine of History* 2 (1906): 165; John Tipton, "John Tipton's Tippecanoe Journal," *Indiana Magazine of History* 2 (1906): 172, 175–77, 180; John to Levina Patterson, February 18, 1813, in Howard and Howard, eds., "The Letters of John Patterson,"

106; John C. Parish, ed., *The Robert Lucas Journal of the War of 1812 during the Campaign under General William Hull* (Iowa City: State Historical Society, 1906), 15, 24–25, 34.

49. Darnell, *Journal,* 35.

50. Ibid., 16.

51. Tipton, "Tippecanoe Journal," 175.

52. Cushing diary, in Lindley, ed., *Fort Meigs,* 98–99, 136. One soldier wrote his wife about his first fight at Fort Niagara in 1812. The two sides fired cannon at one another for a few hours, with two killed and three wounded, and two more killed when an American cannon exploded. "The seign loket awful but i was with out fear." John to Levina Patterson, November 26, 1812, in Howard and Howard, eds., "The Letters of John Patterson," 104.

53. Eleazer D. Wood, "Journal of the Northwestern Campaign of 1812–13," in Cullum, *Campaigns of the War of 1812–15,* 388, 390.

54. Cushing diary, in Lindley, ed., *Fort Meigs,* 136–37.

55. Benson J. Lossing, *Pictorial Field-Book of the War of 1812* (New York: Harper, 1868), 251–96.

56. Cushing diary, in Lindley, ed., *Fort Meigs,* 85–87.

57. Orderly book, 2d U.S. Artillery, in Lindley, ed., *Fort Meigs,* 58–59, 68–69, 71, 76.

58. Ibid., 47. See also ibid., 55, 58.

59. John to Levina Patterson, April 25, 1813, in Howard and Howard, eds., "The Letters of John Patterson," 108. He died of unknown causes shortly thereafter.

60. Cushing diary, in Lindley, ed., *Fort Meigs,* 86, 92, 105.

61. Darnell, *Journal,* 7.

62. Tipton, "Tippecanoe Journal," 176.

63. Orderly book, 2d U.S. Artillery, in Lindley, ed., *Fort Meigs,* 67.

64. Tipton, "Tippecanoe Journal," 179.

65. Orderly book, 2d U.S. Artillery, in Lindley, ed., *Fort Meigs,* 68.

66. Ibid., 77,

67. Tipton, "Tippecanoe Journal," 170–72, 174–75.

68. Darnell, *Journal,* 32. See also Wood, "Journal," in Cullum, *Campaigns of the War of 1812–15,* 362–412; Statement of David Harvey, in Ernest Cruikshank, ed., *Documentary History of the Campaigns on the Niagara Frontier in 1812–14,* 9 vols. (Welland, Ont.: Tribune, 1902–1908), 4:249.

69. Darnell, *Journal,* 40. "The waste of life was also very great from malaria, privations, exposure, excessive fatigue, and the want of competent surgeons, instruments and medicines. Our hospitals did more for the enemy than our arms." Cullum, *Campaigns of the War of 1812–15,* 102n.

70. John to Levina Patterson, January 20, 1813, in Howard and Howard, eds., "The Letters of John Patterson," 105.

71. Wood, "Journal," in Cullum, *Campaigns of the War of 1812–15,* 403.

72. E. Wayne Carp, *To Starve the Army at Pleasure: Continental Army Admin-*

istration and American Political Culture, 1775–1783 (Chapel Hill: University of North Carolina Press, 1984).

73. Darnell, *Journal,* 26, 38–39. See also White, *History of the American Troops,* 13–14; Tipton, "Tippecanoe Journal," 174, 176.

74. Quoted in General Smyth to General Dearborn, November 9, 1812, Cruikshank, ed., *Documentary History,* 4:188.

75. Naylor, "The Battle of Tippecanoe," 169.

76. White, *History of the American Troops,* 8. See also Cullum, *Campaigns of the War of 1812–15,* 101n.

77. Darnell, *Journal,* 45. There is the occasional comment from the other side indicating an equivalent dissatisfaction. William Dunlop wrote, "One of the great drawbacks of the service in Canada was that we got the rubbish of every department in the army." But he was comparing the Canadian forces with his experiences in Europe; once he saw what the Americans had, he altered his opinion. Dunlop, *Recollections,* 63.

78. Darnell, *Journal,* 37, 41.

79. Orderly book, 2d U.S. Artillery, in Lindley, ed., *Fort Meigs,* 69.

80. Darnell, *Journal,* 7, 10.

81. John to Levina Patterson, February 20, 1813, in Howard and Howard, eds., "The Letters of John Patterson," 101. See also John to Levina Patterson, April 25, 1813, ibid., 108; General Porter, General Orders, November 2, 1814, in Cruikshank, ed., *Documentary History,* 2:283–84; Alfred Brunson, *A Western Pioneer; or, Incidents of the Life and Times of Reverend Alfred Brunson,* 2 vols. (Cincinnati: Hitchcock and Walden, 1872–1879), 1:100–108.

82. It was a good thing for Jackson that he did not actually have to fire, as "the musket he had used so effectively was too ancient a weapon to be fired." Robert V. Remini, *Andrew Jackson and the Course of American Empire, 1767–1821* (New York: Harper and Row, 1977), 199.

83. General Izard to the Secretary of War, November 2, 1814, in Cruikshank, ed., *Documentary History,* 2:284.

84. White, *History of the American Troops,* 8, 10. See also General Smyth to General Dearborn, November 9, 1812, Cruikshank, ed., *Documentary History,* 4:188.

85. John Lovett to Joseph Alexander, November 4, 1812, in Cruikshank, ed., *Documentary History,* 4:181.

86. Livingston to General Smyth, November 4, 1812, ibid., 180.

87. Statement of David Harvey, ibid., 249–50; see also 232–33.

88. General Smyth to General Dearborn, November 9, 1812, ibid., 186–87.

89. See, e.g., Darnell, *Journal,* 42; White, *History of the American Troops,* 11–15.

90. Darnell, *Journal,* 40.

91. Tipton, "Tippecanoe Journal," 171.

92. Dunlop, *Recollections,* 33–35.

93. Howard and Howard, eds., "The Letters of John Patterson," 101.

94. John to Levina Patterson, undated [1813], ibid., 107. See also John to Levina Patterson, February 18, 1813, ibid., 106; Brunson, *A Western Pioneer*, 1:113–14, 151–52.

95. Cushing diary, in Lindley, ed., *Fort Meigs*, 103.

96. Ibid., 104–5, 109–10.

97. Wood, "Journal," in Cullum, *Campaigns of the War of 1812–15*, 379.

98. Quoted in Cullum, *Campaigns of the War of 1812–15*, 106.

99. Wood, "Journal," in ibid., 377, 383.

100. Tipton, "Tippecanoe Journal," 177.

101. In general see the Orderly book, 2d U.S. Artillery, in Lindley, ed., *Fort Meigs*.

102. Cushing diary, in Lindley, ed., *Fort Meigs*, 103. See also Tipton, "Tippecanoe Journal," 174–77, 182; General Smyth to General Dearborn, November 9, 1812, in Cruikshank, ed., *Documentary History*, 4:187.

103. General Tannehill to General Smyth, December 7, 1812, Cruikshank, ed., *Documentary History*, 4:285.

104. Tipton, "Tippecanoe Journal," 178.

105. Cushing diary, in Lindley, ed., *Fort Meigs*, 109.

106. Wood, "Journal," in Cullum, *Campaigns of the War of 1812–15*, 362–63.

107. White, *History of the American Troops*, 5–6.

108. See, e.g., Tipton, "Tippecanoe Journal," 170–84.

109. Tipton, "Tippecanoe Journal," 171. Keeping weapons clean was a major problem for the troops; a musket or rifle could get so dirty that it was dangerous to use. "A rifle is by no means suited for a day's fighting; when it gets foul from repeated firing it is difficult even to hammer the ball down, and the same foulness which clogs the barrel must injure the precision of the ball." Dunlop, *Recollections*, 69.

110. General John Stricker to General Smith, September 15, 1814, in Nathaniel Hickman, ed., *The Citizen Soldiers at North Point and Fort McHenry, September 12 and 13, 1814* (Baltimore: J. Young, 1858), 89–90.

111. General Orders, September 19, 1814, ibid., 92.

112. Ibid., 90, 96.

113. Cullum, *Campaigns of the War of 1812–15*, 144–45, 150; Skeen, *Citizen Soldiers*, 106; *Niles' Weekly Register* 4 (June 19, 1813): 261; *Military Monitor* 1 (June 28, 1813): 350; General Brown to Governor Daniel D. Tompkins, June 1, 1813, in Cruikshank, ed., *Documentary History*, 5:283–87; Richard G. Carlson, ed., "George P. Peters' Version of the Battle of Tippecanoe (November 7, 1811)," *Vermont History* 45 (1977): 41.

114. Skeen, *Citizen Soldiers*, 98; General Amos Hall to Governor Tompkins, July 4, 1812, Buffalo and Erie Historical Society, Buffalo, N.Y., reel 2; Van Rensselaer to Governor Tompkins, July 23, 1812, Cruikshank, ed., *Documentary History*, 3:142. On the Niagara frontier in 1812 there were no artillerymen and no artillery heavier

than a six-pounder. At most, there was sufficient ammunition for ten rounds each for 1,000 men. Howard and Howard, eds., "The Letters of John Patterson," 100.

115. General Van Rensselaer to Governor Tompkins of New York, August 31, 1812, in Howard and Howard, eds., "The Letters of John Patterson," 102; Lossing, *Pictorial Field-Book*, 384–85.

116. Theodore Crackel, "The Battle of Queenston Heights, 13 October 1812," in Charles Heller and William Stofft, eds., *America's First Battles, 1776–1965* (Lawrence: University Press of Kansas, 1986), 33–56.

117. Cullum, *Campaigns of the War of 1812–15*, 69. On other militia units refusing to cross into Canada, see Parish, ed., *Robert Lucas Journal*, 27.

118. Quoted in Skeen, *Citizen Soldiers*, 101. The War Department made no effort to coordinate their attacks in 1812, with the result that the British commander, General Brock, was free to move his whole force against Hull at Detroit and then shift it east to defeat Van Rensselaer at Queenstown. Cullum, *Campaigns of the War of 1812–15*, 75–77.

119. Skeen, *Citizen Soldiers*, 101; Inspection Reports of Captain William King, attached to General Smyth, to Speaker of the House Langdon Cheves, February 8, 1814, *Annals of Congress*, 13th Cong., 2d sess., appendix, Docs. 11 (2487), 18 (2483–84).

120. Cushing diary, in Lindley, ed., *Fort Meigs*, 115. William Dunlop offers a good example of the inexperience of American troops: "I once saw a solder of the 32nd take two American sentries prisoners, by placing his cap and great coat on a bush, . . . waited till both of their firelocks were discharged" at the coat, and then took them prisoner. Dunlop, *Recollections*, 69.

121. Cushing diary, in Lindley, ed., *Fort Meigs*, 111.

122. Darnell, *Journal*, 11, 19–20. See also Cruikshank, ed., *Documentary History*, 3:283.

123. John to Levina Patterson, February 20, 1813, in Howard and Howard, eds., "The Letters of John Patterson," 106.

124. Darnell, *Journal*, 29.

125. Cullum, *Campaigns of the War of 1812–15*, 207.

126. Quoted, ibid., 207. From the other side, William Dunlop described how at the battle of Chrysler's Farm the Americans were "driven off by the bayonet." Dunlop, *Recollections*, 19.

127. Quoted in Cullum, *Campaigns of the War of 1812–15*, 215. General Brown was wounded later in the battle and General Ripley withdrew, leaving the British artillery behind. Ibid., 218. See also the evaluation by Brown and Jesup of the bayonet charge by the Americans at the Siege of Fort Erie in 1814 (ibid., 252–53), and William Dunlop's dismissal of the Americans as having "no more idea of a bayonet being pointed at them than they had of being swallowed up by an earthquake." Dunlop, *Recollections*, 76.

128. Cullum, *Campaigns of the War of 1812–15*, 107–9. On this theme see Bellesiles, *Arming America*, 208–304.

129. Hazard et al., eds., *Pennsylvania Archives*, 2d ser., 12:726–41.

130. Sapio, *Pennsylvania and the War,* 188; U.S. Congress, *American State Papers: Documents, Legislative and Executive, of the Congress of the United States,* Class V: *Military Affairs,* 7 vols. (Washington, D.C.: Gales and Seaton, 1832–61), 1:511.

131. Sapio, *Pennsylvania and the War,* 185; see also Hazard et al., eds., *Pennsylvania Archives,* 2d ser., 12:617–27, 641–45.

132. Cushing diary, in Lindley, ed., *Fort Meigs,* 89. See also General Andrew Jackson to the secretary of war, February 18, 1815, in Cullum, *Campaigns of the War of 1812–15,* 335.

133. Snyder to Brigade Inspectors, August 25, 1812, in Cruikshank, ed., *Documentary History,* 3:208.

134. Ibid., 4:187–88, 225–26, 267–71.

135. Josiah Robinson to Colonel Solomon Van Rensselaer, December 2, 1812, ibid., 4:266–67; Skeen, *Citizen Soldiers,* 194, 259.

136. General Smyth to George McClure et al., December 3, 1812, in Cruikshank, ed., *Documentary History,* 4:270–71.

137. Statement of Bill Sherman December 3, 1812, ibid., 4:247. See also the newspaper accounts on these events, ibid., 281–85; *Niles' Weekly Register* 3 (December 19, 1812): 252.

138. Cullum, *Campaigns of the War of 1812–15,* 69; Statement of William Winder and Samuel Angus, December 13, 1812, Cruikshank, ed., *Documentary History,* 4:303; Buffalo *Gazette,* December 15, 1812, in ibid., 303–8.

139. New York *Evening Post,* December 10 and 24, 1812, in Cruikshank, ed., *Documentary History,* 4:238, 282–84.

140. Buffalo *Gazette,* December 8 and 22, 1812, ibid., 4:291–95, 335.

141. Secretary of War to General Dearborn, December 19, 1812, ibid., 4:330.

142. Cullum, *Campaigns of the War of 1812–15,* 294–96.

143. Edward D. Ingraham, *A Sketch of the Events Which Preceded the Capture of Washington* (Philadelphia: Carey and Hart, 1849), 44–45.

144. Cullum, *Campaigns of the War of 1812–15,* 299.

145. Ibid., 285–87; John R. Elting, *Amateurs, to Arms! A Military History of the War of 1812* (New York: Da Capo Press, 1995), 198–243.

146. Cullum, *Campaigns of the War of 1812–15,* 289.

147. Madison to Anna [her sister], August 23, 1813, "Her grand-niece," *Memoirs and Letters of Dolly Madison* (Boston: Houghton Mifflin, 1887), 110.

148. John S. Gallagher, "Memoirs," in John S. Williams, *History of the Invasion and Capture of Washington, and of the Events Which Preceded and Followed* (New York: Harper, 1857), 368–70. Gallagher says this even while recording that the British Captain Gordon held that his forces lost seven men on all his ships during the twenty-three days he was on the Potomac.

149. Darnell, *Journal,* 25–26.

150. White, *History of the American Troops,* 7.

151. Ibid., 15–16.

152. Dunlop, *Recollections,* 84.

153. Cullum, *Campaigns of the War of 1812–15,* 116–17.

154. Darnell, *Journal,* 26–27.

155. Quoted in Cullum, *Campaigns of the War of 1812–15,* 133.

156. Brown to General Joseph G. Swift, September 12, 1816, quoted in ibid., 137.

157. Quoted in the *National Intelligencer* (Washington, D.C.), February 16, 1815.

158. *Annals of Congress,* 13th Cong., 3d sess., House 1155–57, 1167, 1174, 1184–85, 1191, 1194; Senate, 233–34, 238–43, 250, 253, 258–59, 274; Appendix, 1966–67.

159. *Annals of Congress,* 13th Cong., 3d sess., House, 538, 1200–1201.

160. Ibid.

161. *Annals of Congress,* 13th Cong., 3d sess., Senate, 287, 291–92, 297–98; House, 1266–67, 1271–73. The regular army was reduced to 6,000 in 1821. *Annals of Congress,* 16th Cong., 2d sess., House, 1789–99; Skeen, "Calhoun, Crawford, and the Politics of Retrenchment," *South Carolina Historical Magazine* 73 (1972): 141–55.

162. Bellesiles, *Arming America,* 261–304.

163. George S. Pappas, *To the Point: The United States Military Academy, 1802–1902* (Westport, Conn.: Praeger, 1993), 99–322.

164. *National Intelligencer* (Washington, D.C.), March 3, 1815. See also "Wallace" in ibid., April 1, 1815; Albany *Argus* March 7, 1815.

165. *Niles' Weekly Register* 8 (March 4, 1815): 417–19.

166. Robert Meriwether et al., eds., *The Papers of John C. Calhoun,* 25 vols. (Columbia: University of South Carolina Press, 1959–), 1:81.

167. Speech on Merchants' Bonds, December 8, 1812, ibid., 1:144.

168. Speech on the Revenue Bill, January 31, 1816, ibid., 1:324.

169. Dunlop, *Recollections,* xii.

170. Ibid., 13–14, 16–17, 19–20.

171. On the memory of the American Revolution, see Michael Kammen, *A Season of Youth: The American Revolution and the Historical Imagination* (New York: Knopf, 1978); Robert C. Cray Jr., "Major John André and the Three Captors: Class Dynamics and Revolutionary Memory Wars in the Early Republic, 1780–1831," *Journal of the Early Republic* 17 (1997): 371–97; Robert E. McGlone, "Deciphering Memory: John Adams and the Authorship of the Declaration of Independence," *Journal of American History* 85 (1998): 411–38.

172. Young, *The Shoemaker and the Tea Party,* 55.

173. John William Ward, *Andrew Jackson: Symbol for an Age* (New York: Oxford University Press, 1955); Steven Watts, *The Republic Reborn: War and the Making of Liberal America, 1790–1820* (Baltimore: Johns Hopkins University Press, 1987).

174. John S. Rensselaer, *Proceedings of the Convention of the Soldiers of the War of 1812, in the State of New York* (Albany, N.Y.: Joel Munsell, 1857), 7.

175. Ibid., 22–23.

9

The Making of an Atlantic State System

Britain and the United States, 1795–1825

Eliga H. Gould

"Unlike the Axis blueprint of a New World Order," wrote the Roosevelt confidant Forrest Davis on the eve of the United States' entry into the Second World War, "the Atlantic System is old, rational, and pragmatic." In search of an alternative to Fascist Europe—"a sterile prisonhouse inhabited by robotlike heroes and faceless subject races"—Davis had no trouble imagining a "community of . . . self-governing peoples around the Atlantic basin," nor did he doubt that the origins of this regime lay in "the liberal revolutions of the eighteenth and early nineteenth centuries." Among the Atlantic world's progenitors, Davis mentioned the three "Presidents of the Virginia succession," as well as John Quincy Adams, British foreign secretary George Canning, and Simon Bolívar, "who brought independence to one-quarter of South America." More than anything else, however, Davis's was an Anglo-American condominium, one based on Britain's acceptance of the United States' growing power as articulated in the Monroe Doctrine. "While the admonishing declaration came from Washington," wrote Davis, "the power of enforcement lay with the British fleet."

> Canning, with truthful arrogance, could boast in Parliament that he had "called the New World into being to redress the balance of the Old"; the Latin republics were able to consummate their independence in the lee of British sea power and American assertion; and this country rounded out its self-allotted portion of North America undisturbed.[1]

Even allowing for Davis's propagandistic intent, little in this idealized characterization would satisfy current practitioners of Atlantic history. Though hardly an institution of "faceless races," African slavery occupies a well-established place in contemporary literature on the early modern Atlantic, as fundamental to scholarship on the United States (and its colonial predecessors) as to that on the empires of Britain, Spain, France, Portugal, the Netherlands, and Denmark.[2] Similarly, "British sea power and American assertion" generally rank near the bottom of scholarly accounts of Latin America's wars for independence, although the Spanish Empire's demise posed daunting challenges for governments around the Atlantic littoral.[3] Even Davis's rendition of the bilateral discussions that preceded the Monroe Doctrine looks suspect to modern eyes. Notwithstanding Britain's changing priorities after 1815, American distrust remained pronounced through the Civil War, and historians today attribute the Atlantic world's integrated character not to the diplomatic understanding of the 1820s and the efforts of "forefathers" like Canning and Monroe but to social and economic forces whose pattern was set during the three centuries that preceded the age of revolution.[4]

In one crucial respect, however, Davis's remarks contain an element of truth. Although the "great flirtation"—as Bradford Perkins dubbed the Anglo-American exchange of 1823—proved short-lived, the Monroe Doctrine capped an extraordinary thirty-year period during which Britain and the United States worked by fits and starts to fashion the rudiments of an Atlantic state system.[5] Encompassing the Jay and Pinkney treaties (1794–95), the Franco-American Quasi War of 1798–99, the British Orders in Council and Jefferson's Embargo Act (1808), the United States' acquisition of Louisiana (1803) and East and West Florida (1819), and the War of 1812, these years witnessed a gradual retreat (on both sides) from the old colonial order, which held the Atlantic to be a zone of contested sovereignties, diminished legalities, and warring imperialisms. In its place, the two English-speaking empires sought to erect an international regime that mimicked key features of the European state system—a community believed to be ordinarily at peace, animated by mutually beneficial trade and shared respect for the rule of law, and governed by treaties between states that recognized each other's legitimacy. Most important of all, the Atlantic system forged during the first quarter of the nineteenth century was one that remained, in important respects, distinct from Europe. At first little more than a prescriptive flourish, the inception of this state system ultimately carried implications of the first importance, both for the United States and the British Empire and for the Western Hemisphere's other nations and peoples.

Beyond the Line

To America's founding generation, it was a commonplace that the United States occupied an international sphere distinct from Europe. "America has a hemisphere to itself," wrote Thomas Jefferson in 1813. "The insulated state in which nature has placed the American continent" meant "that no spark of war kindled in the other quarters of the globe should be wafted across the wide oceans which separate us from them."[6] As Mercy Otis Warren remarked in the closing pages of her *History of the American Revolution* (1805):

> It will be the wisdom . . . of the American government, forever to maintain with an unshaken magnanimity, the present neutral position of the United States. The hand of nature has displayed its magnificence in this quarter of the globe, in the astonishing rivers, lakes, and mountains, replete with the richest minerals and the most useful materials for manufactures.[7]

In part, this sense of isolation reflected a desire to avoid taking sides in the wars of the French Revolution; more loftily, Americans imagined theirs as a new world where men and women might shed the corrupt ways of the old. But whatever purpose they were meant to serve, assertions of the Western Hemisphere's distinctiveness usually carried expansionist overtones and endorsed the idea that the United States was free to practice slavery, wage war on Indians, and acquire territory along its borders, without becoming embroiled in the wars and diplomacy of Europe.[8]

Although firmly yoked to the Republic's idealized self-image, this perception had its origins in the brutal calculus spawned by Europe's early modern age of expansion, especially the expansion of Great Britain. Into the middle years of the eighteenth century, the British—in common with both the American colonists and their European rivals—assumed that what Edmund Burke called the diplomatic republic of Europe did not extend (at least fully) into those parts of the world that lay beyond the so-called lines of amity, the imaginary quadrant formed by the Tropic of Cancer and a prime meridian that bisected the Atlantic somewhere west of the Azores.[9] As developed by European adventurers during the sixteenth and seventeenth centuries, the doctrine of autonomous spheres made it possible for Europeans to wage war in the Atlantic, Indian, and Pacific oceans, while maintaining peace (or "amity") in Europe. Occasionally, governments reversed this relationship with wartime pacts of colonial neutrality, in effect permitting subjects beyond the line to pursue nonbelligerent activities that appeared inimical to metropolitan interests. More typically, though, Europeans recognized distinctions between the two zones by concluding "truce[s] to be observed in Europe"—in the words of the seventeenth-century jurist Samuel Pufendorf—while continuing hostilities "in the East or West Indies."[10] As Oliver Cromwell allegedly said on learning that English forces had captured French Acadia in 1655, it was well known that "everyone could act for his own advantage in those quarters."[11] From the standpoint of the maritime powers, Europe was a zone of law, the world beyond a place of chronic war and irregular violence.

Ironically, this bifurcated geography was an expression of imperial weakness, not strength. Although the doctrine of autonomous spheres clearly served Britain's colonial and maritime interests, it also reflected the empire's character as a loose-knit consortium of forts, factories, and colonies, over which the metropolitan institutions of crown and Parliament exercised what Jack Greene has called a "negotiated authority."[12] Constraints on the imperial authority of the British state were especially conspicuous with respect to the colonies of settlement, most of which—including the Canadian and West Indian colonies that remained loyal during the American Revolution—possessed jealously independent assemblies with broad legislative and fiscal powers over their own affairs. Although it sprang from different sources, the autonomy of the British Empire's non-European inhabitants was also pronounced, as was evident from agreements like the Covenant Chain with the Iroquois, the colonial treaties with Jamaica's Maroons (1739) and St. Vincent's Black Caribs (1773), and the alliances that British slave traders negotiated with the native kingdoms on Africa's western coasts. Despite the involvement of the Royal Navy and, increasingly, the British army, Britain's expansion was heavily indebted to the collaboration of such groups, many of whom—European creole no less than Indian and African—subscribed to "irregular" norms of war and diplomacy and over whom metropolitan officials exercised limited control.[13]

Compounding this imperial decentralization was the absence of clear, universally recognized European jurisdictions in the extra-European world, which tended to draw people on the margins of the great overseas empires into local acts of violence and undeclared warfare. Although contested borders and disputed titles were hardly unknown in Europe proper, such conflicts were practically the norm in the wider Atlantic, especially in open water and "unoccupied" land where rival governments maintained extensive, overlapping claims but where they often lacked the resources to take actual possession. In the half century between the Peace of Paris (1763) and the Congress of Vienna (1815), Britain's disputed claims along its colonial borders repeatedly brought it to the brink of war with the region's other powers, including France over Senegal and the Turks and Caicos Islands (1764), Spain over the Falkland Islands (1770) and Honduras Bay (1770 and 1786), and—intermittently after 1783—the United States over the border with British North America.[14] At times, such conflicts involved territory whose main function (as Samuel Johnson wrote of the Falkland Islands) was to supply "a station for contraband traders, a nursery for fraud, and a receptacle of theft."[15] Even when the issues at stake were minor, however, Britain's relations with its imperial rivals reinforced perceptions of the western and southern Atlantic as a zone beyond Europe's pale, international space where Europeans and non-Europeans alike could engage in behavior that would have been unthinkable closer to home.

If the violence that the British and their European rivals periodically visited on each other could be appalling, a third distinction between Europe and the extra-European world was the brutality with which Europeans treated the region's indigenous peoples. Despite their self-professed regard for the liberties of Europe, the British readily seized chunks of territory throughout the wider world, including—during the *annus mirabilis* of 1759 and the ensuing Peace of 1763—the eastern half of North America, the so-called ceded islands in the Caribbean, Senegal and Goree on Africa's West Coast, and the Indian province of Bengal. Although Britain's power in Asia depended on a series of sophisticated and highly technical treaties with potentates like the Mogul emperor, British and colonial authorities regarded most of America and parts of Africa as "empty space" from which settlers were free to expel native inhabitants, by force if less coercive means proved inadequate.[16] Despite the legal hostility to owning slaves in both Britain and Western Europe, jurists throughout the British Atlantic also held that it was entirely legitimate to purchase enslaved men, women, and children on the coasts of Africa and to keep them in perpetual bondage in North America and the Caribbean. As Lord Chief Justice Mansfield famously declared in the *Somerset* case (1772), metropolitan slavery was "odious" and could only be supported by "positive" laws that England lacked, but he went out of his way to remind his audience that the institution was "authorized by the laws and opinions of Jamaica and Virginia."[17] Often compounded by wars between European empires, the brutalization of African slaves and Indians ultimately reinforced perceptions of the outer Atlantic as a place fundamentally different from Europe.

The upshot was a system of politics—we might almost say an ancien régime–where Europe's maritime powers subscribed in varying degrees to the principle that "might makes right beyond the line," with governments tolerating or, on occasion, deliberately promoting extra-European acts of war and piracy even as they maintained cordial relations at home. Nowhere was this division more apparent than in what Sir William Blackstone called the British "maritime state," the cornerstone of which was the regulation of colonial trade.[18] Although historians have tended to emphasize the integrative effects of transatlantic commerce, the laws regulating Britain's merchant marine drew a series of distinctions between trade in European waters and trade that had an extra-European point of origin or destination.[19] Foreign commerce originating in European ports was subject to a variety of tariffs, many calculated to make foreign imports prohibitively expensive; however, metropolitan merchants were free to ship goods into or out of any port on the British mainland and to do so in vessels belonging to other nations.[20] Through agreements like the celebrated Methuen Treaty (1704) with Portugal or the short-lived Eden Treaty (1786) with France, Britain also suspended the more onerous duties on goods such as wine, olive oil, and cloth. In the words of the preamble to the Eden Treaty, such concessions transformed "contraband trade" into "lawful commerce"; more idealistically (if less justifiably), some envisioned closer economic relations between European nations as preparing the way for "a system of universal peace."[21]

Outside Europe, however, both Britain and its European rivals prohibited foreigners from trading with their possessions. According to the British navigation laws, colonial planters and merchants had to ship "enumerated goods" like tobacco, rice, and sugar through British ports before being exported again for sale in Europe. Unless granted a special exemption, as in the West Indian Free Ports Act (1766), the commerce of Britain's possessions in Africa, the Caribbean, and North America also had to travel in British ships, which could be built anywhere in the British Empire but were required to be manned by crews that were at least three-quarters British.[22] These regulations served two distinct (though related) purposes. The first was to impose a kind of undeclared warfare on the commerce and manufacturing of Britain's European rivals—what David Hume termed a deliberate attempt to "reduce all our neighbouring nations to the same state of sloth and ignorance that prevails in MOROCCO and the coast of BARBARY."[23] The second was to encourage the British shipping industry, which supplied the Royal Navy with able-bodied seamen and was therefore vital to its ability to dominate the treacherous waters of the western and southern Atlantic.[24] It was not hard to find cosmopolitan writers like Hume and Adam Smith who lamented the first objective, but the second commanded broad support. Indeed, before 1776, even American patriots accepted the parliamentary taxes and regulations upon which Britain's maritime supremacy—and, therefore, their own overseas trade and domestic prosperity—depended.[25] Whereas it was just possible for British trade in Europe to be conducted on mutually beneficial terms, Britain's commerce in the world beyond took place in a brutally competitive zone where superior force was the only certain safeguard against the depredations of friend as well as foe.

Although the British Empire was a spectacular beneficiary of the doctrine of two spheres, Britons and Americans were well aware of political and economic forces tending to forge closer ties between Europe and the wider world, especially in the North Atlantic. As an English pamphleteer remarked in 1755, European outposts in Asia and Africa were generally too small and too dependent on "the Potentates of those Spheres" for colonial tensions to "affect the Tranquility of *Europe*." North America, on the other hand, was the "only *real Seminary* of Commerce and Navigation, in the Universe," making it the one region, "beside *Europe*," where local conflicts could precipitate a general war between Britain and its European rivals.[26] In the years following the Seven Years' War, Britons throughout the empire elevated perceptions of the North Atlantic's unified character to near-doctrinal status.[27] Writing in 1764, the former governor of Massachusetts, Thomas Pownall, opined that Britain and America stood on the brink of a new era, one where "the spirit of [transatlantic] commerce . . . will form the general policy, and rule the powers of Europe."[28] Benjamin Franklin was no less expansive, arguing that the North Atlantic's commercial unity made Britain's far-flung empire a more integrated "nation" than the most centralized of its land-based rivals:

> While our strength at sea continues, the banks of the Ohio . . . are nearer to London, than the remote parts of France and Spain are to their respective capitals; and much nearer than Connaught and Ulster were in the days of Queen Elizabeth. No body foretells the dissolution of the Russian monarchy from its extent, yet I will venture to say, the eastern parts of it are already much more inaccessible from Petersburgh, than the country on the Mississippi is from London.[29]

Obviously, the American Revolution dashed hopes that the British Empire might become a greater British nation of the sort imagined by Franklin and Pownall. Nonetheless, the sense of transatlantic unity that fed such visions remained a conspicuous feature of Anglo-American discourse. As Thomas Paine remarked in *Common Sense* (1776), declaring political independence from Britain did not mean that America was opting out of the transatlantic economy. "The commerce by which she hath enriched herself," wrote Paine, "are the necessaries of life, and will always have a market while eating is the custom of Europe."[30] Notwithstanding the success of the United States' quest for political independence, many Britons agreed with Paine's assessment, though they generally envisioned the erstwhile colonies as economic satellites, not equal partners. Indeed, starting in 1783, Britain placed American merchants trading with the British mainland—though not with the rest of the British Empire—on the same footing as those of its most favored trading partners in Europe.[31] In anticipation of the likely benefits, Caleb Whitefoord allegedly told his French counterpart at the Paris peace conference in 1782 that the United States might someday "form the greatest Empire in the world," but he was sure "that Great Empire wou'd be English."[32] As Lord Sheffield wrote in 1784:

> Every account from America says, that British manufactures are sell-
> ing at a considerable profit, while other European goods cannot ob-
> tain the first cost. Every day's experience shews, that this country,
> from the nature and quality of its manufactures, and from the ascen-
> dancy it has acquired in commerce, will command three-fourths of the
> American trade.[33]

Despite the Atlantic world's genesis in acts of piracy and irregular war-fare, it had become sufficiently unified by the eighteenth century's closing years for writers around its northern rim to imagine a community of shared political, economic, and cultural interests. Without this development, the American Revolution could not have been the event of global significance proclaimed by British writers as varied as Richard Price, Thomas Pownall, and Josiah Tucker, nor could it have initiated the "age of democratic revo-lution" that convulsed much of Europe, most of Latin America, and the French Caribbean island of Saint Domingue.[34] In the words of an Indepen-dence Day sermon preached at the Baptist meetinghouse in Providence, Rhode Island, in 1793:

> Has not united America led the way? And may she not boast, with an
> honest pride, of the influence of her example in exciting the attention
> of many nations to their natural and civil rights? With what freedom
> of thought—with what enlightened and ardent philanthropy, has she
> inspired many of the nations of Europe![35]

Even as Britons and Americans affirmed the integrated character of the Atlantic world, however, they continued to acknowledge key elements of the old divisions. Indeed, for many decades after the Revolution, the United States remained deeply implicated in the social, political, and economic practices of the colonial era. Not only did every state outside New England permit slavery within its borders, but both the federal government and a number of states also continued to engage in protracted and bloody warfare with Indian nations in the West. Equally important, despite the colonies' decisive role in triggering the European wars of 1756–63 and 1778–83, American writers and politicians spoke as though the north-south axis of the old lines of amity was once again a diplomatic reality. "We . . . dwell in a distant part of the world, far removed from any allies, and very little interested in the politics of Europe," observed a New England divine in 1793.[36] As Alexander Hamilton assured British ambassador George Hammond, "it was the settled policy of [the American] government . . . to avoid entangling itself with European connexions."[37] In the oft-quoted words of Washington's "Farewell Address" (1796), the United States sought to cultivate good commercial relations with "foreign Nations," but it desired to maintain "as little *political* connection as possible":

> Europe has a set of primary interests, which to us have none, or a very remote relation. Hence she must be engaged in frequent controversies, the causes of which are essentially foreign to our concerns. Hence therefore it must be unwise in us to implicate ourselves, by artificial ties, in the ordinary vicissitudes of her politics, or the ordinary combinations and collisions of her friendships, or enmities.[38]

Although the Western Hemisphere had become something other than a zone of chronic war between European colonists and their proxies, it remained, in important respects, a place distinct from Europe.

The British Ocean

Given this persistent sense of difference, it was unclear how far the United States or its immediate neighbors (should they become independent) had a claim to diplomatic parity with the states of Europe. From an American standpoint, of course, there was no question that the Declaration of Independence was, among other things, a bid to join the community of nations, which in practice meant the sovereign nations of Europe.[39] In the years following the American Revolution, however, two obstacles—both related to Britain's posture toward the newly independent Republic—made it hard to give an unambiguous endorsement to the United States' aspirations. The first was the British government's dogged refusal to modify the Navigation Acts in the colonies; the second was the perceived weakness of the federal government and the widespread uncertainty it encouraged in both Britain and the British Empire over the United States' long-term viability. As the dominant maritime power in the Western Hemisphere, Britain was in a position to influence American affairs in both these areas, giving its actions a significance for the new Republic second only to those of Americans themselves, and that exceeded that of any of the region's other European powers.

In terms of the United States' maritime interests, Britain's stance on the Navigation Acts was especially important. Because of the intercolonial trade that flourished before 1776, the Revolution prompted writers on both sides of the Atlantic to contemplate revising the commercial regulations that governed trade between the British Caribbean and the United States. Under pressure from the West India lobby, the British government made limited allowances in the Jay Treaty (1794), opening the islands' carrying trade to and from the United States to American ships of less than 70 tons and permitting free trade along Canada's inland border.[40] On the whole, though, Britain responded to the situation after 1783 by reaffirming what Lord Sheffield called the "wisdom of our ancestors" in barring foreign ships from the most lucrative portions of the colonies' carrying trade.[41] Despite the Jay Treaty's endorsement of free trade along the interior border between Canada and the United States, British negotiators made clear that the provision did not "extend to the admission of [American] Vessels . . . into the Sea-Ports, Harbours, Bays or Creeks" of British North America.[42] In the words of the maritime historian J. H. Parry, "The United States . . . offered an example, for some years the only example, of a country outside Europe in which European merchants—specifically British merchants—could trade freely, extensively and profitably, without a European government, or corporation chartered by one, assuming any responsibility for administration or defense."[43]

Because of this persistent mercantilism—on the part of Britain's European rivals no less than Britain itself—much of the United States' commerce with ports elsewhere in the Western Hemisphere remained technically illegal, being classified as contraband under the navigation laws of the region's various colonial powers. This did not prevent American merchants from doing business throughout Latin America and the Caribbean. Indeed, at the outbreak of the War of 1812, the United States possessed a merchant marine second only to that of Britain, much of it—according to critics in the British press—based on carrying the goods of Britain's enemies under the "cover" of American neutrality.[44] Nonetheless, as Jefferson wrote in the Washington administration's *Report on Foreign Commerce* (1793), "the system of prohibitions, duties and regulations" embraced by all the European empires in America made them reluctant to enter into "friendly arrangements" with the United States, exposing its navigation (and, therefore, its maritime defense) to encroachments by rivals.[45] Significantly, in protesting Britain's attempt to bar American ships from carrying food to France and its dependencies during the 1790s, Secretary of State Edmund Randolph felt compelled to remind the British ambassador that, "although the United States be without the European circle," it was not excluded from the "modern" law of nations. "Would not the nations of Europe deem the United States indecently refractory," asked Randolph, "if they should assume the privilege of dispensing with any prevailing modification of that law?" To adopt a different course would be to imply that the American states could be denied the fundamental rights of nations "because they are sovereignties of a recent date, and in the western hemisphere."[46]

Although Randolph spoke rhetorically, the ambiguity in the United States' relationship to Europe remained a recurring problem in Anglo-American diplomacy and opened the way for Britain to claim the right—in fact if not in law—to determine what part of its overseas trade was legitimate and what was not. While Europe remained at peace, this power was largely dormant. With the outbreak of the French Revolution, however, American merchants became vulnerable to the British doctrine known as the Rule of the War of 1756, which held that the king's warships and privateers could take as lawful prizes neutral vessels engaged in wartime colonial trade from which the belligerent powers' commercial regulations would ordinarily have excluded them.[47] For much of the 1790s, the government refrained from full enforcement of its "maritime rights," permitting American merchants to carry specified noncontraband goods to and from the colonies of France and its allies. Nonetheless, the mere existence of the Rule of 1756 enabled Britons to argue that the prosperity of the American Republic was the result not—as Jefferson and the Democratic Republicans would have it—of the United States' position as a nation "separated by a wide ocean from the nations of Europe" whose produce rendered its "commerce and friendship useful to them and theirs to us" but of British indulgence, even protection.[48] On several occasions, the British government offered to convoy American ships sailing for Europe, and during the Franco-American Quasi War of 1798–99, it permitted unarmed merchantmen to travel under the protection of the Royal Navy, which sometimes acted in concert with American warships.[49] In view of this collaboration, many Britons assumed that, without Britain's naval supremacy, the armed vessels of the French Republic and Empire would soon decimate the United States' merchant marine. As the *Times* wrote in 1811, "The Alps and the Apennines of America are the British Navy. If ever that should be removed, a short time will suffice to establish the head-quarters of a Duke-Marshal at

Washington, and to divide the territory of the Union into military prefectures."[50]

By the second decade of the nineteenth century, of course, Britain's protecting hand had come to seem a good deal less benign. In a prize case involving the American merchant ship *Essex* (1805), the British greatly expanded the Rule of 1756, making it legal for British warships and privateers to seize American ships conveying Spanish colonial goods via U.S. ports to Europe. Two years later, following the Napoleonic decrees that placed Europe off-limits to British ships (and British goods in American ships), the British government carried its resentment against American profiteers still further, issuing the notorious Orders in Council of November 1807 that required neutral ships, most of which belonged to the United States, to obtain special British licenses before carrying goods to and from the ports of France and its European satellites. To Americans—then as now—these restrictions amounted to gross infringements of the United States' rights as a neutral power, and many detected in the Orders in Council, in particular, what Alfred Thayer Mahan described as "literally, and in no metaphorical sense, the reimposition of colonial regulation."[51] In terms of Britain's stated goals, Mahan exaggerated; however, Americans agreed that the government's actions threatened to reduce the United States to the status of a British satellite. As a meeting of Philadelphia Republicans resolved in May 1812, Britain's actions left Congress no choice but to declare war; otherwise, "our sovereignty is servility, our commerce a colonial trade, our persons exposed to pillage, our property to piracy, our boasted institutions to piles of theoretical ruins, and peace itself, that most desirable of all political enjoyments, a contumely and a curse."[52] "I am told," remarked Britain's ambassador Augustus Foster on learning of the motion, that "the assembly ... amounted to but 2,000 persons principally composed of Irishmen of the lowest order, Negroes, and Boys."[53] If so, those in attendance spoke for a broad swath of the American public.

The second area where British attitudes clashed with American aspirations was over the viability of the United States as a federal republic. Of course, Americans did not need the British to remind them of the Union's fragility. In the quarter-century between Washington's First Inaugural and the Treaty of Ghent (1814), the Republic's most serious crises all involved regional challenges to the federal government, including the Whiskey Rebellion (1795), the opposition to the Alien and Sedition Acts (1798), and the Burr Conspiracy (1807). Although hostility to excessive concentrations of power was generally associated with Jefferson's Republicans, Federalists were no less willing to invoke the dangers of over-mighty government when it suited their purposes. During the Embargo of 1808, defiance of federal authority in the party's eastern strongholds was widespread, and, following the outbreak of the War of 1812, the governors of Massachusetts, Connecticut, and New Hampshire openly refused to place their militias under the command of the United States Army.[54] Yet to most Americans—including New Englanders in more sanguine moments—the looseness and divided sovereignty that made such contentions possible was one of the United States' principal strengths. In the words of a Republican resolution from 1812, America's federal union was essentially a peaceful construct, an empire "without foreign or domestic wars, without taxation, without any more of the pressure of government than was absolutely necessary to keep the bands of society together."[55] While hinting at the possibility of secession, even the Federalist delegates to the Hartford Convention (1814) expressed their desire to preserve some "form of confederacy . . . among those states which shall intend to maintain a federal relation to each other."[56]

To the British, on the other hand, federalism encouraged behavior that was neither pacific nor desirable. In particular, British diplomats, politicians, and other observers objected to the way the federal government's weakness enabled the American states—or, what was worse, private individuals acting at their behest—to conduct their own foreign policy, often in open defiance of international customs and agreements. Because of Britain's support for the *junta* opposing Napoleon's puppet regime in Spain, the government took particular exception to the incursions of Georgia and Louisiana into Spanish West Florida during the early 1800s, noting in its official response to the War of 1812 the United States' "ungenerous conduct" toward Britain's "intimate ally."[57] The invasion of Florida, however, was only one episode in a larger series of grievances, including the commissioning, arming, and manning of French privateers in American ports; running hostilities with Britain's Indian allies in the West; and tensions along the northern border with Canada. As Ambassador Hammond complained in 1794, the federal government seemed incapable of "restraining *unauthorized* acts of *individual* aggression" across its borders, and he mentioned, in particular, adventurers from Vermont and New York "who erect buildings within the posts now occupied by his Majesty's forces, imprison or compel to fly persons settled under the authority of his Majesty's officers, and . . . [hold] judicial courts, *surrounded by armed men.*"[58] On learning three years later of a French plot to invade Lower Canada from Vermont, Hammond's successor, Robert Liston, could only hope that the United States would take "every measure that the nature of a Federal Government will permit to prevent the Assembling or Arming of Troops within the Territory of the Union."[59]

In fairness, of course, the British government's ability to regulate hostile behavior on the part of its own subjects and allies in America was often no better. During the Indian wars of the 1790s and again on the eve of the War of 1812, Whitehall was forced to disavow unauthorized aggression by both indigenous leaders and, occasionally, colonial agents. Likewise, American merchants frequently had reason to complain of the freelance depredations of West Indian privateers and the colonial prize courts that legitimated their irregularities.[60] To note similarities between the British Empire and the United States, however, was to underscore the manifold ways in which the American Republic continued to partake of the ethos of the European Atlantic empires, and as such remained outside Europe's metropolitan concert. Significantly, British observers never failed to comment on the American slave system, which was both the most vivid sign of the Republic's colonial, extra-European origins and the clearest indication of the licensed violence that its federal structure still sanctioned. "How much to be deprecated are the laws which suffer such abuses to exist!" wrote Isaac Weld on visiting Virginia's Northern Neck during the 1790s.[61] In the words of an English pamphlet from 1796, ostensibly written to dissuade young men from emigrating to Virginia and Kentucky, even poor whites in America felt slavery's detrimental effects, laboring under indentures whose terms exposed them to "every species of brutal insolence and overbearing tyranny."[62]

Of the abuses that federalism appeared to encourage, none was more troubling in British eyes than the liberal naturalization laws that conferred American citizenship on British subjects, especially able-bodied seamen. Although the naval impressment controversy that preceded the War of 1812 was partly an abstract—and irresolvable–debate over whether citizenship was transferable or inborn and indefeasible, it owed much of its acrimony to British outrage over the discretion that insisting on a fundamental right to change allegiance placed in the hands of American magistrates, notaries, customs officials, shipmasters, and even ordinary sailors, all of whom were beyond the control of the federal government. According to an anonymous Foreign Office minute drafted shortly before the outbreak of the War of 1812,

American Seamen are in the constant habit of *selling* their Certificates [of citizenship] to British Seamen. . . . it not infrequently happens that a man with a fair complexion, produces a certificate describing a half-cast, and the West Indian Mulatto, is not infrequently described with blue eyes, and long sandy hair.[63]

To Americans, the ability to transfer one's allegiance was among the fundamental rights of mankind and a crucial bulwark of their own liberty. But when applied to the thousands of British and Irish mariners who sought employment—and, frequently, refuge—in American ships, the apparently indiscriminate granting of United States citizenship directly threatened the Royal Navy's ability to man its ships in the western Atlantic, which in turn supplied the pretext for extraordinary measures like stopping American ships on the high seas, violating the territorial waters of the United States, and forcing any sailor into the king's service who could not prove American birth.

Taken together, Britain's treatment of the United States—both as a maritime nation situated in waters that its navy dominated, and as a government with insufficient authority over its subordinate districts and citizens—placed limits on how far the new Republic could aspire to parity with the independent states of Europe. American objections notwithstanding, the result was to perpetuate the Western Hemisphere's character as a zone regulated not by relations between states that recognized each other's independence and legitimacy but by chronic war between the proxies and colonies of Europe's imperial powers. As every American schoolchild knows, the human costs of the United States' inability to make a clean break with its own proxy status were considerable. The newspapers, memoirs, and diplomatic correspondence of the period are full of accounts like that of William Jessup, master of the New York ship *Mercury,* who was flogged on board a British frigate after objecting when the captain ordered his crew to cut away the ship's sails, saying "they would do to make trowsers."[64] As Samuel Leech, an American native serving on the HMS *Macedonian* at the outbreak of the War of 1812, later recalled, the warship's officers tried to keep the commencement of hostilities with the United States secret to prevent impressed American citizens from giving "themselves up as prisoners of war, and claim[ing] exemption from that unjust service, which compelled them to act with the enemies of their country."[65] Even Americans who were less resentful of Britain's de facto lordship freely acknowledged its existence. "Shield, still Britannia, shield from harm, / The Nations with thy naval arm," implored a Federalist pamphlet in 1799.[66] Significantly, on setting sail for American waters in 1812, Admiral Sir John Borlase Warren carried instructions authorizing him to open negotiations with any state in the

Union; the expectation, of course, was that New Englanders might be willing to conclude a separate peace.[67] Although such plans came to naught, they are a reminder of the extent to which the western Atlantic's legal geography was a matter yet to be settled.

Separation and Equality

By the time President James Monroe articulated the doctrine that bears his name, things had changed significantly. Taking as his cue the success of the various Latin American wars of independence, Monroe declared in his message to Congress in 1823 that the United States would regard any attempt by the Holy Alliance of Russia, Austria, Prussia, and France "to extend their system to any portion of this hemisphere"—meaning the reestablishment of the Spanish Bourbon monarchy and empire in Central and South America—"as dangerous to our peace and safety." While affirming that America had no wish to interfere with "the existing colonies or dependencies of any European power," the president effectively recast the Western Hemisphere as an autonomous system of states with rights comparable to those of metropolitan Europe.[68] Although Monroe was not the first American politician to speak in this way, the United States' appointment of ministers to Columbia, Buenos Aires, Chile, and Mexico (though not Haiti) gave his words a force that previous utterances had lacked. Most striking of all was the widespread recognition that he spoke with Britain's tacit approval.[69] In Britain, some commentators bridled at the unilateralism of Monroe's pronouncement, preferring the image of British sponsorship conveyed in Canning's formulation; however, most agreed that a "New World" had indeed been called into being and that the United States was destined to play a major role in its affairs. "Happily . . . for us and for the interests of mankind," wrote the pro-American *Edinburgh Review* in 1824, "the Government of the United States has interposed to settle this question; and has earned the lasting admiration and gratitude of all freemen, by setting limits to the progress of despotism, and affording liberty effectual protection in all the vast and fertile regions of the Western World."[70] Though hardly a terminus, the Monroe Doctrine marked a crucial milestone in the creation of an Atlantic state system.

In view of the difficulties that had bedeviled their relations, well might people ask how Britain and the United States had reached this point, less than a decade after the War of 1812's conclusion. Ironically, the answer lies partly in the rationale that the British used to justify their high-handed policies during nearly a quarter century of war with Revolutionary and

Napoleonic France. Where Jeffersonian Republicans, in particular, perceived a string of assaults on American sovereignty—by some accounts stretching back to the Washington administration's humiliating acceptance of the Jay Treaty—the British insisted that their restrictions on America's merchant marine were necessary to avert a French universal monarchy and thus served the interests of independent nations everywhere, including the United States. As George Hammond, Britain's minister to the United States, told Alexander Hamilton during a conference in 1794, neutral powers "must expect to suffer some inconveniences . . . in a war like the present[,] in which . . . all the dearest interests of society were involved, and which was a contest between government and disorder, virtue and vice, and religion and impiety."[71] Two decades later, the Liverpool ministry struck practically the same note, insisting in its rebuttal to the American declaration of war that, because the government was "contending against France, in defense not only of the liberties of Great Britain, but of the World," the United States had no basis for opposing measures that were vital to the survival of both nations. "From their common origin," the manifesto pointedly noted, "from their common interests, from their professed principles of freedom and independence, The United States were the last Power in which Great Britain could have expected to find a willing Instrument and Abettor of French tyranny."[72] Although Britain's maritime strategy entailed short-term American sacrifices, the objectives they were meant to serve demonstrated that the government respected—and was committed to upholding—the Republic's independence.

One would not want to read too much into the ostensible reasons for policies that resulted in the impressment of American seaman, the wholesale confiscation of neutral cargoes, or the flogging of a ship's master on the deck of a British frigate. Nonetheless, the government's position on relations with the United States reflected a widespread sense, first articulated during the American Revolution and frequently reiterated during the wars with Revolutionary and Napoleonic France, that the destruction of the great European Atlantic empires—especially Spain's—and the erection of independent states in their place might serve Britain's commercial and strategic interests. As Thomas Pownall wrote in his posthumously published *Memorial to the Sovereigns of Europe and the Atlantic* (1803), France's dominance of the European mainland meant that "Britain must now commence *a new system in a new era*," which Pownall envisioned as a permanent Anglo-American alliance that would eventually include Haiti and the liberated "Spanish provinces of South America."[73] Pownall had a well-deserved reputation for unrealistic abstractions, but his ideas found at least an echo in the prediction of Edward Thornton, Britain's *charge d'affaires* at the time of the Louisiana Purchase, that an American alliance with the former "mother country" would transform the "Western World."[74] As these words suggest, even people with the experience and apparently favorable disposition of Thornton and Pownall found it difficult to conceive of the United States as Britain's diplomatic equal. Their prognostications took for granted Britain's preeminence, and Pownall clearly conceived of his Atlantic Federation as a successor to the "grand marine empire" that the American Revolution had partly demolished.[75] Yet both regarded the Republic as a worthy treaty partner, and they seemed to anticipate the day when the two English-speaking empires would interact on terms of parity.

If this recognition of the United States as a regional power and, conceivably, strategic partner was one reason for the understanding of the 1820s, another was the willingness of Americans to return the favor and to accept the British Empire's continued dominance in the western Atlantic. Not surprisingly, this acceptance was largely tacit. Despite strenuous American attempts to arrive at a clear statement on impressment and the Orders in Council, the Treaty of Ghent was silent on both issues, leaving Britain's rights intact on the two principal grievances that had prompted Congress to declare war in 1812.[76] At times, though, Americans—even Anglophobe Republicans—could be surprisingly forthright both about Britain's continued supremacy and about the potential benefits.[77] As Jefferson wrote Monroe during the international discussions that preceded the President's declaration of 1823:

> Our first and fundamental maxim should be, never to entangle ourselves in the broils of Europe. Our second, never to suffer Europe to intermeddle with cis-Atlantic affairs. . . . One nation, most of all, could disturb us in this pursuit; she now offers to lead, aid, and accompany us in it. By acceding to her proposition, we detach her from the bands, bring her mighty weight into the scale of free government, and emancipate a continent at one stroke, which might otherwise linger long in doubt and difficulty. Great Britain is the nation which can do us the most harm of anyone, or all on earth; and with her on our side we need not fear the whole world.[78]

Although they could have been written by any number of Federalists before 1815, Jefferson's words were remarkable in view of the acrimony that had long subsisted between the two nations.

Told in this manner, the story of the Anglo-American relationship—and of the evolving structure of the Atlantic state system as a whole—is one of interaction between governments, of statements by party hacks and theorists, and of actions by political and military leaders of various denominations. But the changing relationship of the 1820s gained added momentum from the commercial unity that had first impressed British and colonial writers half a century earlier. In Britain, this integration was evident before the War of 1812 in the connections between the disruption of British trade with Europe and America, the depression that silenced the cotton mills of Lancashire, and the labor unrest about which Edward Thompson wrote so evocatively in his history of the English working class.[79] During the Embargo of 1808, the same complex set of relationships characterized household production in America. Although Jefferson placed great stock in homespun's potential to make the nation less dependent on English manufacturing, women who produced cloth at home often did so not to escape Britain's "empire of goods" but to participate more fully, modeling their patterns on Lancashire's factory-made originals, selling their own coarse cloth for finer textiles from Europe, and supplying basic domestic needs with homemade fabric so they could afford to wear the latest British fashions in public.[80] If anything, the relationships engendered by the transatlantic grain trade were even more extensive and inescapable. While American corn helped Britain avoid the demographic catastrophe forecast by Thomas Malthus, England's hungry cities supplied the markets that enabled Jefferson's yeoman farmers to open western Pennsylvania, upstate New York, and the Midwest to commercial agriculture.[81] Although hardly a sufficient cause, economic ties helped facilitate the Anglo-American entente after 1815 and made it a tangible reality for ordinary men and women around its shores.[82]

Yet the old divisions remained. Even as Britain and the United States began to forge closer diplomatic and economic relations, there was no question that America occupied a sphere with customs and interests distinct from those of Europe. This was especially apparent in three aspects of American public life: the entrenchment and spread of southern slavery, the dispossession of Indian land, and the likelihood that the Republic would continue encroaching on land claimed by neighboring states to the west and south. In each area, the United States' departure from European norms continued to create difficulties in its relations with Britain, which was itself still an Atlantic power by virtue of its colonies in North America and the West Indies. At no point, however, did the differences threaten a serious diplomatic breach. When Britain attempted to insert language in the Treaty of Ghent guaranteeing the rights of Indians living within the jurisdiction of the United States, American negotiators managed to kill it; on the repeated occasions when Britain proposed a convention to permit the Royal Navy to search suspected American slave ships, Washington refused; and when the hero of New Orleans, Andrew Jackson, executed two British subjects in Spanish Florida during the Seminole War (1817–18), the Liverpool ministry let the matter drop.[83] In effect, the normalization of international relations in the western Atlantic occurred without displacing the long-standing notion that Europeans beyond the line could do things that Europeans in Europe could not.

All this is to say that Forrest Davis was only partly correct in taking the pronouncements of Canning and Monroe in 1823 at face value. The reconceptualization of the Americas as an Atlantic system of states was certainly a development of the first importance. It was, however, also a development that preserved key features of the Atlantic world's historic divisions. In a sense, the international transformation wrought by the great democratic revolutions had the same effect on the structure of the extra-European Atlantic that Alexis de Tocqueville attributed to the Revolution in France.[84] Although men and women throughout the revolutionary Atlantic—including in counterrevolutionary Britain—did call a "New World into being" during the late eighteenth and early nineteenth centuries, that world was less a repudiation than a restatement and, in some cases, an intensification of key features of the old order. The United States in 1825 was more democratic than British America had been fifty years earlier, and it was unambiguously independent, possessing all the rights of a European nation. But it was also in a zone clearly distinct from Europe, with fewer obstacles to the exploitation of slaves, the removal of Indians, and expansion beyond its borders. To paraphrase Jefferson's letter of 1813 to Alexander von Humboldt, America did indeed have "a continent to itself," and its people had every intention of developing it without European interference or supervision.[85] The more things change, the more they remain the same.

Notes

1. Forrest Davis, *The Atlantic System: The Story of Anglo-American Control of the Seas* (1941; Westport, Conn., 1973), xi–xiv. Davis held that the interests of this transatlantic community were "essentially in conflict with those of Central and Eastern Europe."

2. See esp. Robin Blackburn, *The Making of the New World Slavery: From the Baroque to the Modern, 1492–1800* (London, 1997); David Eltis, *The Rise of African Slavery in the Americas* (Cambridge, 2000).

3. Jaime E. Rodríguez O., "The Emancipation of America," *American Historical Review* 105 (2000): 131–52.

4. Bradford Perkins, *The Creation of a Republican Empire, 1776–1865,* vol. 1 of Warren I. Cohen, ed., *The Cambridge History of American Foreign Relations* (Cambridge, 1993).

5. Ibid., 162.

6. Jefferson to Alexander von Humboldt, December 6, 1813, in Merrill D. Peterson, ed., *Thomas Jefferson, Writings* (New York, 1984), 1312.

7. Mercy Otis Warren, *History of the Rise, Progress, and Termination of the American Revolution,* 2 vols., ed. Lester H. Cohen (1805; Indianapolis, 1989), 2:697.

8. Robert W. Tucker and David C. Hendrickson, *Empire of Liberty: The Statecraft of Thomas Jefferson* (New York, 1990); Jack P. Greene, *The Intellectual Construction of America: Exceptionalism and Identity from 1492 to 1800* (Chapel Hill, N.C., 1993); Peter S. Onuf, *Jefferson's Empire: The Language of American Nationhood* (Charlottesville, Va., 2000).

9. Max Savelle, *The Origins of American Diplomacy: The International History of Angloamerica* (New York, 1967), 21, 210–15; Ian K. Steele, *The English Atlantic, 1675–1740: An Exploration of Communication and Community* (New York, 1986), chap. 10; Elizabeth Mancke, "Early Modern Expansion and the Politicization of Oceanic Space," *Geographical Review* 89 (1997): 225–37.

10. Samuel Pufendorf, *On the Law of Nature and Nations* (1688), trans. C. H. Oldfather and W. A. Oldfather, vol. 2 of *De Jure Naturae et Gentium,* Publications of the Carnegie Endowment for International Peace (Oxford, 1934), 1318. See also Max Savelle, *The Origins of American Diplomacy: The International History of Angloamerica, 1492–1763* (New York, 1967), 210–15.

11. Ian K. Steele, *The English Atlantic,* 190.

12. Jack P. Greene, *Negotiated Authorities: Essays in Colonial Political and Constitutional History* (Charlottesville, Va., 1994), chap. 1.

13. This and the next two paragraphs draw on Eliga H. Gould, "Zones of Law, Zones of Violence: The Legal Geography of the British Atlantic, circa 1772," *William and Mary Quarterly* 3rd ser., 60 (2003): 471–510.

14. Nicholas Tracy, "The Gunboat Diplomacy of the Government of George Grenville, 1764–1765: The Honduras, Turks Island, and Gambian Incidents," *Historical Journal* 17 (1974): 711–31, and "The Falkland Islands Crisis of 1770: Use of Naval Force," *English Historical Review* 90 (1975): 40–75; Frank Griffith Dawson, "William Penn's Settlement at Black River on the Mosquito Shore: A Challenge to Spain in Central America, 1732–1787," *Hispanic American Historical Review* 63 (1983); Perkins, *A Republican Empire.*

15. [Samuel Johnson], *Thoughts on the Late Transactions Respecting Falkland's Islands* (1771), in Donald J. Greene, ed., *Political Writings,* vol. 10 of *The Yale Edition of the Works of Samuel Johnson* (1977), 354.

16. Anthony Pagden, "The Struggle for Legitimacy and Image of Empire in the Atlantic to ca. 1700," in Nicholas Canny, ed., *The Origins of Empire: British Overseas Enterprise to the Close of the Seventeenth Century,* vol. 1 of *The Oxford*

History of the British Empire (Oxford, 1998), gen. ed. William Roger Louis, 34–54.

17. Somerset v. Stewart, 20 How. St. Tr. 1 (1772), in Helen Tunnicliff Catterall, ed., *Judicial Cases concerning American Slavery and the Negro,* Carnegie Institution of Washington (Washington, D.C., 1926), 14, 15; see also David Eltis, "Europeans and the Rise and Fall of African Slavery in the Americas: An Interpretation," *American Historical Review* 98 (1993): 1399–1423.

18. William Blackstone, *Commentaries on the Laws of England,* 4 vols. (1765–1769), ed. Stanley N. Katz et al. (Chicago, 1979), 1:405–9.

19. For integrative tendencies, see esp. Bernard Bailyn, "The Idea of Atlantic History," *Itinerario* 20 (1996); David Hancock, *Citizens of the World: London Merchants and the Integration of the British Atlantic Community, 1735–1785* (Cambridge, 1995).

20. Ralph Davis, *The Rise of the Atlantic Economies* (Ithaca, N.Y., 1973), 190–92.

21. Treaty of Navigation and Commerce between Great Britain and France, September 26, 1786, in Joel H. Wiener, ed., and J. H. Plumb, intro., *Great Britain: Foreign Policy and the Span of Empire, 1689–1971,* 4 vols. (New York, 1972), 1:126; *A Short Vindication of the French Treaty, from the Charges Brought against It in a Late Pamphlet* (London, 1787), 48.

22. Davis, *The Rise of the Atlantic Economies,* 190–92. David Hancock suggests that the free port system, which permitted limited trade in foreign ships between the British West Indies and the colonies of friendly European powers, was a departure from British mercantilist principles (*Citizens of the World,* 38); for its underlying consistency with those principles, see Dorothy Burne Goebel, "British Trade to the Spanish Colonies, 1796–1823," *American Historical Review* 43 (1938): 290–91.

23. David Hume, "Of the Jealousy of Trade" (1758), in Eugene F. Miller, ed., *Essays: Moral, Political, and Literary* (Indianapolis, 1985), 331. See also Paul Langford, *A Polite and Commercial People: England, 1727–1783* (Oxford, 1989), 174: "Trade with European powers was essentially a form of undeclared warfare."

24. Daniel Baugh, "Maritime Strength and Atlantic Commerce: The Uses of 'a Grand Marine Empire,'" in Lawrence Stone, ed., *An Imperial State at War: Britain from 1689 to 1815* (London, 1994), 185–223.

25. Eliga H. Gould, *The Persistence of Empire: British Political Culture in the Age of the American Revolution* (Chapel Hill, N.C., 2000), 123–28.

26. *A Letter from a Member of Parliament to His Grace the Duke of———upon the Present Situation of Affairs* (London, 1755), 15–16.

27. Gould, *The Persistence of Empire,* 53–69, 110–36; Stephen Conway, "From Fellow-Nationals to Foreigners: British Perceptions of the Americans, circa 1739–1783," *William and Mary Quarterly,* 3rd ser., 59 (2002): 77–89.

28. [Thomas Pownall], *The Administration of the Colonies* (London, 1764), 4.

29. [Benjamin Franklin], *The Interest of Great Britain Considered, With Regard*

to her Colonies, and the Acquisitions of Canada and Guadaloupe (London, 1760), 41.

30. Thomas Paine, *Common Sense* (1776), in Jack P. Greene, ed., *Colonies to Nation, 1763–1789: A Documentary History of the American Revolution* (New York, 1975), 276.

31. Bradford Perkins, *The First Rapprochement: England and the United States, 1795–1805* (1955; Berkeley, Calif., 1967), 76.

32. "Anecdotes of the Negotiations," in W.A.S. Hewins, ed., *The Whitefoord Papers: Being the Correspondence and Other Manuscripts of Colonel Charles Whitefoord and Caleb Whitefoord from 1739 to 1810* (Oxford, 1898), 187.

33. John [Baker Holroyd], Lord Sheffield, *Observations on the Commerce of the American States,* 2nd ed. (1784; New York, 1970), 263–64.

34. Eliga H. Gould, "American Independence and Britain's Counter-Revolution," *Past and Present,* no. 154 (February 1997): 107–41; R. R. Palmer, *The Age of the Democratic Revolution: A Political History of Britain and America, 1760–1800,* 2 vols. (Princeton, 1959, 1964); Jaime E. Rodriguez O., "The Emancipation of America," *American Historical Review* 105 (2000): 131–52.

35. Enos Hitchcock, *An Oration, in Commemoration of The INDEPENDENCE of the United States of America. Delivered . . July 4th, 1793* (Providence, R.I., 1793), in Ellis Sandoz, ed., *Political Sermons of the American Founding Era, 1730–1805* (Indianapolis, 1991), 1180.

36. Peter Thacher, *A Sermon, Preached before the Ancient and Honorable Artillery Company, June 3, 1793* (Boston, 1793), in Sandoz, ed., *Political Sermons,* 1144.

37. Hammond to Lord Grenville, Philadelphia, August 3, 1794, Public Record Office, FO 5/5, 181.

38. John Rhodehamel, ed., *George Washington, Writings* (New York, 1997), 974.

39. Peter S. Onuf, "A Declaration of Independence for Diplomatic Historians," *Diplomatic History* 22 (1998): 71–83.

40. John E. Crowley, *The Privileges of Independence: Neomercantilism and the American Revolution* (Baltimore, 1993).

41. Sheffield, *Observations on the Commerce of the American States,* 5.

42. Wiener, ed., *Foreign Policy and the Span of Empire,* 1:318.

43. J. H. Parry, *Trade and Dominion: The European Oversea Empires in the Eighteenth Century* (London, 1971), 277.

44. James Stephen, *War in Disguise* (London, 1805); Kenneth Bourne, *Britain and the Balance of Power in North America, 1815–1908* (Berkeley, Calif., 1967), 3.

45. *Report on the Privileges and Restrictions on the Commerce of the United States in Foreign Countries* (December 16, 1793), in Peterson, ed., *Jefferson, Writings,* 443, 444.

46. Randolph to George Hammond, Philadelphia, May 1, 1794, in *The Memorial of Mr. Pinkney* (Philadelphia, May 12, 1794), 17–19; for the Anglo-American

debate over the "modern" law of nations generally, see Peter S. Onuf and Nicholas G. Onuf, *Federal Union, Modern World: The Law of Nations in an Age of Revolutions, 1776–1814* (Madison, Wisc., 1993).

47. For the rule's origins, see Richard Pares, *Colonial Blockade and Neutral Rights, 1739–1763* (Oxford, 1938).

48. "Third Annual Message," October 17, 1803, in Peterson, ed., *Jefferson, Writings,* 516.

49. Perkins, *The First Rapprochement,* 96–98.

50. *Times,* December 16, 1811, quoted in Bradford Perkins, *Prologue to War, 1805–1812: England and the United States* (1961; Berkeley, Calif., 1974), 5.

51. Perkins, *Prologue,* 199–204; A. T. Mahan, *Sea Power in Its Relations to the War of 1812,* 2 vols. (1905; New York, 1968), 178.

52. "The Citizens of the First Congressional District of Pennsylvania, to Their Fellow-Citizens, the People of the United States," *National Intelligencer* (May 26, 1812).

53. Foster to Lord Castlereagh, May 26, 1812, FO 5/86, 65.

54. Paul A. Varg, *New England and Foreign Relations, 1789–1850* (Hanover, N.H., 1983), chap. 4.

55. "The Citizens of the First Congressional District of Pennsylvania, to their Fellow-Citizens," *National Intelligencer* (May 26, 1812). On federations as "pacific," see Onuf, *Jefferson's Empire.*

56. "Report of the Hartford Convention," in John C. Miller, ed., *The Young Republic, 1789–1815* (New York, 1970), 180.

57. Wiener, ed., *Foreign Policy and the Span of Empire,* 1:333.

58. Hammond to Lord Grenville, March 10, 1794, FO 5/4, 134–35.

59. Robert Liston to Lord Grenville, January 25, 1797, FO 5/18, 59.

60. On Indians, see, e.g., George Beckwith to Henry Dundas, January 14, 1793, FO 5/2, 98–100; on West Indian privateers and prize courts, see George Hammond to Lord Grenville, April 28, 1795, FO 5/9, 146–55; Hammond to Governor of Bermuda, April 9, 1795, ibid., 160–61.

61. Isaac Weld, *Travels through the States of North America . . . during the Years 1795, 1796, and 1797,* 2 vols. (London, 1799), in Miller, ed., *The Young Republic,* 214.

62. *Look before You Leap; or, a Few Hints to Such Artisans, Mechanics, Labourers, Farmers, and Husbandmen, as are desirous of Emigrating to America* (London, 1796), xxxii.

63. "Minute respecting impressment of American Seamen," February 21, 1812, FO 5/104, 107.

64. "The Petition of William Jessup," July 4, 1796, FO 5/14, 94.

65. Samuel Leech, *Thirty Years from Home; or, A Voice from the Main Deck,* 15th ed. (Boston, 1843), in Dean King and John B. Hattendorf, eds., *Every Man Will Do His Duty: An Anthology of Firsthand Accounts from the Age of Nelson* (New York, 1997), 304.

66. Perkins, *The First Rapprochement*, 96.

67. Lord Castlereagh to Lords of Admiralty, August 12, 1812, 77–78.

68. President James Monroe, "Seventh Annual Message," December 2, 1823, in Stanislaus Murray Hamilton, ed., *The Writings of James Monroe*, 7 vols. (New York, 1898–1903), 7:325–42.

69. Bradford Perkins, *Castlereagh and Adams: England and the United States, 1812–1823* (Berkeley, Calif., 1964), chap. 17; Ernest R. May, *The Making of the Monroe Doctrine* (Cambridge, Mass., 1975).

70. *Edinburgh Review* 39, no. 78 (January 1824): 487.

71. Hammond to Lord Grenville, April 17, 1794, FO 5/4, 179.

72. "British Declaration Relative to the Outbreak of the War with the United States," January 9, 1813, in Wiener, ed., *Foreign Policy and the Span of Empire*, 1:333.

73. Thomas Pownall, *Memorial Addressed to the Sovereigns of Europe and the Atlantic* (London, 1803), 50, 73.

74. Thornton to Lord Hawkesbury, February 17, 1803, FO 5/38, 93–102.

75. Pownall, *Memorial*, 68.

76. Perkins, *Prologue to War*, 339.

77. Kinley J. Brauer, "The United States and British Imperial Expansion, 1815–60," *Diplomatic History* 12 (1988): 19–37.

78. Jefferson to Monroe, October 24, 1823, in Peterson, ed., *Jefferson, Writings*, 1481–82.

79. E. P. Thompson, *The Making of the English Working Class* (London, 1963).

80. Laurel Thatcher Ulrich, *The Age of Homespun: Objects and Stories in the Creation of an American Myth* (New York, 2001); T. H. Breen, "An Empire of Goods: The Anglicization of Colonial America, 1690–1776," *Journal of British Studies* 25 (1986): 467–99.

81. Joyce Oldham Appleby, *Capitalism and a New Social Order: The Republican Vision of the 1790s* (New York, 1984); Charles Sellers, *The Market Revolution: Jacksonian America, 1815–1846* (New York, 1991).

82. For the Latin American dimensions, see Peggy K. Liss, *Atlantic Empires: The Network of Trade and Revolution, 1713–1826* (Baltimore, 1983), chaps. 7–9.

83. Perkins, *Castlereagh and Adams*, 91–92, 289–90; Hugh B. Soulsby, *The Right of Search and the Slave Trade in Anglo-American Relations, 1814–1862* (Baltimore, 1933).

84. Alexis de Tocqueville, *The Old Regime and the Revolution*, ed. and intro. by François Furet and Françoise Mélonio, trans. Alan S. Kahan (Chicago, 1998).

85. Jefferson to Alexander von Humboldt, December 6, 1813, in Peterson, ed., *Jefferson, Writings*, 1312.

About the Contributors

C. J. Bartlett is emeritus professor of international history at the University of Dundee. He is the author of numerous books and articles, including *Great Britain and Sea Power, 1815–1853* (1963) and *"The Special Relationship": A Political History of Anglo-American Relations since 1945* (1992).

Michael A. Bellesiles is the author of *Revolutionary Outlaws: Ethan Allen and the Struggle for Independence on the Early American Frontier* (1993) and *Arming America: The Origins of a National Gun Culture* (2000). He is currently working on a book about General John Burgoyne's campaign in America.

Stephen Conway is a professor in history at University College London. He is the author of *The War of American Independence, 1775–1783* (1995) and *The British Isles and the War of American Independence* (2000).

Julie Flavell has published in leading academic journals including the *Historical Journal*, the *William and Mary Quarterly*, and the *English Historical Review*. She was a lecturer in the Department of History at the University of Dundee between 1992–2002. She is a fellow of the Royal Historical Society.

Eliga H. Gould is the Class of 1940 Associate Professor at the University of New Hampshire, where he teaches British and American history. He is the author of *The Persistence of Empire: British Political Culture in the Age of the American Revolution* (2000), and he is currently working on a book-length study of the legal geography of the English-speaking Atlantic between 1776 and the 1820s.

Bob Harris is a reader in history at the University of Dundee and the author of two books: *Politics and the Nation: Britain in the Mid-Eighteenth Century* (2002) and *Politics and the Rise of the Press: Britain and France, 1620–*

1800 (1996). He is currently working on a volume of essays on Scotland in the era of the French Revolution.

P. J. Marshall is emeritus professor of imperial history at the University of London. He is the author of many books and essays on the British Empire in the eighteenth century. He has edited volume two of the Oxford History of the British Empire, *The Eighteenth Century* (1998), as well as the *Cambridge Illustrated History of the British Empire* (1996).

Gene A. Smith is professor of history at Texas Christian University in Fort Worth, Texas. He is the author or editor of numerous publications, including *Filibusters and Expansionists: Jeffersonian Manifest Destiny, 1800–1821*, with Frank L. Owlsey Jr. (1997); Arsène Lacarrière Latour's *Historical Memoir of the War in West Florida and Louisiana in 1814–15: With an Atlas* (1999); *Thomas ap Catesby Jones: Commodore of Manifest Destiny* (2000); and *A British Eyewitness at the Battle of New Orleans: The Memoir of Royal Navy Admiral Robert Aitchison, 1808–1827* (2004).

Margaret Stead gained her doctorate in history from the University of Leeds in 1997. Her article on the raising of the 72nd Regiment, Royal Manchester Volunteers, was published in the *British Journal for Eighteenth-Century Studies* (2000). She is coauthor, with Geoffrey Stead, of *The Exotic Plant: A History of the Moravian Church in Britain 1742–2000* (2003).

Peter Way is associate professor and chair of the History Department at Bowling Green State University. His book, *Common Labour: Workers and the Digging of North American Canals, 1780–1860* (1993), won the 1994 Frederick Jackson Turner Prize from the Organization of American Historians.

Index